REVISIONING
EUROPE

CINEMAS OFF CENTRE SERIES
Darrell Varga, series editor

ISSN 1912-3094 (Print) ISSN 1925-2927 (Online)

The Cinemas Off Centre series highlights bodies of cinematic work that, for various reasons, have been ignored, marginalized, overlooked, and/or obscured within traditional and dominant canons of film and cinema studies. The series presents cutting-edge research that provokes and inspires new explorations of past, present, and emerging cinematic trends by individuals and groups of filmmakers from around the world.

No. 1 · **Filming Politics: Communisim and the Portrayal of the Working Class at the National Film Board of Canada, 1939–46,** by Malek Khouri

No. 2 · **Rain/Drizzle/Fog: Film and Television in Atlantic Canada,** edited by Darrell Varga

No. 3 · **Revisioning Europe: The Films of John Berger and Alain Tanner,** by Jerry White

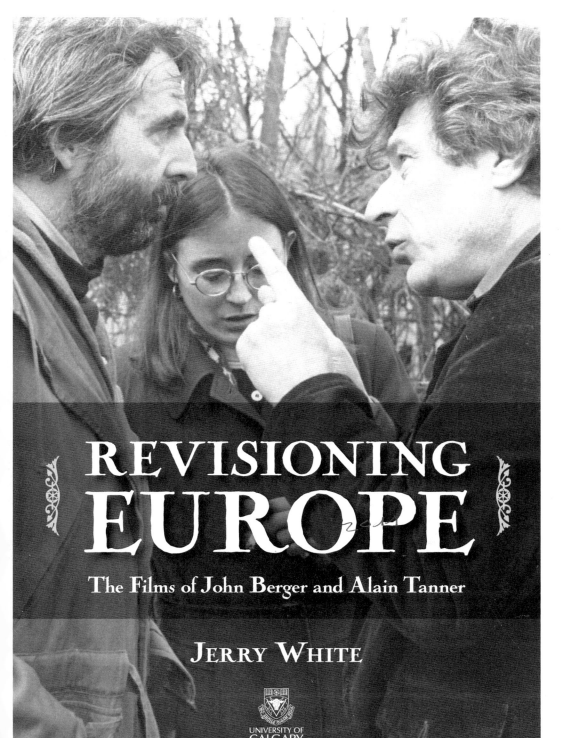

REVISIONING
EUROPE

The Films of John Berger and Alain Tanner

JERRY WHITE

UNIVERSITY OF
CALGARY
PRESS

CINEMAS OFF CENTRE SERIES
ISSN 1912-3094 (Print) ISSN 1925-2927 (Online)

University of Calgary Press
2500 University Drive NW
Calgary, Alberta
Canada T2N 1N4
www.uofcpress.com

LIBRARY AND ARCHIVES CANADA CATALOGUING IN PUBLICATION

White, Jerry, 1971-
    Revisioning Europe : the films of John Berger and Alain Tanner / Jerry White.

(Cinemas off centre series 3)
Includes some text in French.
Includes bibliographical references and index.
Issued also in electronic formats.
ISBN 978-1-55238-550-0

    1. Berger, John—Criticism and interpretation. 2. Tanner, Alain—Criticism and interpretation. 3. Politics in motion pictures. 4. Motion pictures—Political aspects—Europe—History—20th century. 5. Motion pictures—Political aspects—Switzerland—History—20th century. I. Title. II. Series: Cinemas off centre series ;3.

PN1995.9.P6W45 2011   791.43'6581094   C2011-908169-5

The University of Calgary Press acknowledges the support of the Government of Alberta through the Alberta Multimedia Development Fund for our publications. We acknowledge the financial support of the Government of Canada through the Canada Book Fund for our publishing activities. We acknowledge the financial support of the Canada Council for the Arts for our publishing program.

This book has been published with the help of a grant from the Canadian Federation for the Humanities and Social Sciences, through the Aid to Scholarly Publications Program, using funds provided by the Social Sciences and Humanities Research Council of Canada.

Government of Alberta ■   Canadä   Canada Council for the Arts   Conseil des Arts du Canada

Printed and bound in Canada by Marquis
♻ This book is printed on FSC Silva paper

Cover image: John Berger and Alain Tanner, during the shooting of *Jonas qui aura 25 ans en l'an 2000*. Courtesy Cinémathèque Suisse (Lausanne).

Cover design, page design, and typesetting by Melina Cusano

For Jerry and Cathy White,
with fond memories of a great week in Fribourg.

Table of Contents

Acknowledgments   ix
Introduction   1
1: Berger and Tanner before Berger and Tanner   49
2: La Salamandre   89
3: Le Milieu du monde   117
4: Jonas qui aura 25 ans en l'an 2000   149
Conclusion   185

Appendix 1: "Télé-Aphorismes," by Alain Tanner   209
Appendix 2: "Vers Le Milieu du monde," by John Berger   225

Bibliography   231
Sources for the films on video   237
Index   239

Acknowledgments

I should begin by thanking the University of Alberta. This book was written during a sabbatical leave that they generously granted me in 2009–10, and I am certainly grateful for that. I am also grateful to the Department of English and Film Studies, which has been a great place to work; my chairs Garrett Epp and Susan Hamilton have been a major reason for that.

About half of that leave was spent in Switzerland. I am grateful to Maria Tortajada of the Section de cinéma, Université de Lausanne, for helping me secure an appointment as Professeur invité in that program during my time in the country. Claude Hauser (Université de Fribourg) helped clarify a lot of my sense of the history of Jura; the Fribourg contingent of the Association suisse de littérature générale et comparée took me as one of their own, and I have fond memories of their colloquia. Claude Zürcher, archivist at Télévision Suisse Romande (Geneva), was very generous with his time and effort, responding to all of my queries either with news that he had found what I asked for and put it online, or that he had searched vigorously but without success.

Marcy Goldberg (Universität Zürich) has been a huge help on this project, and I feel very lucky to have such an expert in Swiss cinema among my circle of friends. Gareth Evans (Go Together Press, London) also helped a great deal with this project, putting me in contact with John Berger, suggesting fascinating routes for new research, and generally offering a lot of moral support.

Both John Berger and Alain Tanner were good enough to speak with me on the phone about this project, and both very kindly provided permission to translate and reprint the material in the appendices. John Berger was especially good to both suggest and then support the very curious task of my translating back into English a text that he had originally written in English, agreed to have translated into French, and then lost the original of.

Darrell Varga (NSCAD University), in his capacity as series editor for "Cinemas Off Centre," was the lighthouse that brought the manuscript safely into the port of the University of Calgary Press. He was a constant correspondent during the writing process, reading these chapters as I finished them and providing detailed, uncompromising criticism on each one.

I owe him a considerable debt for his work. I am also grateful, of course, to UCP's Donna Livingstone and Judy Powell for their support.

I want to take this opportunity to thank Julia Lesage, now retired from the University of Oregon and one of the founding editors of *Jump Cut*. She was my beloved mentor as an undergraduate, and I could not have possibly had a better role model of the engaged critic and teacher. In the pages that follow I have a lot of arguments with *Jump Cut* writers, but in a way they feel like a family feud with distant cousins that I have never met. Everything I know about political film criticism I learned from Julia and *Jump Cut*.

Almost this entire book was written either at the Bibliothèque cantonale et universitaire Fribourg or just down the line at the Bibliothèque nationale suisse (Berne), and I cannot imagine better workspaces. No small amount of the reading for this book was done at Fribourg's Auberge du Chasseur, and the mother-daughter proprietors of that place, Catherine and Olivia Brunisholz, have no idea how much they helped. Ellen Hertz Wero (Université de Neuchâtel) allowed us to rent 32 Grand Fontaine, an address that now forever lives in my memory as a wonderful place to live and work. Really, I lack the words to describe the singular city of Fribourg, so I will rely on Jacques Chessex, who writes in his 1987 novel *Jonas* that "À Fribourg j'avais découvert la neige baroque, le froid du soir peuplé d'anges et d'appels de cloches, le latin précis et soyeux des officiants, la science multiple et rigoureux, la foi, le don, la sainteté." So it was for us.

Sara Daniels, as always, deserves the biggest thanks of all.

INTRODUCTION

"The subject is European, its meaning global." – John Berger, *A Seventh Man* (7)

What constitutes political cinema? What debt does it owe simply to politics, or simply to cinema? How can its formal patterns really reflect political concerns? The 1970s were dominated by such debate among film critics and theoreticians, a lot of whom were strongly hostile to narrative, to say nothing of pleasure, and a lot of whom were under the spell of Bertolt Brecht. A lot of that is, in retrospect, easily caricatured as quaint, and these sorts of questions have faded from the main stream of Film Studies (at least in English and French). But two people active in these '70s debates never succumbed to pious, over-simplified equations of narrative identification or visual pleasure with oppression. They were neither film theorists nor film critics, although throughout their work they evince a keenly acute sense of the philosophical and aesthetic stakes of cinema and politics. They worked together only briefly, but the films they made together offered a vision of a political cinema whose rigour and accessibility remains, in many ways, unmatched. "They make one of the most interesting film-making teams in Europe today" Vincent Canby wrote in the *New York Times* on 2 October 1976.

I am talking, of course, about the English writer John Berger and the Swiss filmmaker Alain Tanner. The most well-known of their collaborations, *La Salamandre* (1971), *Le Milieu du monde* (1974), and *Jonas qui aura 25 ans en l'an 2000* (1976), are crucial parts of postwar European cinema and deserve a central place in its history. No doubt that the struggles that these films evoked and, in their small way, participated in, are by and large over. But Berger and Tanner's work still needs to be recovered and re-explained in terms of a world cinema that has, in the last decades, been as transformed as the political landscape of Western Europe. I want to argue in this book that the films they made together offered a vision of a political cinema that was unsentimental about the possibilities of revolutionary struggle, unsparing in its critique of the failures of the European left, but still optimistic about the ability of radicalism, and radical art as well, to transform the world.

I will examine each film, and both artists, in their turn, but some elements run throughout the discussion. The first is that these films, like the work Berger and Tanner did on their own, are both forward-looking and historically aware. The second is that the films are aesthetically innovative while still remaining close to conventions of narrative filmmaking. In this way they are actually defined by a richly complex dialectic between conservative and progressive elements, on the level of both form and content. And thus we arrive, I believe, at the nub of the matter. These films are seminal because they embody a considered and tentative experimentalism, forgoing polemics in favour of argument. This rigour, and this humility, is what points the way forward for political cinema. The fact that the political cinema of the last decades shows little sign of this sensibility makes it no less urgent to think of Berger and Tanner's work as a viable path for political cinema to follow.

By way of introduction I want to explain a few important historical and theoretical elements that frame that argument about the nature of the political cinema these two artists created together. I will talk briefly about the "Nouveau cinéma suisse" in the context of similar "New Waves" of the 1960s. I will also sketch out the landscape of 70s theorizing about cinema and political action. I want to do this because it would be very easy to place these three films in contexts like these, and I think that's a bit too simple. These films are defined by a complex combination of narrative convention and innovation; while Berger and Tanner do a lot of what 70s theorists saw as aesthetically progressive, they never fully abandoned cinematic conventions such as narrative, identification, etc. Their work together is preoccupied with the inherent tension between collective action and individual liberty, and this is a conundrum that is, not to put too fine a point on it, seminally Swiss. Another aspect of their work that is seminally Swiss is their tendency to see the mountains not as some repository of timeless values but as a politically unstable border zone. This has a lot to do with the "separatist" conflict in Jura that strongly marked Swiss politics in the 1960s and 70s, and I will explain the way that they both implicitly and explicitly engage with that conflict. I will also try to place their work in the context of Switzerland by offering an analogy between Berger, Tanner, and two important figures of two different generations of Swiss literature: Charles-Ferdinand Ramuz (Switzerland's most celebrated French-language writer of the first half of the twentieth century) and Jacques Chessex (who came to be synonymous with the explosion of creativity in French-speaking Switzerland starting in the 1960s). That tension between individual liberty and collective responsibility was a central conundrum of the Enlightenment as well, and that is finally what I want to point out about Berger and Tanner. They are heirs to what Tzvetan Todorov has recently elegized as "L'Esprit des Lumières."

The fact that you can fit Berger and Tanner's work into "70s counter-cinema" and "Nouveau cinéma suisse" but that you also need to do more to really understand the work is at the heart of the kind of political cinema they were trying to build. They didn't seek to reject the political discourse that emerged in the wake of the 1968 strikes. They understood that the radicals of that period were, at their best moments, richly aware of the ideological and political importance of form and the potential that cinema and its allied arts had to serve as agents of social transformation. Indeed, Berger and Tanner sought to avoid the leftist pieties that marked 1968 while still *building* on its radical and largely unachieved possibilities. Similarly, I don't believe that their films constitute a rejection of Swiss culture. Very much the opposite is true, despite what both Berger and Tanner have said in print and to me personally. I believe that their films show that they saw what was radical in Switzerland's distinctive political culture, and I also believe that they understood how those distinctive qualities could be *built* that into their vision of a renewed European left. My verb there is key. Berger and Tanner were not nostalgic, nor were they cynics, nor were they pious scolds. Through the films they made together, and throughout the work they have done individually, they have tried to be builders.

Not nouvelle, and only partly nouveau

Although it is not a particularly well-known movement within the world of anglophone film studies, the flowering of cinema in 1960s and '70s French-speaking Switzerland did create a certain amount of excitement in the francophone world. This excitement was generated as much by the films of the movement as by the ways in which it changed the institutional situation of Swiss cinema, especially in French-speaking Switzerland. Martin Schaub, in his history *L'Usage de la liberté: le nouveau cinéma suisse 1964-1984*, recalls that during this period imported (mostly Hollywood, although some German and French) films accounted for 98.7 per cent of the films shown in Switzerland in 1960 and 99.8 per cent in 1964. He says that "it seems to me essential to recall the colonization which had a hold on all of the media of this period; just as elsewhere, it dominated music, fashion, and even literature" (8).[1] Tanner was a key part of the first sustained challenge to this cinematic imperialism, although the films that he actually made during this period are different in important ways from the work of his contemporaries.

Aside from Tanner, the best known members of "Le nouveau cinéma suisse" are probably Claude Goretta and Michel Soutter. Goretta had known Tanner when they had both lived in England during the 1950s, and the two had made a film together – the semi-vérité short *Nice Time* (1957)[2] – which had been an important part of Britain's "Free Cinema" movement. Goretta went on to make feature films, including *Le Fou* (1969) and *L'Invitation* (1971), as well as *Jean-Luc Persecuté* (1966), an adaptation of the Ramuz novel. He now is a widely respected figure in Swiss cinema. That's also true of Soutter, who began by making a well-received short in 1965 called *Mick et Arthur*, a jaunty piece that owes a lot to Godard's *À bout de souffle*. He followed that with 1971's feature *Les Arpenteurs*, a much more downbeat work about a mysterious woman and her hapless suitors, one whose subject matter shares a lot with Berger and Tanner's *La Salamandre*, released the same year and also starring Jean-Luc Bideau. *Les Arpenteurs* became one of the signature works of the moment.

Like a lot of the "New Waves" of the 1960s, much of the Nouveau cinéma suisse was strongly influenced by France's Nouvelle Vague of the 1950s and 60s. This is most true of Soutter, whose films are very much about the restlessness of youth and the pleasures of alternating between improvization and alienation in a way that would be very familiar to François Truffaut or to the Jean-Luc Godard of the early 1960s. But this is not true of Tanner's films, which are quite different from the work of the French New Wave. When *La Salamandre* was released in 1971, Tanner recalled in an interview with Guy Braucourt that when he showed his first feature-narrative film *Charles mort ou vif* (1969) to French audiences, "it was received as an 'incredibly exotic' film!" (7).[3] Part of this, no doubt, is easily ascribable to the actors' accents. But a more important element of this "exotic" quality has to do with the fact that the film's characters, when faced with the alienation of bourgeois society, retreat not to a café in a hipster metropolis like Paris but to the Jura mountains, a territory whose politics and history are genuinely distinctive, genuinely unstable, and generally unknown to people outside of Switzerland. I will return to the matter of Jura, and of the "esprit jurassien" that I think is hiding just below the surface of Tanner and Berger's work together, in due time. Suffice it to say for now that there is a great deal in Tanner's films that is at odds with the nouvelle vague sensibility, and among his contemporaries, he is the least influenced by that most famous of French-language film movements. Tanner recalled to Christian Dimitriu how his time in 1958 Paris was basically unpleasant:

> For me it was a bit of a shock to live in Paris after London. The generosity and warm friendship of my London circle was all over. In Paris it was everyone for themselves and knives drawn. It was a closed world, and more and more the New Wave was, for me, who had come out of a very politicized community, a bit too "right wing anarchist." I worked a bit on the *Cahiers du cinéma* but everyone was on their guard. (99)[4]

To see the *Cahiers* group cast as "anarchistes de droite" certainly goes against a lot of main-line, especially English-language histories of the period. But the fact is that *Cahiers* group were very slippery politically. Richard Brody's recent biography of Godard, for instance, is fairly explicit about the sometimes frighteningly reactionary elements of the young Jean-Luc, going so far as to recall how as a child in WWII Switzerland he "cheered on the advances of the German army and lamented its reversals" (6), and how the novelist interviewed by the Jean Seberg character in *À bout de souffle* is named for the right-wing philosopher and novelist Jean Parvulesco, who Brody calls "his Geneva friend" (62). Hélène Logier has followed this Parvulesco connection up in great detail, chronicling the essays on the New Wave that Parvulesco wrote for the Falangist film magazine *Primer Plano* during the Franco era, essays that argued that the New Wave's films were "profondément imprégnés d'idéaux d'extrême droite," profoundly impregnated by the ideals of the extreme right (130). She wrote that in one essay Parvulesco published in 1960, "According to him, the members of the New Wave were impregnated by an 'intellectual fascism.' Their philosophy was nihilism. They put the mentality of youth up on the screen, having a great love of freedom and fascinated by death, violence, and crazy love.... He felt that the films of the New Wave were anti-conformist, anti-communist, anti-democratic and anti-socialist" (134).[5] John Hess argued something similar (although slightly more gentle) about the entire *Cahiers* group of the 1950s in his massive critique of their legacy (published in the first two issues of the radical American film magazine *Jump Cut*), writing that "*La politique des auteurs* was, in fact, a justification, couched in aesthetic terms, of a culturally conservative, politically reactionary attempt to remove film from the realm of social and political concern, in which the progressive forces of the Resistance had placed all the arts in the years immediately after the war" (19). André Bazin's role as a wise father figure trying to instil some reason into his passionate young charges is well known, but there is a political aspect to this as well. Bazin was, after all, a Jacques-Maritain-inflected left Catholic, a Personalist, and a lot of his attempts to counter some of the cinephilic-auteurist enthusiasm in the pages of the magazine clearly evince a strong trace of the spiritually inflected left politics that defined the work of Maritain and his fellow travellers (that said, Hess sees Personalism as part of the problem when it comes to the politics of the 1950s *Cahiers*). Putting this in more generational than explicitly political terms, upon the 1972 release of his *Retour d'Afrique* Bernard Weiner pointed out in the pages of *Jump Cut* that "Tanner is not part of the 'youth explosion' of film makers. He's 45 and paid his dues in England nearly two decades ago (working in the Free Cinema movement, and later as an editor at the BBC)" (4). It really is a mistake to think of Tanner as some sort of south-eastern adjunct of the French New Wave.

At the institutional level, however, Tanner is inseparably linked to his contemporaries in the Nouveau cinéma suisse. He had been active in agitation for a properly constituted federal film body as early as 1962. He recalled the beginnings of his agitation and organization in his 2009 memoir *Cine-mélanges*:

> I summarize: in 1962, a law to support filmmaking came into effect [a referendum calling for federal support of filmmaking had passed in 1956], to be applied by a federal commission, then in formation. Of 27 members, no filmmakers. The various filmmakers who worked in the country, no more than five or six, asked to be given at least one seat on the commission. But, in order to do that, you had to represent an association. We hastily created l'Association suisse des réalisateurs, in which I took the lead and then the chairmanship. *In extremis* the administration accepted to give us a spot and I found myself among the members of this newly elected body.
>
> The nightmare began…. We had closely followed the emergence of new filmmaking practices in France, Czechoslovakia, Quebec, Poland, Brazil, and elsewhere. The cinema was in an energized state all over the world, and of this the 26 other members of the Commission fédérale du cinéma apparently knew nothing. (22–23)[6]

The law was nevertheless modestly successful in that it created some support for indigenous cinema, particularly in French-speaking Switzerland, including the weekly newsreel *Ciné-Journal Suisse*. This was no mean feat; up to this point most filmmaking in Switzerland had been done in German. Tanner, in *Ciné-mélanges*, states polemically that "In French-speaking Switzerland, there had never been any cinema" (129); elsewhere in that book he writes of the 1960s that "during this period, there was absolutely nothing in Switzerland" (42).[7] Freddy Buache's massive history *Le Cinéma Suisse : 1898–1998* tells a slightly different story, although it is clear that Swiss filmmaking in French was, until the 1960s, a pretty marginal affair. But Buache doesn't see the 1962 law as having changed all that much, writing in *Le Cinéma Suisse* that it "is terribly restrictive, in that it only foresees supporting 'documentary, cultural or educational' films ... and that it excludes works of fiction" (32).[8] His overall assessment is that "The delayed birth of Swiss cinema was thus primarily less a financial problem than a problem of the intellectual and spiritual climate" (16).[9] One attempt to remedy this spiritual and intellectual crisis was Tanner's creation of a collective of filmmakers. In 1968, he founded, with Goretta, Soutter, Jean-Louis Roy and Jean-Jacques LaGrange (replaced, Buache notes, by Yves Yersin in 1971), the production collective known as Le Groupe cinq, the Group of Five. "The date was not just an accident," Tanner recalled the survey he answered as part of Antoine de Baecque's book *Cinéma 68*, published by the *Cahiers du cinéma* in 2008. "We could thus get our hands on a tool, in fact, a branch of television. We had no desire to create a film industry, to make commercial films.... But in the spirit of the times, we could invent everything from scratch: the means of production, the working relationships between the technicians, who were all very young" (108).[10] This new means of production was solidified in Groupe cinq's agreement with Société Suisse de Radiodiffusion (SSR), the public French-language television channel (now TSR, Télévision Suisse-Romande) to support the work of each member of the group, in exchange for broadcast rights. For those engaged with Swiss cinema, Groupe cinq is legendary, and it was certainly a big deal at the time. A 1974 issue of the Swiss film review *Cinema* was devoted entirely to the group, reprinting (in both French and German) interviews with and essays about the key members. That dossier recalls that the first two accords were for four films in 1969–70 with SSR contributing CHF 60,000 per production, and then for three films in 1971–72 with SSR contributing CHF 80,000 per production; Tanner's *Charles mort ou vif* was part of the first accord, and his *Retour d'Afrique* (which he made in between *La Salamandre* and *Le Milieu du monde*) was part of the second. The key provision of the agreement was control. Claude Vallon recalled in that *Cinema* dossier that "the principal advantage that the accord between Groupe cinq and television offers (especially for Tanner) is precisely to be able to not have to worry about control over the production. Once the subject is agreed upon, the director is the producer of his own film, and he spends the full CHF 60,000" (6).[11] Part of what was emerging here, then, was indeed a cinéma d'auteur along the lines of what had emerged in French cinema in the 1960s. Tanner has certainly acknowledged this nouvelle vague connection in his memoirs, even though elsewhere he had spoken in less-than-admiring terms about those glory days. Czechoslovakia, Quebec, Poland, and Brazil were just as important, if not more important, to Tanner and the reforms he was part of. Less than a simple cousin of the French nouvelle vague, Tanner was part of an international reconsideration of the connections between the artist, the state, and the political landscape that formed them.

During this period John Berger was reconfiguring his own work as a novelist and critic along lines that were very close to Tanner's sensibilities. Berger had begun his career as a painter in the 1950s, but shortly thereafter he began writing art criticism for various London papers and soon became disenchanted by his potential as an artist. His switch to criticism, and eventually to poetry and novels, was informed both by an intense socialist commitment and desire to recuperate the mantle of realism, both in aesthetic and political terms. His first books bear out these dual aesthetic and political commitments very clearly: the novel *A Painter of Our Time* (1958) and the art reviews and essays collected in *Permanent Red* (1960). Whereas Tanner spent the 1960s trying to forge a space where filmmakers could work independently, during this period Berger was thinking in more theoretical terms about the connection between art and collective action. Distinguishing the criticism he wanted to write from faddish, trend-setting reviewing, he wrote in the introduction to *Permanent Red* that "proper criticism is more modest. First, you must answer the question: What can art serve here and now? Then you criticize according to whether the works serve that purpose or not. You must beware of the believing that they can always do so directly. You are not simply demanding propaganda" (15). Propaganda, for Berger, was an insidious, although characteristic element, of modernity. "I am a modern painter, and I am so because I have lived all my life with propaganda – the problem of facing other men as a man" his protagonist Janos Lavin says in *A Painter of Our Time*. "I would like to write about this some time. I know about it. But now we are going to the cinema" (142). That novel imagined a socialist Hungarian painter living in London right before the 1956 Soviet invasion; straddling the traditional and the radical, he finds himself inescapably at the margins of the gallery world. His problem is not political in the conventional sense; although he is an anti-Stalin socialist, his difficulties come neither from the anti-communists in Britain nor the commissars in the east. Rather, he is a humanist, someone who wants to protect the individual conscience, a conscience that also calls people to do right by the collectives of which they are inevitably a part, from the ravages of a materialistic bourgeois society. Berger's manifesto from this period – one that defines, however unconsciously, the critical work he was doing in books such as *Permanent Red* as well as *The Success and Failure of Picasso* (1965) and *The Moment of Cubism* (1969) – seems to me to be voiced by Janos:

> What we mean by Socialism can be clearly defined in economic terms. But the effects, the changes in man that Socialist economic relations can bring about, are so numerous that each can make his own list.
>
> I live, work for a state where the more honest the son the less the mother need fear; where every worker has a sense of responsibility, not because he is appealed to but because he has responsibility; where the only élite are the old; where every tragedy is admitted as such; where women are not employed to use their sex to sell commodities – finally this is a much greater degradation than prostitution; where the word freedom has become unnecessary because every ability is wanted; where prejudice has been so overcome that every man is able to judge another by his eyes; where every artist is primarily a craftsman; where every Imperialist leader has been tried by his former victims and, if found guilty, been shot by a contingent of his own General Staff whose lives have been spared for this purpose. (117)

It may seem too simple to assume that a character in a novel is speaking for his author, but the correspondence with Berger's own thought here is quite strong. Discussing Gramsci's question "what is a man?" in *Permanent Red* (published two years after *A Painter of Our Time*, although collecting essays written throughout the 1950s), Berger first points out that the question really means "what can a man become?" and then writes that "Up to about 1920 artists could answer this question confidently without necessarily being socialists. Since then, if they are to reach a satisfactory answer, socialism has become increasingly necessary for them" (209). I don't know of anywhere in his critical writing where he mentions the responsibility of workers, the élite of the old, or the prospect of firing squads for imperialists, but the matter of women's sex being employed to sell commodities, and indeed women's sexuality *as* commodity, is a veritable obsession, running most strongly throughout his two most widely read books of the 60s and 70s: *The Success and Failure of Picasso* (which appeared five years after *A Painter of Our Time*) and *Ways of Seeing* (1972). On the matter of artists and craftsmanship, a short essay in *Permanent Red* simply called "The Glut" laments the degree to which there is just too much art in galleries, and seems to long for the ethic of the craftsperson: "their artists clearly haven't the essential creative imagination to have anything to say. Many of them might be excellent craftsmen if they were working under another artist's direction – but that is a different question" (50). There is enough correspondence between this passage and Berger's work overall, and especially the work Berger was doing at basically the same time, to make an assumption of rough correspondence seem more than warranted.

This passage from *A Painter of Our Time* is, of course, supremely optimistic verging towards the romantic, and that sort of philosophical optimism seems to be no small part of what Berger brought to the "Berger-Tanner" relationship. *La Salamandre* is about a pair of friends, one a politically committed Geneva journalist who takes on a lot of hack work, and the other a slightly dreamy novelist who lives in the countryside with his wife and daughter. It is not hard to imagine that having an autobiographical character: Tanner, the founder of the Groupe cinq, the guy who gets people jobs doing *engagé* cultural work; Berger, the writer who relentlessly seeks a rigorously utopian version of socialism. This combination of the hard-headed detail work and the pensive dream-work would also come together for Tanner, in a most unlikely place: the streets of Paris in May 1968. Berger's writing of that period seems to provide a template for the way both men understood those events.

Cinéma selon les soixante-huitards

"One day, in a discussion with a class at a film school, I asked the students the following: 'Do you know why we say that continuity cutting is "rightist" and that montage is "leftist"?' Silence rang out. Thirty years earlier, somebody would have had the answer and today, it's like I had been speaking Chinese."[12] – Alain Tanner, *Ciné-mélanges* (48)

"The need for self-conscious 'shockers' is the natural complement to the handing out of 'inoffensive' platitudes." – John Berger, reporting on the "Free Cinema" program of documentaries, which included Tanner and Goretta's *Nice Time* (1957), for *Sight and Sound* (12)

The place "les événements" of May 1968 in the historical imagination of the Euro-American left is practically sacrosanct. And furthermore, the period's impact on Film Studies – first in French via the *Cahiers du cinéma* and later in English, mostly via *Screen* – is formidable, more so even than in sociology or literary studies.[13] I confess that I have always found this a little strange. I don't doubt that 1968 was a year full of political instability in the capitalist and communist spheres alike. Furthermore, there is no doubt the alliance between workers and students that characterized the best moments of the strikes of May 1968 in Paris was a very exciting realization of leftist idealism. Nor is there any doubt the "États généraux du cinéma," an event held as a kind of sidebar to the strikes that declared a new place for cinema in a rebuilt society, was evidence that, in Tanner's words, "Le cinéma était en état d'ébullition dans le monde."[14] But the immediate aftermath of May '68 was not characterized by a transformation of western capitalism; it was not even characterized by a change of the political scene in France. However unstable his government may have seemed at the height of the strikes, Charles de Gaulle's UDR, it cannot be said often enough, not only won election of June 1968 but massively increased its share of deputies in the Assemblé nationale (it held nearly three-fourths of the seats at the end of the election, a feat without precedent in post-Revolutionary French history). Tanner told Lenny Rubenstein in a 1975 interview that "One mustn't forget that there were ten million strikers, but nobody was prepared to seize power; the political structure was taken by surprise, as if in a play" (103). Thus it seems obvious that glorifications of the period are to be avoided. Rather, May '68 and its immediate aftermath need to be approached just as Berger and Tanner have done throughout their films, their writings, and their interviews on the subject, not only through the simple subject matter work they did together, but also through their sense of what was really important about those days, as well as interventions on the degree to which formal matters can be politically transformative. Jim Leach writes that "The difficulties in keeping alive the spirit of May in a hostile environment are central to all of Tanner's films" (16), but it's important to understand just what part of that "spirit of May" did indeed remain throughout Berger and Tanner's oeuvre.

One way that this spirit of May manifests itself in Berger and Tanner's work is at the level of form, and this is a matter that I will return to again and again throughout my discussions of *La Salamandre*, *Le Milieu du monde*, and *Jonas qui aura 25 ans dans l'an 2000*. The connection of formal practice to revolutionary idealism was, during this period, a crucial matter for Tanner, and for Berger as well. Tanner recalls in *Ciné-mélanges* that:

> In the 1960s and 70s, I read a lot of theoretical work on cinema, as well as that of Brecht on the theatre, which you could apply perfectly to our work. We were in the period where folks were trying to deconstruct the traditional narrative that reigned in dominant cinema, and to then reconstruct it along another schema, which is to say to pull out the elements of the story, to put them back in order and in perspective, so that they could clearly create their meaning, according to the rules of the now relevant dialectic, rather than those of classical dramaturgy. (82)[15]

It is crucial to note, however, that Tanner never fully abandoned this classical sensibility, never crossed over fully into the realm of the anti-narrative militant cinema in the way that, say, Jean-Luc Godard did during his Dziga-Vertov period. Those films, most of which Godard co-directed with Jean-Pierre Gorin and all of which they signed under the name "Groupe Dziga Vertov," were not narrative in any way. Instead they integrated interviews, direct address to the camera, extremely artificial single-shot sequences, etc. It is the part of Godard's work where he stands the furthest from conventional cinema. He didn't make that many films like that, and he made them all pretty close together; in all they are *Pravda* (1969), *British Sounds*

(1969), *Vent d'est* (1970), *Lotte in Italia* (1970, and *Vladmir et Rosa* (1971). Until recently they had been basically impossible to see, although they are now available as part of DVD set called "Godard: El Grupo Dziga Vertov," issued by the invaluable Barcelona-based company Intermedio (they have Spanish subtitles only). None of these films have been released on DVD in France or North America, and despite Intermedio's good efforts they still strike me as excellent examples of Tanner's sardonic remark in *Ciné-mélanges* that "All the militant films of that period have become invisible today."[16] They are invisible today in large part because so many of them are so intensely dated, wedded inseparably to the fleeting moment of revolutionary idealism that produced them. Tanner argues that something similar is true of the films that he made with Berger, as I will discuss in due time. But I think that Tanner is being too hard on himself with that assessment because I agree with Jim Leach's sense that "Tanner's response to cinematic and political difficulties foregrounded by the failure of the May revolution was neither to break completely with the existing cinematic models nor to adapt the 'popular' genres to new political ends" (21). The three feature films that Berger and Tanner made together are excellent examples of this sort of "middle course" between combative obscurantism and bland commercialism, between the Groupe Dziga Vertov and a commercial film about politics such as Costa Gavras' *Z*,[17] which is exactly the way that Dimitriu formulates his cinema: "Tanner, lui, se situe quelque part entre les deux" (32).

This hanging on to popular forms is, of course, the heart of an actual Brechtian practice – that is to say that it follows the writings and plays of Bertolt Brecht himself. It's easy to lose sight of this if you read some of the writings or see some of the films of his more diehard advocates. Trying to explain the self-awareness of *Jonas* in her *New Yorker* review of the film, Pauline Kael wrote that "I hesitate to invoke the word 'Brechtian' because, except for a few sixties films by Godard, that has generally meant a didactic pain" (76). I cannot help but chuckle with some recognition at that assessment, but I think it is important to pay closer attention to critics like the late Robin Wood, who writes that:

> Brecht's plays (at least those which I am familiar with), never *cleanly* dissociate themselves from the basics of "Realist" theatre:

they retain strong narrative lines, with identifiable and evolving characters, and they don't wholly preclude a certain degree of identification. The principle of "alienation," or, as I prefer, distanciation ("making the familiar strange"), operates to counter this without obliterating it (to do so altogether seems virtually impossible within a narrative work): the plays operate on a fine balance between sympathetic involvement and analytical (or critical) distance. (13, italics his)

This is completely consistent with the experience of seeing Brecht's plays performed, an experience that will always include a fair bit of realist representation. The narrative line of, say *Threepenny Opera*, is just as strong as its eighteenth-century predecessor, John Gay's *Beggar's Opera*, and it no more obliterates spectacle than Gay's work does; it just insists that its narrative, and its sense of spectacle, be understood for what they are. Moreover, this acceptance of narrative illusionism is consistent with Brecht's own writings, so important to Tanner (and, as we will see in the discussion of *Une Ville à Chandigarh* in the next chapter, to Berger) during this period. Defending epic theatre from charges that it's boring, Brecht said in a 1949 dialogue with Friedrich Wolf (published in 1952, as part of the East German publication *Theaterarbeit*) that "It is not true, though it is sometimes suggested, that epic theatre (which is not simply undramatic theatre, as is also sometimes suggested) proclaims the slogan: 'Reason this side, Emotion (feeling) that'" (*Brecht on Theatre*, 227).[18] Brecht's practice is a genuinely populist one, an approach to aesthetics that integrates the real power of popular forms (such as realist-illusionist spectacle) at the same time that it tries to move *beyond* them. It does not go to the side of popular forms; it helps them to move forward. But it does so by rejecting the simplicity both of "light" entertainment *and* audience-flattering liberal reformism. Indeed, Tanner was quite explicit about his hostility to the latter in a 1978 interview he gave to *El Pais's* Fernando Trueba and Carlos S. Boyero; echoing Jean Narboni's denunciation of *Z* in the *Cahiers du cinéma*, he told them that "For me the films of Tavernier or Costa Gavras are the worst in all of cinema. This commercial, consumption cinema, which falls along the lines of Hollywood but with leftish political ideas, seems to me detestable" (12).[19]

When Tanner recalls reading theoretical material during the 60s and 70s, he is clearly referring to the reborn *Cahiers du cinéma*, a magazine that in the wake of 1968 vigorously threw off its traditional mantle as a haven for intense cinephilia and adopted a series of militant positions that often had a distinctly Maoist, but also frequently Brechtian, flavour. And Jean-Louis Comolli, then co-editor of the magazine, was clearly an important figure for Tanner. When Lenny Rubenstein asked him about the slow pace of *Le Milieu du monde*, he replied that "There have been studies published in France, by Jean-Louis Comolli amongst others in *Cahiers du cinéma*, about the relations between ideology and technique. I did a lot of research as to the language in this film, and my presentation of the theories may be schematic" (99). I take Jim Leach's point that "Tanner's political perspective corresponds more closely to that of the *Positif* critics than to that of the New Wave filmmakers" of *Positif*'s arch-rival magazine, the *Cahiers du cinéma* (15). But by the time we arrive at 1968 the only new-waver still actively contributing to the *Cahiers* was Jacques Rivette, who was always something of a maverick in the group. And anyway, Leach is referring here to the 1950s *Cahiers'* advocacy of André Bazin's belief in the aesthetic and spiritual supremacy of a cinema based on long takes and mise-en-scène. Tanner was indeed impatient with this, just as he was impatient with the scene he discovered in 1950s Paris overall. The situation of the 1968 *Cahiers* is significantly different, and much closer to Tanner's overall political outlook, especially during the period of the late 1960s and 70s. For the most part the "anarchistes de droite" had either changed their politics dramatically (as Godard did) or stopped writing for the magazine (as Truffaut had, although he remained on the board). Texts by Jean-Louis Comolli and Jean Narboni, who together edited the magazine from 1966 to 1971, were seminal in changing the magazine's orientation towards explicitly political work, especially their two-part "Cinéma/idéologie/critique," published in nos. 216 and 217 (October and November 1969). The first part of that essay was translated in 1974 and is still widely used in English-language undergraduate courses as an example of the militant criticism of the 1970s.[20] It is in part one of the essay that the two famously declared that "*tout film est politique*," and that moreover, the realism of classical Hollywood was always political in, ahem, a certain way. "But the tools and techniques of filmmaking are a part of 'reality' themselves, and furthermore 'reality' is nothing but an expression of the prevailing ideology. Seen this light, the classic theory of cinema that the camera is an impartial instrument which grasps, or rather is impregnated by, the world in its 'concrete reality' is an eminently reactionary one" ("Cinema/Ideology/Criticism," 30).[21] Tanner wrote in exactly these terms in a text based on interviews given around the release of *Le Milieu du monde*. He wrote there that "It has today become evident that the technique of a story is inseparably linked to its ideology, and not only to the story itself.... It [the ideology] corresponds exactly to the type of relations established by an industry looking for the biggest audience possible" ("Le pourquoi dire," 14).[22] The key connection here is via form; the problem of ideology is in the "*technique* du récit" and not just the subject matter of the film. Tanner affirms this early in the same text when he says, simply "Le contenu est tout entier dans la forme" (13), a formulation he would return to in interviews again and again. This matter of form is a crucial one for the film theory that emerges in the wake of May 1968; overall, it is really an attempt to reclaim the mantle of formalism for a political project that had been renewed by the idealism of those days of May.

The most ambitious of this material is probably the massive text simply titled "Montage," published in no. 210 (March 1969), which its introduction describes as "not a debate, nor a round table, nor a collection of articles, nor a single discourse in many voices, but a 'montage' of critical fragments" (17).[23] Its "authors" (I tremble in using the word!) were Narboni, Jacques Rivette, and Sylvie Pierre, and the films they discussed included work by Sergei Eisenstein, Dziga Vertov, D.W. Griffith, Kenji Mizoguchi, Jean Rouch, Pierre Perrault, Alain Resnais, Phillipe Garrel, Godard, Straub-Huillet, Vera Chytilova, Fernando Solanas, and John Cassavetes. But a lot of this theoretical work has, like Godard's Groupe Dziga Vertov films, taken on the air of the dated. Its persistence is practically an anthropological issue, a matter of its ability to illustrate a more idealistic and committed time in film criticism and aesthetics. What was all that stuff about montage being leftist but continuity editing being reactionary? Ah yes, every film is political....

It's easy to be so dismissive, but Tanner was a serious intellectual and it's clear that he was reading pretty widely in this material. Because if you do read widely then there is some very intellectually nourishing stuff to be found. Comolli wrote a great, two-part essay (published in *Cahiers du cinéma* 209 and 211, February and April 1969) called "Le détour par le direct" that enunciates very clearly the political excitement that was part and parcel of the rise of lightweight camera gear in the late 50s and 60s and which, like the "Montage" text, draws on a *very* wide range of films to illustrate not only a technical shift but an ethical, political, and theoretical one as well; I'll have cause to discuss both essays in more detail in the next chapter, when I talk about the television films Tanner made in collaboration with Berger. Indeed, the sheer cinematic voraciousness of the "Montage" essay is an fine example of this theoretical moment's intellectual vitality, as is Sylvie Pierre's refreshingly hard-nosed assessment that "what you can, on one hand, call in Eisensteinian montage 'progressive' is paradoxically that which is most dictatorial: movements from one shot to another that preclude the spectator from ever escaping reason, because of the need to put the shot in a position of reflexive distance" (25).[24] This is valuable for understanding the relationship that Tanner and Berger's films have with 70s film theory for two reasons. One is that, as Jim Leach says, "'Brechtian' cinema is normally associated with 'montage' … and this approach is not absent from Tanner's films. But their basic unit is the shot-sequence, which is more usually associated with a contemplative cinema based on a Bazinian respect for the integrity of time and space" (42). But Tanner, in his "pourquoi dire" text, written for the published screenplay of *Le Milieu du monde*, distinguishes between "le montage à l'intérieur d'une scène ou simplement entre les scènes" (17), noting that in that film he was attached to the second. Both are montage, though, different enunciations of the same belief in complexity, dialectics, and, as Tanner writes there, "un travail de déconstruction à opérer sur le langage traditionnel" (17). I will discuss this "montage of long takes" in more detail in the chapters on the feature-narrative films Berger and Tanner made together, especially *Le Milieu du monde* and *Jonas*. Furthermore, as Sylvie Pierre helps us to understand, montage is, in some forms, just as oppressive, just as manipulative, as découpage, just as long takes can, chez Tanner and Berger, be self-reflexive and politically charged in a way that is fully consistent with the "spirit of montage" that Narboni, Rivette, and Pierre were trying to explore in their text. This insight of Pierre's is also important for Berger and Tanner's cinema because it presents reason as something that must, from time to time, be escaped from. *La Salamandre, Le Milieu du monde,* and *Jonas* are self-aware, challenging films, but they are not didactic, not dictatorial. They allow for emotion, for humour, for the possibility of occasional escape from reason and into the realm of passion. And that sort of slippage, really, is everywhere present in the *Cahiers* of the late 1960s and 1970s, just as it was in Brecht's own writings and interviews on the theatre. By *ideology*, Comolli and Narboni seem to mean something that is flawed, tentative, *human*. In the second part of "Cinéma/idéologie/critique" they write that *"cinema is an ideological product*; its defining and active field is ideology, and not science" (148; emphasis in the original); elsewhere they write that "A camera filming itself … contributes nothing in the way of science nor theory, or even 'materialist cinema'; the most one can say of it is that it is a reflection of a reflection, the ideology mirrored in itself" (150).[25] This is not exactly a model of lucid reasoning, but it is an attempt to lay out a separation between the cold clarity of science and the tricky, slippery, and ultimately pleasurable actions of the human spirit, of which ideology is a formative part. Furthermore, it is in the second part of Jean-Pierre Oudart's "Suture" essay that we find the statement (appended at the end "pour corriger quelque peu cet extrémisme") that when it comes to reading a film, "something is said which can only be discussed in erotic terms, and which is itself given as the closest representation of the actual process of eroticism" ("Cinema and Suture," 47).[26] This kind of intellectualized eroticism is at the very heart of Berger and Tanner's *Le Milieu du monde*, and it is certainly part of *La Salamandre* and *Jonas* as well. So when one moves beyond the awkward language and occasional self-confessed *extrémisme*, it is possible to find some surprisingly passionate and still very relevant material in the theoretical writings of the late 60s and 70s *Cahiers*. Tanner and Berger's films are greatly enriched for the effort.

Beyond these formal and theoretical innovations that came in its wake, May '68 was also important to Tanner, of course, because he was present for a lot of the strikes themselves. In 1968 he was working as a journalist for SSR, making documentaries all over Switzerland and throughout Europe and elsewhere (Belgium, Wales, Israel). His film on the Paris strikes was called *Le Pouvoir dans la rue*; it was broadcast on 6 June 1968, and its opening voice-over states that its shooting began when the strikes had been on for two weeks (Tanner recalls in *Cine-mélanges* that "J'avais filmé tout le mois de mai 1968 à Paris" [43]). Christian Dimitriu argues that the film is "precious for Tanner, in that May '68 is the realization of a long questioning of society, of himself and his work as a filmmaker, and the beginning of a new creative period. Precious for television and for researchers, because the images are rich in information. The film is formally more sober, with an agile camera, a minimum of tracking shots and zooms, and quick editing" (26).[27]

I take Dimitriu's point here, but to my mind *Le Pouvoir de la rue* is most important precisely because of its sobriety and its tendency to plunge deeply into the details of the how students especially plan to transform their existence (the film centres on actions at and around the Sorbonne). Frédéric Bas is, I believe, a lot closer to the mark when he writes of *La Pouvoir dans la rue* (in his afterword to Tanner's *Ciné-mélanges*) that "This is not to say that the filmmaker was a militant; very much the opposite is the case. In Paris in May '68, he was working as a reporter for Swiss television. He was almost forty years old and he had for quite a while rejected the high priests of the extreme left and their leaden ideologies. Unlike others, he didn't think – and has never thought – that 'the camera is a gun'" (162).[28] Indeed, the film doesn't really go all verité and montagey until towards the end, when we do indeed get fairly visceral and crisply edited footage of night-time confrontations with police. The bulk of it is made up of an examination of the alternative university that students were trying to set up. Those students, as well as sympathetic faculty members, hold forth to Tanner's camera about the degree to which universities are or aren't compatible with the capitalist system, on the power relationships between teachers and students, and the role that students can or can't play in the formation of a fully functioning socialist society. Looking back on his memories of 1968, Tanner told the *Cahiers du cinéma*'s N. Heinic in a 1977 interview that "68 (or really May 68) was a big piece of street theatre.... And what was important, more so than 'les événements,' was the fallout, simply in the way that this theatre staged the hopes and allowed the flowering of hidden desires, which since then have stayed at the surface" ("An Interview with Alain Tanner," 42).[29] He said something very similar thirty years later (and forty years after '68) in *Ciné-mélanges*: "May '68 in Paris was a big *happening*, a big piece of street theatre, playful, a liberation of speech" (128).[30] He basically said the same thing in English, in that 1974 interview with Lenny Rubenstein, where he struck a more sceptical tone: "May '68 in Paris was an enormous event; it may have had no political significance but it was a tremendous happening.

I covered the events for Swiss television – people were performing revolution without being shot at. All the ideas germinating since then show how important May '68 was for cultural and social life." (103). But *Le Pouvoir dans la rue* isn't about idealistic street theatre or performance at all. Instead, it is about the nuts and bolts of organization, the serious ideological and political implications inherent in education, and perhaps most importantly although more implicitly, the need to reconcile ideology – the assumptions that form our view of the world – with politics – the arrangement of resources, responsibilities, and power. It is about putting ideas into action.

Because of the way that *Le Pouvoir dans la rue* visualizes the complexities and ambiguities of ideologically complex political action, it belongs not alongside militant May '68 films liked the famed *ciné-tracts* that were shot and then projected during the strikes themselves, but alongside other Tanner television films such as *Les Trois belgique*. This was a work about events very similar to the strikes of May '68: disputes between Flemish and Walloon students at Université Catholique de Louvain.[31] It opens with protest footage that, if the voice-over were removed, would be indistinguishable from the protests at the Sorbonne in May. And it was broadcast a mere eight weeks before *Le Pouvoir dans la rue*, on 6 April 1968. *Les Trois belgique* is, formally, more conventional than *Le Pouvoir dans la rue*; it includes some talking heads with maps, explaining the geographical and linguistics splits in Belgium, and also has a lot more talking-heads-style debates between ostensibly opposing factions (here represented by a Walloon and a Flemish journalist, both speaking in French). But as these journalists are allowed to speak together and at length, both wind up being fairly self-critical; the Walloon journalist, for instance, notes that Flemings are a majority but have a minority complex, whereas the Walloons are a minority but behave like an entitled majority. Tanner also spends time with a family whose young son is in a bi-lingual school but who tells his interviewers that he rarely speaks Flemish for more than an hour a day, as well as with a Walloon priest assigned to a Flemish parish. The portrait that emerges is one defined by paradox, uneasy but sometimes hopeful attempts at mixing, and most importantly an uncertain future. *Les Trois belgique* is very close to *Le Pouvoir dans la rue*, and just as strongly a part of the spirit of '68, if not exactly of the spirit of May, in that through a sober focus on detail and complexity, it imagines not only the world transformed but also the process of transformation.

I allude here to Berger's famous 1969 essay "The Moment of Cubism," collected in his anthology *The Sense of Sight*. He wrote there that "The Cubists imagined the world transformed, but not the process of transformation" (171). He was picking up there on some of the work that he had done in his equally celebrated and reviled critical biography *The Success and Failure of Picasso* (1965), in which he tried to take account of the degree to which Picasso's true significance has been distorted by the myths that surround him. "The Moment of Cubism" is more broadly philosophical, although like *The Success and Failure of Picasso* it is split between genuine admiration for the radical aspirations of the revolutionaries who are its subject and palatable displeasure with the ways that they have failed to understand that revolutionary idealism in all its complexity and ambiguity. Berger could very well be·talking about the stone-throwing student militants of May '68 when he wrote in "The Moment of Cubism" that "the Cubists – during the moment of Cubism – were unconcerned about the personalized human and social implications of what they were doing. This, I think, is because they had to simplify. The problem before them was so complex that their manner of stating it and their trying to solve it absorbed all their attention" (183). Tanner's televisual representation of May '68 is looking for a way past this kind of absorption, towards an understanding of how these events would affect the lives of individual students and faculty members and how it would affect the everyday lives of the people of France. That concern for "the personalized human and social implications" of politics is a driving force of the films that Berger and Tanner made together, and this kind of engagement with these kinds of unpredictably human rather than systematic matters can also be found, as I have tried to show, in some of the theoretical material that Tanner was reading.

Berger has also addressed the legacy of 1968 explicitly, although the fact that he was doing so five years after the events rather than at the moment of their unspooling accounts for the fact that his tone is more defeated than Tanner's in *Le Pouvoir dans la rue*. Writing in 1973, Berger recalled in an essay called "Between Two Colmars" (collected in *About Looking*) how "In 1968, hopes, nurtured more or less underground for years, were born in several places in the world and given their names: and in the same year, these hopes were categorically defeated. This became clearer in retro-spect. At the time many of us tried to shield ourselves from the harshness of the truth" (127). Berger was actually writing there about Grünewald's sixteenth-century altarpiece depicting the life of Christ, a work of art that he believes embodies a very radical understanding of love, a vision at odds with a technocratic, "normalized" society. This essay, really, is a blueprint for *Le Milieu du monde*, a film that is precisely about the tensions between love, passion, and "normalization," and I will return to the essay in more detail in Chapter 3, by way of explaining just how closely linked to the memories of 1968 that film really is. But the vision of the possibilities of 1968 that Berger lays out in this "Between Two Colmars" text is also im-portant for coming to terms with the way that both Berger and Tanner understood these events and their legacy. No doubt that the possibilities that were released during that year were very radical. But an acceptance of the failure of that idealism comes with its own radical possibilities. "In 1963 the light in the other panels seemed to me frail and artificial," Berger writes of Grünewald's representation of Alsatian peasants fleeing across an empty, dark plain. "In 1973 I thought I saw that the light in these panels accords with the essential experience of light" (132). That kind of rigorous attention to the political, historical, and ethical quality of formal matters is consistent with a lot of idealism that we find in the pages of the *Cahiers* in the period directly following the strikes of May '68. Berger's understanding of the crisis at the heart of these images is transformed not by their subject matter but by his ability to read the image as a semi-abstract portrait of people looking for light *as such*, rather than inadequately realistic depiction of a part of Europe's historical narrative. But the reason that Berger is so valuable for a politically conscious theory and criticism is because he is un-willing to abandon criticism, unwilling to abandon what Susan Sontag, in the slightly cryptic final sentence of her 1964 essay "Against Interpretation," called the erotics of art (14), the sensation that occurs when two bodies – the viewer and the work of art – come into sensual, fully aware contact with one another. The following year Berger wrote in just these terms in *The Success and Failure of Picasso*, arguing that painting "is the most immediately sensu-ous of the arts. Body to body. One of them being the spectator's" (208). Berger's method – in his criticism, his novels, and his films – has always eschewed didacticism, focussing instead on just this fluid, shifting nature of understanding. He has shown throughout his career the insight that he offered upon reviewing one of Tanner's first films for the British film magazine *Sight and Sound* in 1957: cultivating righteous outrage over injustice by trying to "shock" the viewer or reader is a product of the same mindset that tries to normalize social relations by handing out bland platitudes. Art cannot change the world directly; that is mere propaganda. Berger, who like Jonas Lavin, has lived with propaganda for his entire life, rejects such sterilization. For him and Tanner, as for the *Cahiers* critics, "eroticism is the essentially figurative reality of the cinema that unfolds before us."

La Suisse

> "[As] a people, the Swiss are among the least revolutionary in Europe. They do not believe in *ex nihilo* constructions on an empty slate. Their temperament inclines them and their economy obliges them to reform what already exists and 'what's always worked,' rather than expose themselves to the risks of destroying best practices through abuse." – Denis de Rougemont, *La Suisse, ou l'histoire d'une peuple heureux* (135-36)[32]

> "The motif that ties together these diversified forms of inquiry over fifteen centuries is one of an enduring struggle to preserve the special freedom that came to characterize the self-governing alpine community – a struggle that pitted a handful of uniquely autonomous villages against feudalism, ecclesiastical tyranny, empire, corruption, foreign aggression, confederal integration, centralizing federalism, and finally against modernity itself as expressed in the aspirations of materialistic consumer capitalism in its most centralized, egalitarian form." – Benjamin Barber, *The Death of Communal Liberty: A History of Freedom in a Swiss Mountain Canton* (18)

Of course, France was not the only place where one has to look to understand the work that Tanner and Berger were doing together. During the

1960s and 70s both men lived in Geneva – Tanner's family had been established in Geneva for several generations, while Berger had moved there following his then-partner, who worked as an interpreter at the UN. It is a truism in Switzerland the Genèvois tend to look to France, being surrounded on all sides by it as they are. Certainly this is true to some extent of both Tanner – keenly interested in theoretical writing that was basically coming from France, and in the events of Paris 1968 – and of Berger – who now lives in a small alpine village in France, where he has produced major works of literature about the region. But like most truisms, this sense of the non-Swiss-ness of the Genèvois is not really true at all, and not true of the films that Tanner and Berger made either. We can see this in a few key areas: a politics that is caught between individual liberty and the very real demands of collectives; their interest in Switzerland's distinctive landscape and the politics that go along with that landscape; and the explanatory value of making an analogy between their work and that of two great (but very different) Swiss novelists, Charles-Ferdinand Ramuz and Jacques Chessex.

The tension in Tanner and Berger's work between individualist and collectivist sensibilities is, in many ways, at the heart of Swiss political life. Switzerland is made up of twenty-six cantons, to which most political responsibilities are devolved. As federations go, Switzerland is an exceptionally weak one, with the central government having relatively little authority beyond monetary, foreign, and military policy.[33] Denis de Rougemont, in his widely popular history of Switzerland, *La Suisse, ou l'histoire d'une peuple heureux*, imagines a chance meeting of "A peasant yodeler from Appenzell, a socialist worker from Berne, and a comfortable banker from Geneva" at some train station cafe, a meeting which he jokes is basically impossible. Although they would have little to say to each other, de Rougemont argues, "The three each know they are Swiss, not because of some common quality, whether natural, cultural (language, race, religion, character, etc.), which they would indeed be lacking, but because they are placed in the same *grouping* that we have called 'Swiss,' and which they agree to. And when you understand that, you understand federalism" (122).[34] I suspect that this looseness is part of what has led Tanner to say things like "The Swiss do not form a people, and do not have a culture, but attach themselves to a bunch of others" (*Ciné-mélanges* 84),or that "francophone Swiss grouchiness or this unfortunate 'Swissness' doesn't interest anybody anymore, least of all me"

(Dimitriu interview, 109).[35] For his part Berger, when I spoke with him on the phone on 20 October 2009, said that when he was living in Geneva in the 1960s and 70s he was interested in Switzerland just as anyone would naturally be interested in the place where they lived, but that the culture and history of the country were not especially important to his work of the period. And while he said in a 1985 interview with Richard Appignanesi that "it's very easy to knock Switzerland" and that there were some interesting aspects to the country (such as the fact that "this is a civilian people's army, one in which the soldiers keep their own arms, democratically, in their homes"), he finally concluded that "Switzerland, as a country, interests me less" than it did Tanner, whom he saw as having "a love/hate relationship" with the place (302). Indeed, Tanner told Lenny Rubenstein in that 1975 interview that "I think the center of my films will always be Switzerland" (104). But he was quite dismissive about the matter of Swiss identity with me during a phone conversation of 7 November 2009, even more so than he was in *Ciné-mélanges* or his interview with Dimitriu. He told me, in a very kind and jovial way, that the idea of Swiss culture meant absolutely nothing to him and that my desire to read his work as having very Swiss qualities was, basically, ridiculous. When I told him that his attitude towards Swiss identity sounded a lot like the way many English-Canadians, and many English-Canadian filmmakers for sure, talk about Canadian identity, he seemed delighted by the analogy. It is one that had already been offered by James Monaco, thirty-five years earlier, in his interview/article on Tanner about the North American release of *Le Milieu du monde*. Describing the state of French-language Swiss filmmaking in the early 1970s, Monaco wrote that ".The situation is not unlike the relationship between English-speaking Canadian filmmakers and the U.S. film industry, and Geneva may yet become just another training ground for workers in the French film industry" (31).

But just as I reject the idea that there is no English-Canadian identity outside of bland pieties about infinite diversity, I don't accept the idea that there is no Swiss identity outside of everyone agreeing that there is no Swiss identity. Barber writes that "the decentralization of Switzerland presents us with a paradox: in attracting us to the land as a fit subject for study, it repels our attentions with the reality that, by the very nature of its diversity and decentralization, it does not exist.... Diversity is Switzerland's essence, drawing our interest, yet defeating our inquiries" (11–12). But I am not easily defeated, and neither, I hasten to add, is Barber. One crucial aspect of the Swiss experience is the way that its political life has been a non-stop challenge to liberalism: sometimes from the right, and sometimes from the left. Barber argues that this is one of the reasons that those interested in political philosophy have a lot to learn from the Helvetian Confederation. He writes that his task in his study of the canton of Graubünden is to explain "the Swiss vision of political reality that, while it evolved within the familiar framework of Western political history, is strikingly inhospitable to the familiar predilections of Western political theory – at least in its liberal variations" (9). One of these challenges to liberalism, and the one that is most interesting for the purposes of Berger and Tanner's work together, is the way in which the needs of individuals are always held in difficult balance with those of collectives. This is at the very heart of *Le Milieu du monde* and *Jonas*, and it underwrites a great deal of *La Salamandre* as well; it is also an important part of the television work that the two did together. Barber agues that it is at the heart of Switzerland's political culture as well, writing that "in Switzerland, freedom has been understandable only in the context of community" (11). At the macro-political level "community" can be taken to mean canton, or, really, commune (in French, the word "commune" is often taken for city, town, or village), which de Rougemont is at pains to point out is the real basis of the Swiss political system (his history has a section called "La Commune : un petit état" [109–23]). But the word can also mean the sorts of informal collectives that people form for reasons of friendship or shared marginalization (as in *Jonas qui aura 25 ans en l'an 2000*), or simply the connections between strangers and casual friends which must be recognized and maintained in the name of social harmony (as in *La Salamandre*). Each of Berger and Tanner's films are about the quest for individual expression and fulfillment, but they are equally about the ties that (sometimes improbably, sometimes passionately) bind people together, and the dialectics between those ties and those individual quests. What is clear throughout is the inseparability of those two elements of the dialectic. In all of their work together, freedom is only understandable in the context of community.

Another aspect of Berger and Tanner's work together which is inescapably Swiss is the way that they have looked upon the nature of militant political action; it seems to be defined precisely by the seemingly contradictory politics embodied by the two quotes that open this section. In fact these two senses of Swiss politics are not contradictory at all; de Rougemont's belief that the Swiss are Europe's least revolutionary people is quite consistent with Barber's sense of Swiss history as being a constant struggle for freedom. The part of modern Swiss history that illustrates this most vividly was everywhere in the air, at least in Switzerland when Berger and Tanner were starting to work together: Jura.

The Jura mountains are in both France and Switzerland, and on the Swiss side, in the 1960s and 70s, they were synonymous with the spectre of political instability. From the period following the Napoleonic wars until 1974, most of the Swiss Jura had been part of the canton of Berne. Berne, however, is a German-speaking canton, and the population of the Jura is overwhelmingly francophone. Claude Hauser has written an invaluable history of the movement to separate Jura from Berne, which did indeed occur following an initial referendum on 23 June 1974, a series of smaller referenda in the next few years which allowed communes to opt out of the new canton, and a final referendum at the federal level in 1978 (the canton officially came into being on 1 January 1979). In that book *L'Aventure du Jura*, Hauser traces the progression from a basically conservative, sometimes ultra-Catholic semi-nationalism at the turn of the twentieth century to a left-of-centre movement which sought "contacts with 'brother' movements struggling for the defence of French-speaking minorities, be they in Belgium, Italy, or even in Quebec" (92).[36] It is necessary, though, to distinguish between, say, Quebec separatism and Jurassian "separatism." I put "separatism" in scepticism-quotes because, although that is the term (*séparatisme*) that is always used when discussing the push for a canton of Jura that was indeed separate from the canton of Berne, the idea that Jura would separate from Switzerland was more or less never part of the discourse. Indeed, very much the opposite was the case. Jura separatists often stressed their Swiss patriotism, sometimes pointing to the particularly strong tradition of military service in the area. One influential bloc of the movement styled itself as "helvétistes," and it was comprised mostly of young left-of-centre activists and intellectuals; in Quebec of the same era they'd have been péquistes, except that in the Swiss case the idea of leaving confederation was unthinkable.

I remind the reader here that Tanner had, in 1968, made a television film about the French-speaking minority in Belgium in that most *luttant* year of 1968, and I point out now that three years earlier he had also made a film for SSR called *L'Indépendance au loin* (broadcast on 30 September 1965), which dealt with the rise of "separatism" in Jura. Tanner's Jura film is structured basically as a montage, with interviews of a few young "separatists" being cross-cut with an anti-"separatist" cantonal councillor from Berne and the editor of the *Gazette de Lausanne*, who is basically supportive of "Jura Libre" but who has a slightly sceptical tone. Dimitru writes of the film that "what counts is not what is said but what is left out. It's above all through montage that the filmmaker expresses his point of view" (23).[37] I'm not quite sure what Dimitriu is alluding to here, although I suppose it could refer to Tanner's not reporting on the sectarian violence that had characterized a lot of mainstream media coverage of the Jura conflict. The film overall is basically pro-Jura-libre, with the Bernese councillor coming off as slightly uptight and paranoid, especially in contrast with the younger "separatists." But overall it is relatively even-handed and is, like *Le Pouvoir dans la rue*, a very sober analysis of a situation that, in the French and Swiss press of the 1960s and 70s, had been reported in a way that was often quite sensationalistic, emphasizing the violence of the movement (an example of this would be SSR's own report of 5 October 1963 on the bombing of the Berner Kantonalbank in Delémont, which would become the eventual capital of Canton Jura[38]). Tanner presents Jura as a place where identity is genuinely shifting and a struggle against centralization is definitely unfolding. But there are no revolutions here.

In the Switzerland of the 1960s and 70s, the term "Jura" connoted challenges to traditions of Swiss federalism along with an insurgent view of the possibilities of *la Francophonie*. Berger would go on to write about the region in these terms, in a 1978 essay called "Courbet and the Jura" (collected in *About Looking*). Here he is talking about the French side of the Jura mountains, but his view of it is certainly consistent with the significance that it held for most Swiss in the period leading up to the creation of the new canton. "To grow up surrounded by such rocks is to grow up in a region which is both lawless and irreducibly real," Berger writes of Courbet's sense of place as reflected in his paintings (137–38). A bit later Berger writes that "The hunter from the Jura, the rural democrat and the bandit painter came together in the same artist for a few years between 1848 and 1856 to produce some shocking and new images" (140). Is this spirit of rebellion, like the mixture of democracy, banditry, and self-sufficiency that Berger saw coming together in Courbet, so far from the idealism of May '68? I don't think so, and I am struck by the way that Tanner casually invoked the region when he reflected, in 2008, on the way that "les événements" had affected his work. Linking the success of *La Salamandre* to memories of the period, he recalled that "Just before, there was *Charles mort ou vif* which, made 500 kilometres from Pairs, with Jura as its setting, echoing it" (107).[39] *Charles mort ou vif*'s anti-hero Charles Dé not only retreats to the Jura mountains in search of an escape from his captain-of-industry life-style (he owns a successful watchmaker), but also recalls how his *horloger* grandfather was part of an anarchist commune in those mountains in the nineteenth century (Jura is equally famous for its traditions of radical politics and watch-making).

Thus it is not surprising that two of the three films that Berger and Tanner made together have some connection to "the Jura," although not explicitly to the canton of Jura. There is a long section in *La Salamandre* that takes place in an area that the film describes as the mountains on the French border; although this could very well be the canton of Vaud, Neuchâtel, Jura/Berne (this being 1971 a canton of Jura didn't exist yet), or Basel, this can only be the Jura mountains. *Le Milieu du monde* is set in the canton of Vaud, but again, the mountains that loom so heavy over the film's visuals are the Jura. Thus I am not trying to say that Berger and Tanner were dealing explicitly with the specifics of the Jura situation; you cannot glean, from the work they made together, a sense of whether Jura-Sud should or should not remain part of Canton Berne. Rather, their films visualize the mountains, not as some repository of timeless, unchanging purity, but instead as border zones, places where the culture is strongly anti-conformist and the politics, more often than not, quite unstable. To invoke the Jura as the signifier of such volatility is a very Swiss way of seeing the landscape.

Another Swiss author who saw the mountains as the home of a culture that was engaging with modernity head-on was Charles-Ferdinand Ramuz (1878–1947), probably French-speaking Switzerland's most celebrated novelist. Ramuz's place in Swiss letters is roughly equivalent to that of W.O. Mitchell's in English Canada, Dylan Thomas' in Britain, or J.M. Synge's in Ireland. His interest was in rural communities and the landscapes that surrounded them, and he moved beyond the romanticism of the late nineteenth century to offer a poetic but often mournful, and in many ways critical, vision of the ways that modernity was intruding on these places and the people who lived in them. One of his clearest literary heirs is, I would argue, John Berger. Berger's novels have evoked the Alpine peasantry in ways that owe a lot to the richly detailed dialogues of Ramuz, to the ways in which the Swiss master tries to lay out social and cultural realities by patiently evoking his characters as they chew over the details of their everyday lives. Illustrating the alienation of old men in from the village life that they spent a lifetime creating, Ramuz's 1946 short story "Vieux dans une salle à boire" (collected in *Les Servants et autres nouvelles*) describes the following scene:

> — Hey, Gailloud, you've got a son, you've even got two. What do you think of this?
> — They didn't turn out too bad.
> — Yeah, but tell us now, their habits, the way they dress. What do they smoke?
> — Cigarettes.
> — You see; me, the pipe, and you, the cigar. Cigarettes, they cost a lot, they don't last, and moreover, they're stringy. You light your pipe once and you stick it in the corner of your mouth, and you don't have to think about it anymore. What's more, a pack of tobacco costs forty centimes. Lads today spend up to a franc and more for a packet of these paper things that get burned up ten times as fast. Lads today, they smoke while they work. They always have their hands busy. I don't like that so much. You? (*Les Servants et autres nouvelles*, 27)[40]

Berger's 1979 novel *Pig Earth*, which evoked the lives of peasants in a French alpine village, has a very similar tendency to spin out larger themes of alienation and loneliness that stem from a change in everyday patterns of life: in how you spend your money, how busy you keep yourself, and your habits:

My sons won't work on the farm. They want to have free week-
ends and holidays and fixed hours. They like to have money in
their pockets so as to be able to spend it. They have gone to earn
money, and are mad about it. Michel has gone to work in a factory. Edouard has gone into commerce. (He used the term commerce because he did not wish to be harsh towards his youngest
son.) I believe they are mistaken. Selling things all day, working
forty-five hours a week in a factory is no life for a man – jobs like
that lead to ignorance. (74–75)

The analysis of how working patterns have changed in the young is, between
the two authors, basically opposite, even if their analysis of the importance
of money is more or less the same. What is striking, though, is Berger
and Ramuz's shared desire to evoke the spiritual crises of the European
peasantry through detailed accounts of their material existence. Where do
they work, how do they work, and why? How do they choose to spend their
money, and why? These are far from trivial questions, matters added in for
"local colour" or simply to flesh a character out. Berger inherits from Ramuz
an abiding engagement with the uses of realism for the purposes of vigorous, often critical social analysis.

But the Berger-Ramuz connection that is most relevant for the purposes
of a discussion of Berger's work in cinema is certainly that between Berger's
paean to the power of cinema "Ev'ry Time We Say Goodbye" (collected
in *Keeping a Rendezvous*, and originally published in English in *Sight and
Sound* in June 1991) and Ramuz's 1924 novel *L'Amour du monde*. The earlier
work concerns the arrival of cinema in a small mountain town in Vaud, and
the simultaneous appearance of a mysterious man whom the villagers believe is Jesus Christ. "It was towards the end of May; all the windows were
open. The man walked down the street: heads in each place turned to look
out those windows. He was tall, he was handsome, he had broad shoulders;
he had a full beard, he had long hair" (14).[41] This is how Berger, in that
"Ev'ry Time We Say Goodbye" essay, describes Giotto's chapel paintings
of the life of Christ: "Everywhere the expressions and gestures are charged
with intense meaning – like those in silent films. Giotto was a realist and
a great *metteur en scène*. The scenes, which follow one after another, are full
of stark material details, taken from life" (13). That's true of Ramuz's prose

in the passage I just quoted as well as throughout this book, a book that is about the simultaneous convergence of silent cinema and images of Christ. Berger and Ramuz also talk about cinema's power to transport in very similar terms. In "Ev'ry Time We Say Goodbye," we read:

> Imagine a cinema screen being installed in the Scrovegni Chapel and a film being projected on to it. Let's say the scene where the angel appears to the shepherds to announce Christ's birth at Bethlehem.… Watching this film, we would be transported *out* of the chapel to a field somewhere at night, where shepherds are lying in the grass. The cinema, because its images are moving, takes us *away* from where we are to the *scene of action*. (Action! murmurs or shouts the director to set the scene in motion.) Painting brings home. The cinema transports elsewhere. (14)

Sixty-six years earlier, Ramuz had discovered in cinema a very similar power. Early in *L'Amour du monde*, he writes of how at the cinema, "there, we start with a bit of piano, and then a window is opened, at the head of the theatre, on the world" (26).[42] Later on, recalling the sensations of the projector starting up, he writes that:

> Because now, the whole world is ours, if we want; all the centuries are ours, all of space; it's dizzying, but it's good, it makes us turn our heads, but it's good; in the heat, under the low sky, under the dark sky, between the houses with darkened windows; coming out around eleven o'clock, in small groups, man and woman, two or three young people together, girls and boys together, solitary men, solitary women; they are quiet, they talk all of the sudden.… (104)[43]

This collision between the insularity of the village or the chapel is, of course, a sort of echo of the collision between ancient religious imagery of Christ and the modernity of the cinematic image. In Berger's and Ramuz's work alike, this collision is creative, evocative of a world that is struggling to be born, struggling to reveal its riches. It is a rejoinder to critics of either Berger or Ramuz who would paint them as nostalgic or backward-looking, on the basis of passages that I quoted earlier. Both wrote novels that were defined by a dialectic between tradition and modernity, novels that were struggling, however incompletely, to evoke the synthesis that comes about when the two concepts come into collision.

Although one of Tanner's first films was about Ramuz (the poetic 1961 documentary *Ramuz : passage d'un poète*, where we find Tanner's most affectionate treatment of the Swiss landscape), there is a better literary analogy to be made with his work: that of Jacques Chessex (1934–2009). Chessex is a *very* different writer from Ramuz. Whereas Ramuz was a figure stuck between the nineteenth and twentieth centuries, Chessex was very much a child of the twentieth and was writing not about the ravages of modernity but about the ways in which the bourgeoisie – sometimes in Switzerland, sometimes elsewhere – had evolved into a class that was essentially parasitic, unable to create and unable to reflect. I feel some obligation to recall at this point that in our phone conversation of 7 November 2009, Tanner identified (again, in a very pleasant, jovial way) my desire to link him with the work of Jacques Chessex as the single most ridiculous part of my plans for this book. He said that he recalled reading only one novel by Chessex many years ago; he couldn't remember which novel that was, but he said he found it utterly foreign.[44] But like Tanner's disavowal of Swiss identity, I remain convinced that there is a connection in his work to what was going on around him; Chessex, whether Tanner recalls reading him or not, was a very big part of what was going on in French-language Swiss literature during the period that he was working. Schaub, in *L'Usage de la liberté*, has pointed out that "It's at the beginning of the 1960s that the young Swiss literature began to more sharply observe the everyday life of Switzerland, the 'malaise' to use the term that belongs to that moment, even when they choose themes that are not of that period" (8–9), and for him this is indicative of the wider restlessness in Swiss culture, of which the Nouveau cinéma suisse, very much including Tanner, is a part.[45] Schaub then rattles off an entirely German-language list of prominent authors of the period, which wouldn't be so surprising given that his book was originally written in German, except that he also claims that "le mouvement était plus timide en Suisse romande" (9–10). I'm not sure what leads him to say that, for it was during this period in French-speaking Switzerland (generally known as Suisse Romande) that Chessex, who was a youngish novelist (he was four years older than Tanner), was rising to prominence. He remains the only Swiss author to have won the Prix Goncourt, which he was awarded in 1973 for his novel *L'Ogre*. Chessex's books were not usually set "hors du temps," as Schaub writes, but they were sometimes set outside of Switzerland. That is true of his first novel, 1963's *La Tête ouverte*, which I think has a very real kinship with Tanner's work of this period. The novel is about a young man stuck living in a cheap pension near the French seaside, a young man who chafes both at the uprightness of his landlady and at the philistinism of the lower-middle-class people with whom he shares the pension. At one point Chessex reproduces the angry note that the landlady leaves for her slacker boarder: "Sir, This isn't working anymore, I cannot have in my home someone who doesn't come to meals, we prepare only enough for the number of people we have here and after this consideration we have to throw out the food and also we can't make your bed at the same time as everyone else's because you get up at noon. This is to say nothing of the guests who have seen you come in during the night with someone think of the impression that this gives to customers in a respectable and reputable House" (58).[46] As an evocation of the self-confident pettiness of the petite-bourgeoisie this is quite efficient, and its run-on sentences and careless errors in grammar hint at the philistinism of the class as well. Passages like this one lead me, almost viscerally, to the scene in *La Salamandre* where the young journalist Pierre interviews the small-town, petite-bourgeois uncle who the title character has claimed to have shot. He recalls how Rosemonde, a.k.a. The Salamander, had been sent to live with him by her parents at the age of fifteen, "so she could take her classes in the town. And also because it was one less mouth to feed (*pause*). At fifteen, she started hanging around with little hoodlums,... was getting up at ten o'clock in the morning, and, finally, that leads to crime" (*L'Avant-scène cinéma*, 17).[47] That the spectre of sleepy young people would provoke such fear and loathing is a fairly sharp indictment of the state of the middle class in the French-speaking world of the 1960s and 70s. Tanner, like Chessex, sees this sort of neurotic small-mindedness as central to what had to change in Swiss society of the 1960s. But both are equally critical of the way that it was being changed by the youth of the period. Chessex's young anti-hero is self-absorbed and a bit paranoid, and in many ways is little better than the burgers who torment him. Likewise, The Salamander's actions are far from being revolutionary, and really end up signifying little more than the disconnection that lies at the heart of contemporary Swiss life. Both Tanner and Chessex are thus consistent with what Schaub saw as a sensibility that was found in literature and cinema alike: a new attention, not only to the everyday life of Switzerland, but to her relentlessly everyday malaise as well.

What I have been trying to argue here is in no way inconsistent with Tanner's own indictment in *Ciné-mélanges* of the Office fédéral de la culture's desire to create a Swiss cinema that "tried to re-launch the idea of a ridiculous cultural patriotism that now gave us back our winning spirit, exactly like you did for soccer players" (85), or his statement in his interview with Dimitriu that "The Swiss landscape is terribly domesticated, marked out by clean-scrubbed indicators of a nearly hysterical passion for petite-bourgeois values and the order that follows from them" (109).[48] The fact that Berger and Tanner's work is utterly free of the "moral de gagneurs" that Tanner invokes does not mean that it is unaffected by the distinct history and culture of Switzerland, and his and Berger's representation of the Swiss mountains as spaces of political and cultural instability is a direct challenge to the – yes, very Swiss! – notion of a domesticated landscape. One finds throughout their work a palatable tension between individual liberty and shared obligation, between responsibility and agency. The fact that such concepts are held in permanent tension is a big part of the work's connection to Swiss culture. And they are far from the only Swiss artists to see the world in this way, even if they are still offering slightly different analyses or emphases from those of Ramuz and Chessex. Switzerland is a complex country whose distinctive political culture offers, and certainly offered in the 1970s, a very vigorous challenge to liberalism. That Berger and Tanner were offering such a challenge from a critical-left position does not make them any less a part of this Swiss project.

Enlighten me

The way to synthesize all of these concerns that I have argued here are central to the work Berger and Tanner did together is, I believe, to see them as part of the legacy of the Enlightenment. The desire to balance the rational and the emotional, and to do so in a way that requires sustained critical activity on the part of the reader, is a seminal part of the Enlightenment idea. And the desire to marshal this critical activity towards an experience that is educational in the best sense (as in without any trace of reductive didacticism) is as central to the product of the Enlightenment as it is to that of Berger and Tanner. There is no doubt that the shadow of Rousseau, and specifically his 1762 treatise on education, *Émile*, hangs heavy over Berger and Tanner's collective work. Rousseau's *Du Contrat sociale* is one of the many texts quoted in the commentary of *Une Ville à Chandigarh* and is the only non-twentieth-century work that is invoked in this quotation-rich film. But it is especially true, of course, of *Jonas*, a film which is set in Rousseau's hometown of Geneva and its surrounding countryside, which self-consciously evokes *Émile*, and where Rousseau is often evoked explicitly through images of his statue or mentions from the characters. I will deal with the Rousseau connection in the chapter on *Jonas*. But the comparison that I think is more fecund for all of the work Berger and Tanner have done together, and to which I will return, is that of Voltaire, and specifically his 1759 *Candide, ou, l'optimisme.*[49]

Frédéric Bas also poses this *Candide* connection in his afterword to Tanner's *Ciné-mélanges*, which he titles "Tanner ou l'optimisme." He recalls there that *Candide* was one of Brecht's favourite books, partially because its sustained irony offered a blueprint for his ideas about distanciation, but also because it is defined "on one hand, by the innocence and optimism of the characters; on the other, by the horrors of the world. Between these two states, the space that is opened up for the reader is that of a conscience. At the same time, Tanner's cinema evinces a fundamental innocence, freed from the desires of its characters at the same time that it denotes extreme fragility. Tanner, 'cruel and kind, naïve and cunning.' Tanner, ou l'Optimisme" (170).[50] The tension between innocence/optimism and horror has an echo in the tension between tragedy and comedy, a dialectic that is also at the core of all of Tanner and Berger's work and that is explicitly part of *Candide*:

> Imagine every possible contradiction and inconsistency, and you will find them in the government, the law-courts, the churches, and in the whole life of this absurd nation.

"Is it true," asked Candide, "that people in Paris are always laughing?"

"Yes," said the *abbé*, "but they are laughing through vexation; for they complain of everything with loud bursts of laughter, just as they laugh while they commit the most detestable crimes." (99–100)[51]

The contradictions of the state, the political sphere, the marketplace, and the media are the basically parallel concerns of the films Berger and Tanner made together. But it is not only their subject matter that is Voltairian; their sensibility is just as close to their eighteenth-century predecessor. Like Voltaire they approach these collisions between the horrible and the possible, not through didacticism or manipulated outrage, but through humour and pathos. Yes, you often laugh in these films, but you are laughing through vexation, laughing at the most detestable crimes.

This tension between laughter and criticism is something that Tzvetan Todorov places at the heart of the Enlightenment's ideology. He writes in his book *L'Esprit des Lumières* that among Enlightenment thinkers, "Reason is valued as a tool of understanding, not as a motive for human behaviour; it is opposed to faith, not passion" (13).[52] Thus we come back to Sylvie Pierre's ideas about what is really important about montage: it allows occasional escape from reason into the realm of passion. Berger and Tanner's work (and this is true both of the films they made together and their production independent of one another) uses the fragmented aesthetic so often associated with montage as often as it insists on an intense, studied realism. What is consistent throughout, though, is this "spirit of montage," this openness to contradiction and complexity that allows the opening up, in the mind of the spectator, of a third space of synthesis: the space of conscience. Recognizing this "opening up" allows us to see them not only as products of Swiss culture (which I will to continue to argue is the case) but also as the product of a deeply European sensibility. "Thus we can say without exaggeration: without Europe, no Enlightenment; but also, without the Enlightenment, no Europe," writes Todorov (139).[53] This European-Enlightenment heritage begins with Voltaire but also moves through the drafters of the modern Swiss confederation (which, while having roots that go back as early as the thirteenth century is basically a nineteenth-century creation;

the federal constitution that created modern Switzerland was finalized in 1848), through Eisenstein, Ramuz, Brecht, the rebels of 1968, and, indeed, John Berger and Alain Tanner. Their work together was genuinely distinctive, but it also needs to be understood as part of this continuum. To put it in Benjamin Barber's Swiss terms, their innovative filmmaking can only be understood in the context of their communities. Without the richness of both European and Swiss culture and history, no Berger and Tanner; but without Berger and Tanner, European and Swiss culture alike would be nowhere near as rich.

Notes

1 "… il me paraît essentiel de rappeler la colonisation qui pesait sur tous les médias de cette époque, comme d'ailleurs sur la musique, la mode et même la littérature."

2 *Nice Time* deserves a chapter unto itself, in no small part because of this *semi*-vérité quality. Like a lot of early vérité, it feels a lot more direct than it really is. The key element of cinéma vérité, or direct cinema, or whatever one wishes to call the more spontaneous documentary practice of the late 1950s and 1960s, is synchronous sound. And like contemporary films such as Michel Brault and Gilles Groulx's *Les Racquetteurs* (Quebec, 1959) or Robert Drew's *Primary* (USA, 1960), there is actually a fairly small amount of synch sound in *Nice Time*. Like *Primary* or *Les Racquetteurs*, it is mostly comprised of *wild* sound, obviously taken in the same locations as the images but very rarely in actual synchronization with those images. The *aesthetic* gestures of vérité are present in all of these films – long takes, hand-held camera, complex and sometimes over-crowded compositions – but the actual technology of spontaneous sound documentary is clearly still something of a work in progress. I will discuss this transitional quality of Tanner's early films in the next chapter.

3 "Pourtant, lorsque j'ai présenté *Charles* au public français, il a été reçu comme un film « incroyablement exotique »!"

4 "Mais ça était un peu choc de vivre à Paris après Londres. Terminées la générosité, la chaleur amicale des cercles londoniens. A Paris c'était chacun pour soi et le couteau tiré. Un monde clos, et plus la nouvelle vague pour moi qui sortais d'un bain très politisé c'était un peu trop « anarchiste de droite ». J'ai collaboré aux *Cahiers du cinéma* mais tout le monde était sur ses gardes."

5 "D'après lui, les membres de la Nouvelle Vague sont imprégnés d'un « fascisme intellectuel ». Leur philosophie est le nihilisme. Ils mettent en scène la mentalité de la jeune génération, farouchement éprise de liberté et fascinée par la mort, la violence, l'amou fou…. L'auteur considère que les films de la Nouvelle Vague sont anticonformistes, anticommunistes, antidémocratiques, et anti-socialistes."

6 "J'abrège : en 1962, une loi d'aide au cinéma est entrée en vigueur, devant être appliquée par une commission fédérale, alors en formation. Sur vingt-sept membres, aucun cinéaste. Les quelques réalisateurs qui travaillent alors dans ce pays, pas plus de cinq ou six, demandèrent d'occuper au moins un siège dans cette commission. Mais pour ce faire, il fallait représenter une association. En toute hâte, nous avons alors créé l'Association suisse des réalisateurs, dont j'avais pris l'initiative et donc la présidence. L'administration accepta de nous donner *in extremis* un strapontin et je me retrouvai dès lors membres de cette commission fraîchement élue. Le cauchemar commençait…. Nous avons suivi de près l'éclosion de nouvelles cinématographiques en France, en Tchécoslovaquie, au Québec, en Pologne, au Brésil, et ailleurs. Le cinéma était en état d'ébullition dans le monde, et les vingt-six autres membres de la Commission fédérale

du cinéma n'en savait apparemment rien."

7   "En Suisse romande, il n'y avait jamais eu du cinéma.... À cette époque, il n'y avait rien du tout en Suisse." Tanner gives a much more interesting and well-informed discussion of the history of Swiss cinema in the interview he gave to *Cahiers du cinéma* upon the release of *Charles mort ou vif*. He points out there, for instance, that during WWII a Swiss cinema in *Schweizerdeutsch* the Swiss dialect of German, was relatively strong, because the country's borders were sealed off. He notes that this sort of cinema ceased to exist after the war, and that it never really existed in French. See Delahaye, Eisenschitz and Narboni interview, 26.

8   "Tout de suite, on remarque à la lecture de cette loi d'aide qu'elle est terriblement restrictive, puisqu'elle ne prévoit une aide à la réalisation qu'aux films 'documentaires, culturels, ou éducatifs'... et qu'elle excepte les œuvres de fiction."

9   "La naissance d'un cinéma suisse relève donc moins, d'abord, d'un problème financier que d'un problème de climat intellectuel et spirituel."

10 "La date n'est pas un pur hasard. On a alors pu mettre la main sur un outil de travail, en fait, une branche de la télévision. Nous n'avons aucune envie de créer une industrie du cinéma, de faire du cinéma commercial.... Mais dans l'esprit de l'époque, on pouvait tout inventer à partir de zéro : les moyens de production, les rapports de travail avec les techniciens qui étaient tous très jeunes."

11 "L'avantage principal qu'offrent donc (pour Tanner en particulier) les accords Groupe 5 et TV, c'est précisément d'ignorer le contrôle sur la production. Une fois le sujet admis, le réalisateur est le propre producteur de son film et il dispose de 60,000 francs sonnants dans le cas du premier accord passé avec la Télévision en 1968."

12 "Un jour, en discutant avec une classe d'une école de cinéma, je posai aux étudiants la colle suivant : « Savez-vous pourquoi on dit que le découpage est "de droite" et le montage 'de gauche' ? » Silence effaré dans les rangs. Trente ans plus tôt, quelqu'un aurait eu la réponse, et aujourd'hui, c'est comme j'avais parlé chinois."

13 Good introductions to the specifically cinematic legacy of May '68 can be found in both French and English; see Sylvia Harvey, *May '68 and Film Culture* (London: British Film Institute, 1980) and Antoine de Baecque et al., *Cinéma 68*, which I mention a bit later.

14 The conference produced a document, collectively authored by a group led Jean-Louis Comolli, which outlined in considerable detail (there are a number of charts) the role that cinema would play in a revolutionized society. That was published in *Cahiers du cinéma* 203 (August 1968), and was translated into English in *Screen* 13, no. 4 (1972).

15 "Dans les années 1960–70, j'ai beaucoup fréquenté les écrits théorétiques sur le cinéma, et ceux de Brecht sur le théâtre, mais qu'on ne pouvait parfaitement appliquer à notre travail. On était alors à l'époque où l'on cherchait surtout à déconstruire la

narration traditionnelle en vigueur dans la cinématographie dominante, et à la reconstruire ensuite selon un autre schéma, c'est-à-dire à remettre à plat les éléments du récit, à les remettre en ordre et en perspective, afin qu'ils produisent clairement leur sens, selon les règles relévant davantage de la dialectique que celles de la dramaturgie classique."

16 "Tous les films militants de l'époque sont devenus invisibles aujourd'hui."

17 Jean Narboni's review of *Z* in *Cahiers du cinéma* (published in 1969 as "Le Pirée pour un homme") is legendary because it argued that Costa-Gavras' commercially popular and critically acclaimed film was a perfect example of what an emerging political cinema should not be. "Militant?" scoffs Narboni. "Maybe like singers' shows can be, but like them it's mystifying, because it has defined neither an object of study, nor the means to produce it" ["Militant ? Comme peuvent l'être peut-être les spectacles de chansonniers, mais comme eux mystifiant : pour n'avoir pas défini un objet d'étude, ni les moyens de le produire" (55)]. He and Comolli also mention the film in "Cinéma/ idéologie/critique," complaining that it is a bad example of a cinema with political content, "its presentation of politics is unremittingly ideological from first to last" ("Cinema/Ideology/ Criticism," 26–27) ["la politique y étant dès le départ représentée – sans recours – idéologiquement" ("Cinéma/idéologie/critique" 13)].

18 "Es ist nicht der Fall – wiewohl es mitunter vorgebracht wurde –, daß episches Theater, das übrigens – wie ebenfalls mitunter vorgebracht – nicht etwa einfach undramatisches Theater ist, den Kampfruf „hie Vernunft – hie Emotion" (Gefühl) erschallen läßt" ("Formprobleme des Theaters," 254).

19 "Para mí las películas de Tavernier o de Costa Gavras son lo peor que existe en cine. Ese cine comercial, de consumo, que retoma los esquemas hollywoodenses, pero con ideas políticas de izquierda, me parece detestable."

20 Equally exemplary, although not as well known, are the texts on cinema, technology, and ideology that Comolli published from 1971 to 1972. These were in nos. 229 (May–June 1971), 231 (September 1971), 233 (November 1971), 234–35 (December 1971/January–February 1972), and 241 (September–October 1972). They have recently been collected in his collection *Cinéma contre spectacle*, the first half of which is a sort of intellectual memoir, which makes for very interesting reading. "In short, the question of alienation was, for the *Cahiers* group of the 1970s, a *truly* political matter," he writes, explaining that the post-68 break with its past was not as severe as it might seem in retrospect ["Bref, la question de l'aliénation était pour le groupe des *Cahiers* dans les années soixante-dix une question *vraiment* politique" (78)]. Comolli also recalls in that first section that "Ces six articles ont été traduits en anglais (*Screen* 1974, *Film Reader* 1977)" (12n2).

21 "Mais cette « réalité » susceptible d'être reproduite fidèlement, reflétée par des instruments et techniques que, d'ailleurs font partie d'elle, on voit bien qu'elle est idéologique tout entière. En ce sens, la théorie de

la « transparence » (le classicisme cinématographique) est éminemment réactionnaire" ("Cinéma/idéologie/critique," pp. 1, 12). I think this is a very strange translation of this passage; as you can see here, Susan Bennett not only embellishes quite a bit from the original but also imposes some serious changes to Comolli and Narboni's style. It is utterly beyond me how the fairly crisp and clear (if polemical) "la théorie de la « transparence » (le classicisme cinématographique) est éminemment réactionnaire" becomes the florid "the classic theory of cinema that the camera is an impartial instrument which grasps, or rather is impregnated by, the world in its 'concrete reality' is an eminently reactionary one." That would, in a colder translation, simply be "the theory of 'transparency' (cinematic classicism) is eminently reactionary."

22   "Il est aujourd'hui évident que la technique du récit est étroitement liée à une idéologie, et pas seulement le récit lui-même…. Elle [l'idéologie] correspond exactement à un type de relations établi par une industrie à la recherche du plus large public possible."

23   "Ni débat, ni table ronde, ni rassemblement d'articles, ni discours unique à plusieurs voix, mais « montage » de fragments critiques."

24   "Ce en quoi, on peut, par opposition, qualifier de « progressiste » le montage eisensteinien, c'est paradoxalement par ce qu'il a plus dictatorial : les passages d'un plan à un autre ôtent au spectateur toute possibilité d'échapper au raisonnement, à la nécessité de se

mettre par rapport au plan en état de distance réflexive."

25   "… le cinéma est un produit idéologique, son champ de définition et d'exercice est l'idéologie, et non la science" (8).… "Une caméra qui se filme … cela ne donne ni la science, ni de la théorie, ni du « cinéma matérialiste » : tout au plus est-on en droit de dire que, reflet du reflet, l'idéologie se mire en elle-même" (9).

26   "… quelque chose se dit, dans le procès même de ce qui est à la fois la jouissance et la « lecture » du film … dont on ne peut parler qu'en termes d'érotisme, et qui se donne lui-même comme la représentation la plus approchante du procès même de l'érotisme" ("La Suture, Deuxième partie," 55).

27   "Précieux pour Tanner, pour qui Mai 68 est l'aboutissement d'une longue mise en question de la société, de soi-même et de son métier de cinéaste, et le début d'une nouvelle ère créatrice. Précieux pour la télévision et pour les chercheurs, car les images sont riches d'informations. Ce film est formellement plus sobre, avec un caméra agile, un minimum de travellings et de zooms, un montage plus rapide."

28   "… il est à Paris en mai 1968, où il travaille comme reporter pour la télévision suisse. Il a près de quarante ans et il y a bien longtemps qu'il se méfie des curés d'extrême gauche et de l'idéologie de plomb. À la différence de beaucoup d'autres, il ne pense pas – et il ne pensera jamais – que « la caméra est un fusil »."

29   "Car 68 (ou plutôt mai 68) fut un grand théâtre de rue, avec l'intendance en grève qui attendait que

ça se passe. Et ce qui importe, bien davantage que « les événements », ce sont les retombées, dans la mesure justement où ce théâtre mis en scène des espoirs et fit affleurer les désirs cachés, qui depuis sont demeurés à la surface."

30 "Mai 68 à Paris fut un grand happening, un grand théâtre dans la rue, ludique, une libération de la parole."

31 The strife at Université Catholique de Louvain is a sort of microcosm of the struggles Belgium has had with linguistic co-existence. The university had historically (as in since the 1400s) been French-speaking, but starting in the 1960s Flemish-speaking students began agitating for greater linguistic rights. This eventually led to the 1968 split of the university into French-medium and Flemish-medium versions. A famous metaphor for the absurdity of the split is that Université Catholique de Louvain got the library holdings whose call numbers ended with an odd number, with Katholieke Universiteit Leuven taking the even-numbered material.

32 "… dans son ensemble, le peuple suisse est l'un des moins révolutionnaires de l'Europe. Il ne croit pas aux constructions *ex nihilo*, sur table rase. Son tempérament l'incline et son économie l'oblige à reformer ce qui existe et « qui peut toujours servir », plutôt qu'à s'exposer aux risques de détruire le bon usage avec l'abus."

33 This accounts for the important role of the Swiss military as a means of national cohesion. Continuous service is obligatory for all able-bodied male citizens resident in Switzerland from the age of 18 to 30, with officers and specialists serving until the age of 50 (women can serve, but are not conscripted). Everyone does two weeks of training a year and is required to report to that training with what is officially known as their "arme personnelle," which is issued to everyone upon intake and kept, along with ammunition, at home (it must be turned in once a member is discharged from service, although de-mobbed members can opt to have the automatic part of the rifle disabled and keep it for "raisons sportifs"). This comes up explicitly in *La Salamandre* when the mysterious young woman known alternatively as Rosemonde and "The Salamander" seems to have shot her uncle with his own gun – his "arme personelle," which he calls his "fusil militaire" – which as he tells Pierre, the engagé young journalist who has come to interview him, was doubly traumatic since it is a symbol of their liberty. I spent the fall and winter of 2009 and 2010 in the Swiss city of Fribourg, a commune of about 50,000 people with no exceptionally central role in the military, and, except for the week between Christmas and New Year's, not a single day went by without my seeing someone in uniform. Walk through any public square in Switzerland and you will find posted, in German, French, and Italian, the year's mobilization schedules. This, I say especially to my American readers, is what a "well-regulated militia" looks like. John McPhee's wonderful book *La place de la concorde suisse* (New York: Farrar, Strauss and Giroux, 1984) is, despite its title, an English-language discussion of the place of the army in Swiss society that unfolds as an account of a few weeks that McPhee spent with a French-speaking unit.

34 "Un paysan jodleur d'Appenzell, un ouvrier socialiste de Berne et un banquier anglomane de Genève, s'ils se rencontraient par hasard – et j'allais dire par impossible – autour d'un demi de blanc dans quelque buffet de gare, n'auraient pas grand-chose à dire. Mais qu'importe! ... Tous les trois savent qu'ils sont suisses, non pas à cause de quelque qualité commune, soit naturelle, soit culturelle (langue, race, confession, caractère, etc.) qui justement leur fait défaut, mais parce qu'ils sont placés dans la même *ensemble* que l'on a baptisé du nom « Suisse » et qu'ils l'approuvent. Et quand on a bien compris cela, on a compris le fédéralisme."

35 "Les Suisses ne forment pas un peuple, n'ont pas une culture, mais se rattachent à plusieurs autres" ... "Le spleen suisse romande ou la « suissitude » malheureuse, ça n'intéresse plus personne et moi en dernier."

36 "... contacts avec des mouvements dits « frères », luttant pour la défense des minorités de langue française, que ce soit en Belgique, en Italie, ou même au Québec."

37 "... ce qui compte n'est pas ce qui est dit mais ce qui est tu. C'est surtout par le montage que le cinéaste exprime son point de vue."

38 This is a very short news clip (just under a minute) available for viewing at http://archives.tsr.ch/dossier-juralibre/jura-attentat (6 May 2010).

39 "Avant, il y a eu *Charles mort ou vif* qui, réalisé à 500 kilomètres de Paris, avec le Jura au milieu, s'en fait l'écho."

40 "— Voyons, Gailloud, tu as pourtant un fils, tu en as même deux. Qu'est-ce que tu en penses ?

— Ils ne tournent pas trop mal.

— Oui, mais, dis donc, leurs habitudes, leur manière de s'habiller. Qu'est-ce qu'ils fument ?

— La cigarette.

— Tu vois bien; moi, la pipe, et toi, le cigare. Les cigarettes, ça coûte cher, ça ne dure pas et puis c'est nerveux. Une fois que tu as bourré ta pipe et que tu te l'es vissée au coin du bec, tu n'as plus besoin d'y penser. Et puis, un paquet de tabac, ça coûte quarante centimes. Les garçons d'aujourd'hui dépensent dès un franc et plus pour un paquet de ces choses en papier qui est brûlé dix fois plus vite. Les garçons d'aujourd'hui, ça fume en travaillant. Ils ont tout le temps les mains occupées. J'aime pas tant ça. Et toi ?"

41 "On est vers la fin de mai; toutes les fenêtres étaient ouvertes. L'homme s'avançait dans la rue : une tête, de place en place, se penchait hors d'une ces fenêtres. Il était grand, il était beau, il était large d'épaules; il portait toute la barbe, il avait des cheveux longs."

42 "... là, on a commencé par un morceau de piano, puis une fenêtre a été ouverte, au fond de la salle, sur le monde."

43 "Car maintenant le monde entier est à nous, si on veut; tous les siècles sont à nous, tout l'espace; ayant le vertige, mais c'est bon, ayant la tête qui leur tournait, mais c'est bon; dans la chaleur, sous le ciel bas, sous le ciel noir, entre les maisons aux fenêtres

noires, sortant vers onze heures, par petits groupes, l'homme et la femme, deux ou trois jeunes ensemble, des filles et des garçons ensemble; des hommes seuls, des femmes seules; se taisent, parlant tout à coup…."

44 I asked him if this was Chessex's 1987 novel *Jonas*, but he didn't think it was. *Jonas* is a semi-autobiographical portrait of a novelist who winds up back in Fribourg, the city where he had gone to school (Chessex was educated at Fribourg's Collège St-Michel, where his father taught chemistry). Chessex's Jonas returns to that city of giant cathedrals, that home of the country's only bi-lingual university, to get his chops as a writer back, although he ends up mostly prowling the grubby cafés of the lower town. The book's title and its narrative of lost intellectual idealism strongly recall Tanner and Berger's *Jonas qui aura 25 ans en l'an 2000*, and I dare say its revisiting of that narrative is a lot more compelling than Tanner's own return to the character of Jonas, *Light Years Away* (1980), which I discuss in Chapter 5.

45 "C'est au début des années 60 que la jeune littérature helvétique se mit à observer de façon plus aiguë la vie quotidienne suisse, le « malaise », selon le terme consacré du moment, et cela même lorsqu'elle choisissait des thèmes hors du temps."

46 "Monsieur, Ça ne va plus, je ne peux pas admettre chez mois une personne qui vient pas aux repas, on prépare juste pour le nombre alors après avec cette chaleur il faut jeter la nourriture et puis on peut pas faire votre lit en même temps que les autres parce que vous vous levez à midi. Sans compter

que des pensionnaires vous ont vu entrer ici la nuit avec quelqu'un vous pensez l'impression que ça fait sur les clients dans une Maison respectable et réputée."

47 "On me l'a confiée, quand elle avait quinze ans, pour qu'elle puisse suivre ses classes en ville. Et puis aussi parce que ça faisait une bouche de moins à nourrir (*un temps*). A quinze ans, ça se laisse tourner autour par des petits voyous,… ça se lève à dix heures du matin et, pour finir, ça verse dans le crime."

48 "… on essaie de relancer l'idée d'un patriotisme culturel ridicule qui nous redonnait un moral de gagneurs, exactement comme on le fait pour les joueurs de football" …. "Le paysage suisse est terriblement domestiqué, quadrillé par les signes bien nettoyés d'une passion presque hystérique pour les valeurs petites-bourgeois et par l'ordre qui en découle."

49 *Candide*, first published in 1759, has something of a Swiss pedigree. Voltaire had, from 1755 to 1760, a home in Geneva that he called "Les Délices." José Lupin's notes to the version contained in Gallimard's 1972 *Romans et contes* state that "Voltaire definitely wrote *Candide* throughout 1758, at first in Lausanne then around Mannheim…. He published it, anonymously, in Geneva, with the Cramers, in February 1759…. The book was condemned in Geneva and Paris, seized by the police, and its success was confirmed" (552) ["Voltaire a sans doute rédigé *Candide* au cours de l'année 1758, à Lausanne d'abord, puis aux environs de Mannheim…. Il parut anonymement, à Genève, chez les Cramers, en février

1759.... Le livre est condamné à Genève et à Paris, saisi par la police ; et son succès s'affirme"]. It should be pointed out, though, that at this time Geneva was not part of Switzerland; until 1815 it was basically a city-state with some loosely governed countryside outside its pale. This was, of course, part of its appeal for Voltaire; the city's eighteenth century reputation as a sort of model republic seemed attractive, although its harsh clerical authorities gave the lie to this idealism, as Voltaire fairly quickly discovered. Geneva's status as a "late arrival" to the Swiss confederation is part of what leads to the *idée reçu* that Geneva is the least Swiss part of Switzerland. I reject this idea, in no small part because I see Tanner – who is a citizen of Geneva *par excellence* – as a seminally Swiss filmmaker.

50 "... d'un côté, l'innocence et l'optimisme du personnage; de l'autre, les horreurs du monde. Entre ces deux états, l'espace laissé au lecteur est celui d'une conscience. De même, le cinéma de Tanner exprime une innocence fondamentale, libère des désirs des personnages en même temps qu'il en désigne l'extrême fragilité. Tanner, « gentil et méchant, naïf et rusé. » Tanner ou l'Optimisme."

51 "Imaginez toutes les contradictions, toutes les incompatibilités possibles, vous les verrez dans le gouvernement, dans les tribunaux, dans les églises, dans les spectacles de cette drôle de nation. — Est-il vrai qu'on rit toujours à Paris? dit Candide. — Oui, dit l'abbé, mais c'est en enrageant; car on s'y plaint de tout avec de grands éclats de rire; même on y fait en riant les actions les plus détestables" (*Romans et contes*, 200).

52 "La raison est mise en valeur comme outil de connaissance, non comme mobile des conduites humaines, elle s'oppose à la foi, non aux passions."

53 "De sorte que l'on peut dire sans exagération : sans l'Europe, pas de Lumières; mais aussi, sans les Lumières, pas d'Europe."

CHAPTER ONE

BERGER AND TANNER BEFORE "BERGER AND TANNER"

"Working conditions and economic pressures put direct cinema in a political situation, even if the majority of the films in that style don't want to be, or aren't in the first place, political films."
– Jean-Louis Comolli, "Le détour par le direct," part 1 (52)[1]

It is common to speak of Berger and Tanner's collaboration in terms of three films: *La Salamandre* (1971), *Le Milieu du monde* (1974), and *Jonas qui aura 25 ans en l'an 2000* (1976). Berger, in his 1985 interview with Richard Appignanesi, mentions those three, and also mentions their 1966 short documentary *Une Ville à Chandigarh* in passing (298); that's also true of Tanner's interview with Christian Dimitriu (108). But there were other manifestations of their collaboration, and furthermore it is important not to give short shrift to *Une Ville à Chandigarh* by referring to it as though it meant basically nothing to the history of their work together. That most of this collaboration was for television and a lot of it is uncredited or informal accounts for much of its invisibility, even to Tanner and Berger themselves. That is fair enough. Nevertheless, the films *Une Ville à Chandigarh* (1966, directed by Tanner, commentary by Berger), *Mike et l'usage de la science* (1968, "Reportage et réalization: Alain Tanner, avec la participation de John Berger"), and *Docteur B., médecin de campagne* (1968, directed by Tanner) are important parts both of Swiss documentary and of the œuvres of Berger and Tanner themselves. Their formal patterns and political engagements are well worth discussing by way of easing into the better-known (and, yes, more fully realized) films that the two made together. Moreover, this pre-*Salamandre* work constitutes, in its own right, an intellectually vigorous and formally ambitious engagement with the possibilities of television, a medium whose aesthetic and ideological contours were still very much up for grabs in the 1960s. Moreover, this documentary work anticipates a lot of the concerns of those three narrative films, partially on the level of form but more clearly on the level of subject matter and narrative structure. Thanks to the good work of the archivists at Télévision Suisse Romande, almost all of these films are available for viewing on their website (and I give the addresses for each film at the end of this book). They are well worth viewing.

Equally worth viewing is, of course, Tanner's film *Le Retour d'Afrique* (1974), a film that Tanner made between *La Salamandre* (1971) and *Le Milieu du monde* (1974). This is also a film that may seem like it belongs in this chapter, which is basically devoted to "semi-collaborations" between the two. In 1985 Berger told Appignanesi: "There was another film in between, called *Return to Africa*, which I didn't collaborate on.... It was a story that more or less happened to two friends of mine, and I told it to Alain one evening in some detail" (306). *Retour d'Afrique* is a story about an idealistic young couple who plan to give up their bohemian life in Geneva and go to Algeria but can never quite manage to leave, even though they sell all their possessions. As a narrative it is certainly consistent with both Berger and Tanner's interests in the ravages of consumer culture, especially on restless, idealistic youth, and cinematically speaking it features a lot of the meta-cinematic and distancing effects that are common to Tanner's films of this period.

But even though Berger speaks of *Le Retour d'Afrique* as a kind of 'half-collaboration' (he said to Appignanesi that "when two people have collaborated on, say, three and a half films ..." [300]). I have chosen to more or less exclude it because of my sense that the collaboration does not seem to have gone beyond a single, albeit very detailed, conversation. *Une Ville à Chandigarh* and *Mike et l'usage de la science* really do seem to have involved Berger co-creating a work with Tanner. That's definitely true of *Une Ville*, and while the details of collaboration on *Mike* are a bit sketchier, the fact that Berger is actually in the film makes it seem like a far more collaborative affair than *Retour d'Afrique*. Now, admittedly I know of no explicit collaboration between Berger and Tanner at all on *Docteur B., médecin de campagne*, even at the level of a conversation such as the one that gave birth to *Retour d'Afrique*. But it is clear that *Docteur B.* is very close indeed to Berger's 1967 book *A Fortunate Man* (another collaboration with Jean Mohr), both at the level of subject matter and form. Indeed, it is impossible to offer a full account of the workings of *Docteur B.* without talking about *A Fortunate Man*, impossible to really understand that work of Tanner's without talking about that work of Berger's. There is no comparable "twin" in Berger's œuvre for *Retour d'Afrique*.

Tanner, Berger, and Television Documentary

In addition to its second-class status as television documentaries, another reason that this material may not be very well known is because at first glance it seems atypical for both Tanner and Berger. Tanner had very mixed feelings about documentary and television alike, and the period when he became really famous seems to be synonymous with the period when he left both forms. Nobody who knew Tanner's widely circulated work of the 1970s and 80s would necessarily suspect that he had made films like *Une Ville à Chandigarh* or *Docteur B., médecin de campagne*, which are both complex interventions in an emerging cinéma vérité aesthetic. Berger, on the other hand, spent the 1960s and 70s embracing the idea that realism needed to be revitalized, and he is no stranger to television; the catalogue for Gareth Evans' 2005 season devoted to Berger's work notes that "At the heart of John Berger's oeuvre lies a body of work (features, series and documentaries) in film and television" (25). In addition to working collaboratively in film and television, Berger also worked with the Swiss photographer Jean Mohr, with whom he made photo-books about village communities and migrant workers. But nobody who knew Berger's work of this period would necessarily suspect that he had collaborated on a film like *Mike et l'usage de la science*, which is about a thoughtful nuclear scientist from Geneva.

Television was first introduced in Switzerland (by the state) in 1953, and it became, in fairly short order, something of a political battleground. Its origins are as a committee of the Société Suisse de Radiodiffusion (SSR) on television experiments, which was first introduced in 1950 (as the

Commission fédérale pour les questions de télévision); a second committee, on cultural matters (Commission fédérale pour l'étude des questions culturelles touchant la télévision), was introduced in 1952 (this is explained in Rostan, 47). By 1956 the government was trying to write support for television into the constitution, but the effort failed when it, like all proposed constitutional amendments, was put to a public referendum in 1957. François Vallotton recalls how its opponents played on a populist fear of the new medium, including the idea that it meant the end of radio, adopting the slogan "pas un sou de la radio pour la télévision": "not a penny from the radio for TV" (43). Television nevertheless quickly acquired considerable political influence in Switzerland; Vallotton also recalls how during the 1950s, "One journalist had even spoken of Marcel Bezençon, then director of SSR, as the '8th Federal Councillor'" (43).[2] This was due in large part to the network's role in reporting a series of political scandals, such as the decision of the minister responsible for the Départment militaire fédérale, Paul Chaudet, to explain his role in an arms-sale controversy on television rather than on the radio or through the written press. Vallotton summarizes the anxiety that this newfound influence provoked by explaining a Swiss fear of an emerging "télécratie helvétique" (45). This widespread uncertainty about the future of television in Swiss life led to the creation of a new policy for both radio and TV, which both shored up the new medium institutionally and gave it a civically oriented mandate. The policy came into force in 1964. SSR's mandate is laid out in article 13: "The programs broadcast by SSR must defend and develop the country's cultural values and contribute to the spiritual, moral, religious, civic and artistic formation of the listeners and viewers.... The programs must serve the interests of the country, reinforce national unity, and contribute to international understanding" (Rostan 71).[3] This was, as I discussed in the introduction, the year after Switzerland's 1963 Loi fédérale sur le cinéma was introduced. It was thus a period of great tumult, and great possibility, for a publicly-oriented vision of both filmmaking and television.

It is a period that was formative for Tanner: just as he was active in gaining the acceptance and implementation of the 1963 cinema law, he started working for SSR the year after this new policy was put into force. His first work for the station was *Le Droit au logement* (broadcast 4 February 1965), a twenty-minute piece strongly influenced by the John-Grierson-produced

Housing Problems (1935). This was made as part of the series "Continents sans visa," which became important as a venue where national and international issues where held in close balance. Here is how Vallotton explains it:

> In French-speaking Switzerland, the two news flagships "Continents sans visa," as well as "Temps présent," took account of little-known international realities and sensitized the public opinion to the brutality of the North-South relationship. "Continents sans visa" also took on certain hot topics with a show on banking secrecy in 1964, as well as with a "Dossier," directed by Alain Tanner, about "The Swiss Worker" (19 May 1966). This clearly activist broadcast was followed by a similar program on "The Swiss Peasant" and, a year later, "The Swiss Boss." (50)[4]

Despite this sense of excitement surrounding the early days of Swiss television, Tanner has always been clear that working for SSR was, at best, a mixed experience. Dimitriu has written that "The relationship between Tanner and television has always been that of the impossible love between a filmmaker who needs to be able to make images freely, not necessarily documentaries, and an institution that produces them but which upholds the laws of rationalization, and thus of bureaucracy" (22).[5] That desire to create freely is, of course, at the heart of the matter, and Tanner began as an agnostic about documentary and fiction when it came to searching for an environment where he could work as he wished. He wrote, in 1980, a sort of "ABCs" of television called "Télé-aphorismes" (which is reprinted and translated here, as Appendix 1), wherein he laid out his belief in the stages of televisual development. And although that essay is fairly pessimistic overall about the possibilities of the medium, in the entry for "Phases" he hints at what he found in the medium during the 1960s:

> **Phases.** There have been three phases in the development of television, three ways to look at it. The first was a period of creativity, of work, and of a bit of belief. The second was the discovery of what television really is, accompanied by a perverse

gorging on codes and signs, and a sort of third-degree joy in those codes and signs, a joy that goes right on up to understanding, and then to the quick exhaustion of that understanding. The third phase is now: a piece of furniture, with a bit of soccer and some old movies late at night. (31)[6]

Tanner and Berger made the material in this chapter halfway between phases one and two. The first phase, for Swiss television, was really the early experimental days, the days of those SSR committees which, because television had no real institutional status at all, were sustained entirely by hard work and faith in the future. But the immediately post-1964 period was clearly still a creative time, animated by a certain amount of belief as well, belief in television as a genuinely popular medium. But with the preliminary experiments now a fading memory, that belief was now coupled with a fairly rigorous understanding of what television really was, of its codes and signs. These productions – especially *Mike et l'usage de la science* and *Docteur B., médecin de campagne* – are unimaginable in any medium other than television.

That said, Tanner has never seemed entirely at home in documentary, televisual or otherwise. He wrote in *Ciné-mélanges* that:

> I hadn't made a documentary film in thirty years. In fiction, you say "I" and that gives you more free space. In saying "I," you have no obligation to anyone but yourself and the spectators. In documentary, you say "Them" and you have some obligation to them; you're not free to take advantage of them, without their agreement and their participation. But you mustn't make the film on them because that would place you outside and that's not a good place to be. You have to be with them, so that "them" gets changed into "us." This is the good place to work on a documentary. (41)[7]

Tanner was speaking there of making of two films thirty years apart – *L'Identité galloise* (1965), a nineteen-minute documentary he made for SSR, and *Les Hommes du port* (1995), which he produced independently. He argues in *Ciné-mélanges* that the culture of the Welsh miners that he tried to portray in the 1960s was similar in some ways to that of the Genoese dock workers, whose professionalism and incredibly well-organized union is the subject of his elegiac film of the 1990s. This trepidation in speaking as "nous" rather than "je" is a signal of Tanner's respect for the political possibilities of documentary, and his understanding of the ethical pitfalls it presents as well. These ethical pitfalls, as well as these political possibilities, were the subject of a lot of debate in the 1960s, when Tanner was making documentaries in the style that was, really, ground zero for such debate: direct cinema.

This was a movement that Tanner helped to found. Tanner's first film was a short documentary that he co-directed with Claude Goretta in London: 1957's *Nice Time*. Because of its hand-held camera work and interest in the everyday (it is shot over the course of an evening in Piccadilly Circus), it became a signature part of the "Free Cinema" movement. It was shown on the third program of the legendary Free Cinema shows that played that year at the British Film Institute's National Film Theatre, programs that were, I mentioned in the introduction, reviewed for *Sight and Sound* by one John Berger. "Free Cinema" is certainly an important predecessor to cinéma vérité or cinéma direct, but one crucial aspect of that aesthetic that *Nice Time* lacks is extensive use of synchronous sound. That use of synchronous sound, that ability to allow people to talk at length in spontaneous rather than staged situations (which would have been necessary for an earlier generation of heavier, lankier sound recorders and microphones), is a big part of what makes it possible to make films with people rather than just about people, to speak as "nous" rather than "je." Nevertheless, Tanner's first film is part of that international moment of direct cinema that so strongly marks the late 1950s and 60s, and its formal and political idealism is a constant presence in his work before *La Salamandre*.

Geoff Dyer argues that something very similar is going on in Berger's work during this period. He spends a lot of time in his book-length study *Ways of Telling* explaining the importance of a revitalized realist practice for the kind of aesthetics that he saw as a necessary response to the ravages of bourgeois capitalism. To a great extent this was a matter of a Georg-Lukács-inspired distinguishing between a naturalism that makes fetishes of surface details for basically formalist ends and a realism that uses these details to make the social, political, and historical reality of a work of art an integral part of its meaning. Drawing on Berger's reviews for the *New Statesman*, Dyer recalls that he felt in the 1950s that artists worked in a "narrow laboratory atmosphere" that was fully dependent on support from the bourgeoisie, and that this

> … went hand in hand with a social base of the visual arts that had shrunk to the point where they could not contain the broad scope of which Berger hoped they were capable. What Berger had prophesised in painting was, however, occurring in other areas of communication; on literary, drama and television. Berger noted that the works such as *The Lambeth Boys*, *Look Back in Anger*, *The Kitchen*, and *Room at the Top* satisfied "many of my often repeated critical demands." (24)

Berger was noting, basically, the importance of British Free Cinema (*The Lambeth Boys*) and its successors in feature-narrative filmmaking (*Look Back in Anger*, *The Kitchen*, and *Room at the Top*). These British filmmakers translated their use of freewheeling camera work and quotidian subject matter into studies of Britain's underclass, studies that made the simmering rage and lost human potential of that underclass the stuff of politically inflected tragedy (for me the best example of this is Karel Reisz's 1960 film *Saturday Night and Sunday Morning*, a work I am surprised to see missing from this roll call). In this way they are quite distinct from their contemporaries in the French New Wave, whose references, especially in the early 1960s, were mostly based not in their local political reality but in other films, frequently those from Hollywood (which, having been banned during the German occupation of their youth, took on a discernable, if entirely post-facto, subversive edge). The point for the early New-Wavers, after all, was to revolutionize French cinema, which they saw as being trapped in a stale, pretentious literary mindset. This mindset was eviscerated in Truffaut's firey 1954 essay "Une certaine tendance du cinéma français" (first published in the *Cahiers du cinéma* 31, at the same time Truffaut was also writing for the right-leaning magazine *Arts*; it is also reprinted in his collection *Le Plaisir des yeux*). That now-famous polemic castigated the French tendency to glorify the screenwriter at the expense of the director. Both early auteurism and the New Wave were revolutionary challenges, then, but challenges to French cinema, not to French society at large (this changes, especially chez Godard, as the 60s wear on). Dyer goes on to say that "Berger was *for* a reintegration of art and society as part of a larger political project at a time when technological and social changes were causing art to become increasingly self-determining, increasingly grounded in its own logic" (26). In cinema one of the most important technological changes of the 50s and 60s was the emergence of lightweight camera and sound gear. This technology was without doubt a driver of the French New Wave, and it was that technology that enabled the movement to become more self-determining. But its most famous members (Truffaut for sure, Godard until 1965's *Pierrot le fou*) used that self-determination to turn inward, to ground their films in their own logic of Parisian bohemianism and cinephilic knowingness. This formulation is not exactly the "anarchistes de droite" that Tanner recalled creeping him out during his 1958 visit to Paris, but it's close. The technology of direct cinema allowed a new kind of filmmaking to emerge, but the political orientation of such filmmaking varied greatly from place to place, despite aesthetic similarities. Berger saw this emergence as consistent with his own desire for an art that integrated the details of social and political reality into its aesthetic, but what was going on in France was basically inconsistent with this desire.

This is ironic, because at the theoretical level there are two figures that are of inescapable relevance for both Berger and Tanner's ideas about collaboration, aesthetics, and documentary: Jean Rouch and Jean-Louis Comolli. You will recall that I mentioned, in the introduction, Tanner's invocation of Comolli specifically as being important to his filmmaking. He was similarly complimentary about Rouch, specifically in the context of the films – all made for television – that I am discussing here. He told *Positif*'s Laurent Bonnard in 1972 that "Television was the beginning of the experience of synch sound, the handheld camera; it followed Rouch's first experiments, for example. Fiction didn't attract me and dramas didn't interest me at all" (31).[8] As early as 1961 Tanner was proclaiming his love for Rouch: in an interview for *Journal de Genève*'s "Samedi littéraire" that dealt with the three-screen short film *L'École* (a study of school architecture which had been commissioned for the 1962 Venice Trienniel), he said that "In France, my favourite is Jean Rouch. He is on the cutting edge of research into a new language and the discovery of the truth ['de la vérité,' so this is probably

a double-entendre with cinéma vérité, the documentary film movement]"
("Alain Tanner: Trois films").[9] Rouch was a celebrated ethnographic filmmaker (he made many films in Africa during the 1950s) and a very early
adopter of the technology of direct cinema. His cameraman on the famous
1960 film *Chronique d'un été* was the Québécois Michel Brault, who brought
to the production then-cutting-edge camera and sound gear that he had
developed while working at the National Film Board of Canada. In Peter
Wintonick's documentary *Cinéma Vérité: The Decisive Moment*, Rouch recalls
how Brault had brought from Quebec the prized objects of both "micro-
cravats" – lavaliere microphones – and "lentilles interdits" – by which he
meant impossible-to-obtain 60 mm lenses. Rouch used this equipment to
film what he jokingly called his "own tribe": Parisians in their native environs (the city's streets and small apartments). He then showed this footage
back to his subjects and edited in their responses to it by way of a coda for the
film. This is a very good example of what Comolli argued, in the two-part
essay on direct cinema that I mentioned in the introduction, is characteristic of the form: "The traditional divide between 'the action to film' and 'the
action of filming' resolves itself in 'filmed action'" (part 2, 42).[10] For Rouch
this "filmed action" is not only the simple record of young Parisians living
their lives but also the experience of having those lives filmed, of working
together with the camera crew – sometimes explicitly, as at the end, and
sometimes implicitly, as throughout the rest of the film. The technology
that makes this collapse possible is a core part of the film itself, something
that grounds the film inescapably in the moment of 1960s Paris, with all of
its social and political instability but also its sense as a genuine metropolis,
a place where all manner of people interact and collaborate in spontaneous,
unpredictable ways. Without the technology itself, such interaction remains
just a possibility; the technology is constitutive of the political and historical
moment, not simply a neutral tool to record it. "As much as you'd like to
respect the document, you can't help but **fabricate** it," Comolli writes. "It
doesn't pre-exist the reportage, but is instead its product" (part 1, 48–49,
bold in the original).[11] It is a very good example of the kind of realism that
Berger was looking for, an aesthetic, fabricated object which is nevertheless
the product of a social interaction. *Chronique d'un été*'s doing away with the
split between "action à filmer" and "action de filmer" means that it has, in
essence, moved away from using people simply as subject matter, as action

à filmer. Although Rouch's voice is present, speaking in first person on the film's soundtrack, there is a very real way in which he is speaking not as "je" but as "nous," as Tanner believes a documentarian should.

The films that I want to discuss here – *Une Ville à Chandigarh*, *Docteur B., médecin de campagne*, and *Mike et l'usage de la science* – are all significant for the challenges that they pose to the documentary practice of direct cinema, especially as enunciated by Rouch and Comolli. Tanner and Berger are working on these films after Rouch's best work has been shown throughout the francophone world and just before Comolli was writing his theoretical treatise. They proceed from some of the same assumptions Rouch was making and share a lot of the political idealism of Comolli, but they are often coming to very different conclusions about the formal and ethical stakes of documentary cinema. *Une Ville à Chandigarh* is a highly aestheticized work, one that integrates social and historical detail very tightly but which does so in a very self-conscious way that looks at times like direct cinema but which is actually something more hybrid, more between older and emerging documentary forms. *Docteur B., médecin de campagne* looks more like a "conventional" work of direct cinema and helps draw attention to the cinematic quality of Berger's literary work of this period, especially *A Fortunate Man*, the 1967 book to which this film is an obvious companion. *Mike et l'usage de la science* is the oddest of these films: it has few of the stylistic traits of direct cinema, but the film's politics are more consistent with Comolli's sense of direct as inherently oppositional than are the other two films. These three films, then, rather that simple hack-work done for Swiss television before "real" films like *La Salamandre* or *Jonas qui aura 25 ans en l'an 2000*, together constitute a wide-ranging inquiry into a form that was, in the 1960s, at the leading edge of political cinema. And crucially, this inquiry was being conducted not in a "narrow laboratory atmosphere," but in the most widely diffused medium of its day: television.

Une Ville à Chandigarh

Its roots should not fool you. Even though it was partially commissioned by Swiss Air as a tribute to the work of the ultra-rationalist Swiss urban planner Le Corbusier (1887–1965), *Une Ville à Chandigarh* is an aesthetically complex piece of work. It was the place where Berger and Tanner, working together for the first time (Tanner directed the film and oversaw the shooting; Berger wrote the voice-over text, after the fact), were able to outline some of their ideas about modernity, the sound-image relationship, and political art.

As with Tanner's early film *Nice Time* (1957), *Une Ville à Chandigarh* frequently looks and feels like a piece of mid-60s direct cinema, but it is in fact defined by an older ethic of documentary. I mentioned in note 2 of the introduction that, although *Nice Time* has a lot of hand-held camera work, it actually has very little synchronous sound; this is quite typical of documentaries of the 1950s and 60s, the period of transition between post-synched and synchronized sound in documentary. Furthermore, it's typical of Tanner's work of this period, and not only of *Nice Time*. Recalling his first feature-length film, a 1964 documentary about young carpentry apprentices called *Les Apprentis*, he told Dimitriu that "We shot *Les Apprentis* in a basically anachronistic way (although these techniques [of direct cinema] didn't exist in Switzerland), with a big, blimped 35 mm camera, even though it was an ideal subject for a more free-wheeling style" (100).[12] Even a cursory viewing of *Les Apprentis* (available in full at TSR's website) bears this out; there is very little in the way of handheld or genuinely mobile camera work in the film, although there is plenty of synch sound, shot on location. Although *Une Ville à Chandigarh* was actually shot on 16 mm, something very similar is going on aesthetically, if slightly in reverse; there is plenty of camera movement, but little synch sound. The only moment of such sound in the entire film is its concluding shot, which is of a woman singing. She is held in a medium close-up, and the camera does not move at all; whether the camera was blimped I cannot say, but this is just as static an image as those of *Les Apprentis*. There is a lot of hand-held camera work in *Une Ville à Chandigarh*, it's just that the soundtrack is either made up of the text written by Berger or of "wild sound." A sequence showing a Sikh harvest dance is particularly illustrative here. This is an event filled with colour and kinesis, and the camera moves all around the space, more or less holding the dancers in long shot. Tanner is obviously using a wide-angle lens here, and the visual field in all of the images feels open and full of possibility. In short, a classic kind of vérité sensibility is at work here, one that emphasizes dynamic visuals and a sense of spontaneity. But what is missing is the *sound* of vérité. All of the sounds of a parade and dancing are present (in addition to spoken text, which observes how the methods of harvest are far less precise than this dance), but they are not meaningfully in synch with the dancers, not comparable to the concluding sequence where the woman's lips are really moving with the sound of the song. This is the direct cinema of *Les Raquetteurs* (Quebec, 1959), whose soundtrack full of city noises, cheering spectators and barking dogs was almost entirely "built" in an editing studio; it is the direct cinema of *Primary* (USA, 1960), a film whose only really synchronous images are those of politicians giving speeches to one or two almost completely static cameras.

To put it in Swiss terms, this is the direct cinema of *Quand nous étions petits enfants*, Henry Brandt's 1964, feature-length documentary portrait of a small village in the Jura mountains of Neuchâtel. Tanner recalled to Dimitriu that "Inspired by the English experience of 'Free Cinema' and Brandt's film *Quand nous étions petits enfants*, we put into action a plan for a series of medium-length documentaries on subjects that got a bit into the social life of the country" (99).[13] Brandt's work was of enormous importance to Swiss cinema of the 1960s, in a way that is comparable to the importance of the French-language unit of the NFB during the same period. Discussing the 1964 Exposition nationale (for which Tanner had made the documentary *Les Apprentis* as part of the Brandt-produced series "La Suisse s'interroge"), Freddy Buache notes that "I believe that he is the first francophone Swiss filmmaker who was able to make the general public understand the importance and the powers of cinema in modern life. The presence of Henry Brandt's films at the Exposition nationale was a real event" (*Le cinéma suisse*, 13).[14] *Quand nous étions petits enfants* definitely has a lyrical feel to it, being centred mostly around the everyday events of a small village as seen through the eyes of its schoolteacher, Charles Guyot; this is no doubt the reason Buache calls the film a "poème des Travaux" (ibid.). Brandt's eye for landscape is very sharp, but he also has a genuinely kinetic sense; a sequence late in the film that documents winter frolicking is especially vividly realized, and a shot where about a dozen ice-skating kids all holding hands glide towards the camera is truly lovely. But as far as sound goes there is very little that is really synchronous; a lot of it is "wild sound" in the style of *Nice Time* or *Les Raquetteurs*, and some of the dialogue that is "synched" is so awkward that it looks to have been done in a studio after shooting.

By pointing this out I certainly do not mean to speak ill of any of these films. They are each fascinating works of documentary, all indicative of a genuinely kinetic visual consciousness. But their sound-image relationships are quite a bit more complex than a simple matter of "you are there," fly-on-the-wall aesthetics.

It is thus important to take full account of the images of *Une Ville à Chandigarh*'s shifting relationship with its soundtrack. At first, the soundtrack and images work very closely together, but as the film progresses they slowly move apart, only to sometimes come back together again. "This is the tradition of India," the voice-over states at early in the film. "This is what must both be accepted and change. 360 million Indians live in villages, and that is 80 per cent of the population." This is over an extreme long shot of a man pulling a plough through a large, dusty field; it is shot in slow motion. So far we seem to be solidly in the realm of the liberal-reformist documentary about the Third World, and there are a lot of images in first part of *Une Ville* that work like this. But even here, matters are more complicated. The shot that follows this one is very different. It is a close-up of an old man at the plough; it is shot with a telephoto lens, so the man and his plough are in very sharp focus but the limited depth of field makes the crops in the background look distant and blurry. The camera pans back and forth a bit as the man walks side to side, and at one point he fills up nearly the entire frame, with only some green blur in the background. Both he and the camera continue to move, and eventually the camera settles on the face of a younger man, who hovers on the edge of the frame, always in motion. The shot is completely at odds with images like the one of the Sikh harvest dance, inasmuch as the long lenses heighten both the closeness of the people in the image and the distance of the other graphic elements, giving the image a semi-abstract quality. Furthermore, despite the pans side to side there is a kind of illusion of stasis here, generated by the fact that people keep coming in and out of frame. This studied and yet non-figurative imagery is also at odds with the parts of this first section of the film where the voice-over is generally used to explain the images. The explanations are in a more impassioned tone of voice than in a conventional documentary and demonstrate a real admiration for the work that is being done here. But they are fairly straightforward as documentary narration. When the film forgoes voice-over, it moves into very lyrical territory, into an aesthetic pattern that is equally defined by photographic realism and poetry. And at other times, the soundtrack works quite directly against the images. About halfway through the film, the voice-over explains how, even though Indian peasants used to live among their cows, there are no cows allowed in the new city of Chandigarh; there is only a city-owned dairy, at the edge of town. This text is set over a 180-degree pan shot of a small village that is filled equally with cows and people. This shot is followed by a short montage of the countryside as the voice-over explains that there are no shantytowns on the edge of the city because it is all owned by the state. This sort of push and pull between illustration and opposition is what defines more or less the last two thirds of the film.

The transitional part of *Une Ville à Chandigarh* is the sequence in the library. This is comprised of a very long tracking shot and a short montage. As the camera slowly moves up a reading room, keeping patrons in a close-up, the soundtrack is silent. Once we are about halfway up the room, the voice-over simply says that there is something special about libraries, and then goes silent again. But once we are at the end of the room, the film switches to a montage of faces of young women reading, and there is a quote from W.B. Yeats' poem "Long-Legged Fly": "Like a long-legged fly upon the stream / Her mind moves upon the silence." This will become the overall strategy for the film: the use of quotations which have nothing to do with India by way of illuminating some element of the film's visual field.

Berger explained this strategy in his interview with Appignanesi, stating that his desire in writing the text was to eschew conventional description, but that is not exactly what we have in *Une Ville à Chandigarh*. He said there that he and Tanner got to know each other first in London in the 1950s and 60s, and then re-connected a few years later when both were living in Geneva:

> At that time he was occasionally making films for Swiss television. One of these was a thirty-minute film about the architecture of Chandigarh in India, which had been built by Le Corbusier, another Swiss. Alain asked me to write the commentary for this film, which I did. The kind of commentary I wrote, although we didn't realize it at the time, was perhaps a little prophetic of some other things we were going to do. Instead of

writing a descriptive commentary about the architecture, what I used were quotations from poets and political theorists which were played in juxtaposition – sometimes ironic, sometimes confirmative – of what was seen on the screen. (299)

The film's commentary integrates text by Rousseau, Yeats, Le Corbusier, Bertolt Brecht, and Aimé Césaire. And as Berger says, sometimes these citations confirm what is on screen, as with the line from Yeats and the montage of young women reading in a library. And sometimes they are ironic; this is true of a sequence towards the end of the film, when the lines "My son asks me should I learn mathematics / What for, I'd like to say / This empire is ending" are placed over a high-angle long shot of a professor holding forth in a lecture hall and close-ups of students attentively listening (the lines are from Brecht's poem "My Young Son Asks Me"). But in other parts of the film there is, quite literally, descriptive commentary about the architecture. In addition to the commentary about 80 per cent of the population living in villages, this is also true of a sequence late in the film composed of a series of zooms in and out of various parts of Le Corbusier's buildings in Chandigarh; the commentary explains the way in which the spaces were built, how they interact with one another, etc.

This mélange of voices on the soundtrack is notable, of course, for its absence of Indian voices; this is actually key to the film's politics. Berger was a strong advocate for many francophone writers from former colonies, and part of the reason for Césaire's presence on the soundtrack was no doubt that Berger was the first to translate his seminal prose-poem *Cahier d'un retour au pays natal* into English. And that work, it is important to recall here, traced a path that wandered all over Africa, the Caribbean, and France; it was an explicitly nomadic analysis of the fate of the displaced black consciousness. And while Tanner was certainly an internationalist, casually rattling off his cinematic inspirations "en France, en Tchécoslovaquie, au Québec, en Pologne, au Brésil, et ailleurs," Berger was, during this period, more passionate still about forging an internationalism that would include the Third World on equal terms. Reporting for the *New Statesman* on the 1958 Venice Biennale, he wrote that:

Among the 500 or so artists on show at Venice there are perhaps a dozen who were possibly born with no more talent than their fellow exhibitors but who encouragingly remind us that art is independent to exactly the same degree as it discloses reality. There are Kewal Soni, Indian Sculptor; Padamsee, Indian painter; Ivan Peries, Ceylonese painter; Raul Anguiano, Mexican follower of Rivera; Brusselmans of Belgium; Ichiro Fukuzara, Japanese expressionist. And then there is the pavilion of the United Arab Republic.[15] Only occasionally do history and art correspond with one another as directly as they do here; but it remains a fact that this pavilion is the most affirmative and vital of all in the 1958 Biennale. (*Permanent Red*, 49)

What is striking here is the casualness with which these nationalities mingle. India, Ceylon (Sri Lanka), Mexico, Belgium, Japan, and the UAR are, to say the least, in *very* different places in terms of the socio-economic balance of power circa 1950, but they come together in Berger's prose because they have something to tell us about the value of his beloved realist aesthetics. Berger's politics of 1950s and 60s were defined not by nationalist-led liberation movements, then, but by mixtures, by wanderings. His was a Third World politics of Césaire, not Fanon. Thus it is not surprising that a film about India has no Indians on the soundtrack; the cultural condition that he was evoking here went well beyond India, a place that comprises the visual track in its entirety. Tanner's images visualize India as modern in part because it is able to integrate the designs of a European architect into the rhythms of a daily life that is still strongly dominated by tradition. Although he is critical of Berger's text for insufficiently dealing with Indian concepts of life and death, Dimitriu frames this sort of mixture in a basically positive light when he notes that "Throughout the entire film, we see this connection, both formal and semantic, between Indian and European elements. The city is built by and for Indians, but the students wear European clothes. Rupees are converted into francs. The architecture is western, but the music and the sounds are indigenous. This is the optimistic sense of Le Corbusier that is shared by Tanner: it is above all about the search for *joie de vivre*, the aspiration to live in a radiant city, that counts" (20–21).[16] Berger's collage of European and Caribbean voices is part and parcel of the way that the film evokes this optimistic, distinctly modern and, it bears noting, seminally Indian vision of cultural transformation via mixture.

Overall, then, *Une Ville à Chandigarh* is defined by an exceptionally complex form of montage, the putting together of disparate elements in order to create some sort of synthesis not contained in either element alone. Indeed, the film is defined by a kind of "spirit of montage," one that is very close to the project laid out in the "Montage" text by Jacques Rivette, Jean Narboni, and Sylvie Pierre that I discussed in the introduction. It is there that Rivette lays out a distinction between two kinds of filmmakers:

> ... between filmmakers who essentially "make" the film during shooting (and in the preparation for shooting, such as Ford and Renoir), and those for whom this work of writing, or of strategy, and the shooting of footage, is only the accumulation of "matter" (of the material for the film), which is then all put together, and only takes on its shape and makes sense in the editing room (this is as true of Rouch and [Quebec filmmaker Pierre] Perrault as it is for Godard and Eisenstein). (18)[17]

Clearly Berger and Tanner are more in the "Rouch and Perrault" camp than the "Godard and Eisenstein" one, being filmmakers who are interested, especially here, in evoking a complex culture in a way that makes the partial, composite nature of the portrait explicit. Furthermore, the film is defined by a marked tension between "le montage à l'intérieur d'une scène ou simplement entre les scènes," which was the way that Tanner saw the editing of *Le Milieu du monde*. This is definitely how the editing of *Une Ville* operates as well. The film has a lot of straightforward montage sequences – such as the montage of the women's faces, or that sequence of zooms through Chandigarh's buildings. This is le montage à l'intérieur d'une scène. The film's many complex long takes – such as a quite extraordinary sequence where the camera (again using a telephoto lens) holds the dirty face of an older female labourer in a medium close-up as she picks up and drops material on a building site – are in no way incompatible with these sequences. They are elements of a sort of macro-level montage, of montage entre les scènes, as Tanner writes. The film is comprised of juxtaposition between long takes and montage sequences, seemingly disparate elements that sometimes work together and sometimes are put into opposition. This is, of course, a very clear echo of how the voice-over is interacting with the images. It is also, as Berger said in that 1985 interview, prophetic of the things they would go on to do together.

Mike et l'usage de la science

One of the films that *Une Ville à Chandigarh* anticipates is *Mike et l'usage de la science*, a television documentary about a socially committed nuclear scientist (broadcast 12 March 1968). The film as preserved by TSR has no credits on it, and the fiche on the website mentions only Tanner's name. And even though the filmography in Dimitriu's book says that the film's scenario is by Tanner alone, it also has the credit "Reportage et réalization: Alain Tanner, avec la participation de John Berger." Dimitriu writes of the film that "We sense here the very strong influence of John Berger, who collaborated on the scenario.... Mike and his spirit come up again, probably twice as much, in several characters in *Jonas*" (24).[18] *Mike et l'usage de la science* is indeed possessed of a spirit that is very Bergerian (to coin a term that I plan to use again!) in that it is political but in a slightly brooding way and is possessed of a very optimistic view of internationalism. It also presents science as something that is tied to worldly concerns, mostly in the way that it represents, via Mike, a restless, optimistic search for truth. Aesthetically *Mike et l'usage de la science* owes relatively little to direct cinema, and the amount of direct address contained in the film hints at Tanner's burgeoning Brechtianism. As my discussion of *Une Ville à Chandigarh* contained some political discussion but presented that film as being significant for mostly aesthetic reasons, I will discuss the aesthetics of *Mike et l'usage de la science* here but mostly present the film as being important for political reasons.

The film opens with a medium shot of two men engaging in a very broad philosophical discussion in heavily accented French. How can we really understand reality? they wonder. Reality, the man on the right says, is only an abstraction, unless you have the POV of God. The man on the right is John Berger, who will again appear in the film's concluding sequence, when the two continue their discussion to include a debate on the value of making a film about issues of science and responsibility. The man on the left is Michael Pence, a nuclear physicist originally from South Africa who renounced his citizenship to become British, before moving, with his wife and five children, to Geneva. We know this because Pence says all that directly to the camera, in the film's second shot, a medium close-up where he speaks casually and smokes his ever-present pipe.

This is a pretty fair summary of the film's aesthetic pattern overall. There is a bit of handheld camera work when Tanner follows him around his laboratory at the Université de Genève, as well as during a montage sequence that moves between images of him in the lecture hall and shots of one of his younger sons learning his multiplication tables at school. But a very large part of the film is given over to interviews with Mike where he – sometimes with family members – speaks directly to the camera, or to candid but basically static material that, more often than not, uses voice-over rather than (or sometimes in addition to) directly synched sound.

Even though I use the term "film" when discussing *Mike et l'usage de la science* (largely because it was shot on 16 mm), this is, really, the visual pattern of television. Serge Daney, writing nineteen years after *Mike* was broadcast, speculated that "If, finally, TV is our prose (and we'll never speak well enough), cinema no longer has a chance, except in poetry" (90).[19] This poetry-prose split is evocative, especially in the context of a film like *Mike*. There is very little visual poetry, so to speak, in this film. There are some well-executed moving-camera images and the occasional moment of lyricism (a high-angle medium shot of Mike having a mug of tea in bed, for instance), but these are occasional flourishes, the likes of which would be present in any essay written with some sense of style. The film's impact comes mostly from what people say, rather than the images of them saying it. Overall *Mike* is expositional rather than suggestive, prosaic rather than poetic. Tanner echoed Daney's sentiments in his "Télé-Aphorismes" essay, although in a much less optimistic tone. "Television is an art of the mouth," he wrote under the entry for **"Bouche"** [mouth], "and it's not always very appetizing."[20] *Mike et l'usage de la science* is certainly about being an art of the mouth, but this doesn't at all lessen its power to politically engage. If anything, this insistence on the value of talk, and complex, sometimes meandering talk, evinces a patience and seriousness on the part of the viewer that brings us closer to Daney's utopia of "une télé adulte." Tanner complains that the third, decadent phase of television is when it becomes furniture. Here we can see television in a stage that is closer to vegetation, to wild grass; it's everywhere, and it remains rooted in the landscape from which it came. "Television rises to the level of ecology," Daney writes, "because it touches the responsible citizen in us, that is to say, the adult" (189).[21]

So despite the fact that the film isn't much as direct cinema, which Comolli sees as the inherently political form of documentary, it is still as explicitly activist as anything in Berger and Tanner's œuvre. It wasn't that the two were strangers to political filmmaking at this point. Although the politics of *Une Ville à Chandigarh* are a bit opaque, Tanner, for instance, was making television work in the 1960s that was quite engaged with (often militant) struggles of various sorts. I have in mind here not only the films that I discussed in the introduction – *La Pouvoir dans la rue*, about May '68; *Les Trois belgique*, about linguistic strife in Flanders and Wallonia; *L'Indépendance au loin*, about the Jura conflict, etc. – but also films about Wales and Israel. *L'Identité galloise* (broadcast 15 July 1965) is about Welsh nationalism, and it is very similar to *L'Indépendance au loin* in terms of its even-handedness in the face of Tanner's discernable sympathy. The film has a lot of interviews with key figures in Welsh nationalism; it opens with a shot of the pirate radio station Radio Free Wales ("The Voice of Welsh Freedom!"), has an interview with the militant Harri Williams, has footage of a Welsh-language crèche and a Welsh-medium school (where kids are learning French through Welsh), etc. But Tanner gives almost as much screen time to interviews with miners, people in dance halls, on beaches, etc., who awkwardly express a sense of being Welsh but who have little to no interest in nationalism or separatism. The film seems sympathetic to one side of a political struggle, but it's not really a work of advocacy. Much the same is true of *La Troupe de music-hall* (broadcast 16 May 1969), a film Tanner made about the post-Six-Day-War state (and State) of Israel. Again the work is mostly made up of interviews, but the range of political opinions is greater even than in *L'Identité galloise*. The film seems basically sympathetic to Israeli culture, purely by virtue of the ethnic and political diversity that is on display here (a Sabra dance teacher, a kibbutz-dwelling florist whose parents came from Germany, a woman born in Switzerland where her parents were refugees, etc.). But Tanner also seems critical of the current political situation, by virtue of the fact that he asks everyone he interviews how peace can be made with the Arabs and how the problem of Palestinian refugees can be solved. I use the verb "seem" in discussing both films because it is hard to get a sense of their political positions. In many ways the films are defined by the experience of widespread indifference coming up against the idealism of an outsider (as Tanner seems to gradually discover that Welsh people aren't all that interested in Welsh nationalism and have only the vaguest sense of what it means to be Welsh) or the realization that a community of highly committed twentysomethings are living in a country that has entered into a likely intractable political quagmire (as young Israeli after young Israeli offers pained, inadequate responses to the refugee crisis which they, as members of a citizen militia explicitly modelled on Switzerland's, are directly involved in).

There is no such sense of defeat in *Mike et l'usage de la science*. The film presents Mike as tireless; we see him working in the lab, talking of being president of the university's staff association, presenting at an anti-apartheid meeting, playing Beethoven on the piano with his youngest son and skiing shirtless with his two older boys after the three of them quaff a beer on the mountaintop. One image is particularly effective in conveying his relentlessness: a tracking shot that follows him through the halls of the university, with a voice-over that has him holding forth about an early job working as a physicist at a factory in Manchester is what brought him to socialism, since it gave him a sense of the economic roots of racial discrimination. There's a lot packed into that shot: a past in South Africa, a decision to become British, a present-day life as a nuclear physicist at one of Europe's leading universities, a commitment to socialism, a realization that economics doesn't tell the whole story but that telling the whole story requires it, etc. It's a key moment in the film because it presents a guy at the peak of his form, and that peak has a lot to do with being a political animal.

Mike's politics as presented in the film are, like those of Janos Lavin in *A Painter of Our Time*, very close to Berger's own. Mike is someone who was restless in the country of his birth and so chose to emigrate to Geneva. Berger made a similar decision in the 1960s, and to Richard Appignanesi's question of why he lives outside of the UK, he replied that "I've lived outside of Britain now for about twenty years, and I had the idea of leaving Britain long before that, but I didn't quite see the opportunity of doing so. The very simple answer is, I feel far more at home on the continent than I do in Britain" (303). This is not an explicitly political reason for migrating to Europe, and so it is interesting to see that the film presents Mike's movement from South Africa to the UK to Geneva in terms that are not only political. Early in the film Mike recalls (in direct address to the camera) that he renounced his South African citizenship because the political situation had become intolerable. But he also recalls that he came to the UK so he could do *science*. This has a political aspect to it; he tells the camera that many of his friends from South Africa are now in jail or in exile. But during that sequence he also says that living in South Africa faced him with a stark choice: "faire la science ou pas." Not "prison ou pas" or "exil ou pas": Mike's ability to pursue his vocation as a *scientist* was the reason he left South Africa for Britain, eventually coming to Europe, and that very strongly echoes Berger's own literary blossoming once he left London for Switzerland and then for France.

So this film, which begins and ends with an image of John Berger talking philosophy with Mike, has a discernibly auto-biographical character to it: it is a portrait of a man who wants to reconcile his deep political commitments with his equally powerful commitment to something that seems to transcend earthly concerns at the same time it embodies them. Mike's commitment to physics is, really, a lot like Berger's commitment to art and literature. In the lecture that I mentioned earlier as part of a montage sequence with images of his son at school, Mike holds forth on how quantum theory leads both to benefits to humanity and to napalm, both to nuclear energy and to nuclear weapons. What *Mike et l'usage de la science* never shows is Mike discussing how quantum theory leads to more precise or more complex equations. Physics as a purely formal practice holds no interest for him, at least as he is presented by the film. Trying to enunciate what he means by realism, Berger writes in *Permanent Red* that realists "bring into art aspects of nature and life previously ignored or forbidden by the rule-makers. It is in this sense that realists can be opposed to formalists. Formalists are those who use the conventions of their medium (conventions that originally came into being for the purpose of translating aspects of life into art) to keep out or pass over new aspects" (208). *Mike et l'usage de la science* is defined by a desire to explain what aspects of life Mike can translate into physics. A desire for discovery, and a desire for truth, both of which were so crucially important to the idealism of the Enlightenment, is clearly a big part of Berger and Tanner's task here, just as it is for their version of Mike. We have so little influence, Mike and Berger jointly lament in the closing sequence of the film. Ah, but there is one thing we can control, Mike says: "L'esprit scientifique." Understanding that spirit in all its radicalism is what this film is about, and that is a clear continuation of Berger's desire to recover the parallel radicalism of realist aesthetics.

Docteur B., médecin de campagne

Although it is also ostensibly about a man of science, *Docteur B., médecin de campagne* (broadcast 7 May 1968) is a very different film from *Mike et l'usage de la science*. Part of this is about aesthetics; of all the films I am discussing in this chapter, this is the one that is most clearly an example of direct cinema. But it is also about tone, and about politics. Even though this is a film that Berger officially had nothing to do with, it is the television work of Tanner's that is closest to work Berger did elsewhere. For *Docteur B., médecin de campagne* is very clearly influenced by the book Berger did with the Swiss photographer Jean Mohr, *A Fortunate Man* (1967), simply in terms of its subject matter but also in terms of its complex formal pattern. This is quite an extraordinary film, certainly the most complex piece of work that Tanner would do until the features he made with Berger (and really, the most complex film he would make until *Le Milieu du monde*). This is due, in no small part, to the way that it presents the push and pull between the community and the individual as part of the same dialectic as that push and pull between tradition and modernity, and yet still manages, as Berger's book does, to avoid all traces of the folkloric or nostalgic. Politically, it sets the stage for the work that Berger and Tanner would go on to do together in a way that no other film had yet done.

Docteur B. is a portrait of a doctor practising somewhere in the Jura mountains (it is not clear exactly where, although all the cars have Vaud licence plates), and it follows a lot of the then-current patterns of vérité portraiture. There is no voice-over narration (the only non-synchronous sound is of the Doctor's own voice), and there are no interviews with anyone; whenever someone seems to be directly addressing the camera, it is because they are in some situation where they are addressing an audience and the camera is adopting that point of view. We come to know a lot about the Doctor – he is married with five children, he is fairly religious, he thinks a lot about politics, he speaks Italian well enough to have consultations in that language with a local immigrant family, he is a scout leader (who is committed enough to the cause to wear the very silly uniform at meetings), etc. Like all portraiture the picture we get here is fragmented and incomplete, but there is a level of detail and an interest in aspects of everyday life (like those scout meetings) such that the viewer has the sensation of knowing the man quite well. This is true despite the fact that we never actually learn his name.

This push and pull between the very precise and the basically hidden – the Jura, but where? We know he's a scoutmaster but we don't know his surname? – gives the film the weight of allegory. For what Tanner is portraying here is not really a specific man, a specific doctor, but a way of moving through the world that is committed in a broadly humanist way but also deeply rooted to a specific place, a specific community. There are plenty of aspects of *Docteur B.* that encourage such an allegorical reading, many of them visual. Early in the film, for instance, there is a shot out the window taken from the front seat of the doctor's VW Bug as it lopes through the incredibly snowy countryside. On the voice-over the Doctor says that he came to medicine "because of an interest in entering into peoples lives and seeing them *chez eux*."[22] As he explains these reasons for his vocation, the camera holds on the windshield, and as the snow gets thicker and thicker, the entire screen eventually goes completely white. It is a moment of verbalized idealism and visual abstraction, and serves as an indication that, despite the fact that this is a documentary, simple representation of reality is not the film's task. Instead, it is a contemplative study of the relationship between landscape (which here becomes totalizing and pure), personal commitment (which is explained briefly but pithily on the soundtrack) and community (which is implicit here, as we are in this car to follow the Doctor from one *house* call to another). There is a very similar sequence later in the film, where images of his car consumed by blowing snow are accompanied by the Doctor's voice explaining the degree to which medicine is a balance between art and science.

There's no doubt that *Docteur B.* is quite consistent with the formal and thematic concerns of 60s vérité, but the politics that result from this form are not quite those that Comolli alludes to in the quote that opens this chapter. This film is political, and it is about struggle, but I'm not sure that *Cahiers* watchwords of this period such as *cinéma politique* or *luttant* would really apply here. Instead, the theoretical program that the film is connected to by its realist form is that of John Berger. Here the relevant text is not so much *Permanent Red* but the work that he was doing with Tanner's fellow citizen of Geneva, the photographer Jean Mohr. Berger and Mohr saw their work together as something that would use art to try to forge more meaningful connections between people, to try to contribute to a world defined by solidarity rather than atomization. Berger spelled this out in an interview he and Mohr gave to *Screen Education*'s Paul Willis in 1979:

> … individuality is something we all share, and the crucial question is whether we use this individuality in a way which leads to individualism – feelings and emotions of envy, which the consumer society so catastrophically stimulates – or whether one uses it to realise that within one's own individuality, there is precisely the capacity to understand, and sometimes, if that happens to be your craft, to speak for or take pictures for other people's experiences and their individuality. (26)

This desire to see in a picture of an individual some glimpse of other people's experiences, to recover understanding through plunging deeply into people's lives, and doing so *chez eux*, is exactly the subject and the formal strategy of *Docteur B., médecin de campagne*. One aspect that Tanner brings out in his portrait of the Doctor is that he is not some sort of scientist-technician. He is, like Mike Pence, a man of science because he has such a capacity to understand, a capacity he is constantly nurturing and trying to nurture in others. Because while Tanner does show a number of consultations, he also includes sequences where the Doctor gives a talk to teenage boys about sexuality, where he engages in a long talk with a young man about how Swiss youth are increasingly restless with the army and neutrality because they are more able to spend time abroad, and where he tries to get an assembly of pastors' wives to think about the troubles faced by immigrants from Spain, Italy, and Tunisia. These sequences come without any particular segue from the material that is more strictly medical or more strictly personal. Understanding the way that these kinds of subjects blur together is a big part of understanding what kind of individual the Doctor is, a task that Tanner accomplishes without any whiff of what Berger would call individualism.

This dialectic between self and others, between portraiture and community, is at the heart of the text that is my reason for including this film as a "collaboration," Berger and Mohr's *A Fortunate Man* (1967). This came out the year before Tanner made *Docteur B., médecin de campagne*, and the similarities between the two works are considerable, especially on the level form. Both *A Fortunate Man* and *Docteur B.* are examples of the sort of realism that Berger had invested so much effort in theorizing and which was also close to the ideals of cinéma vérité: they are rooted in the material details of the everyday, but are very clearly *works*, aesthetic objects that make an analysis of the world as their creators find it, an analysis that they do not seek to hide behind a cloak of hyper-verisimilitude. Furthermore, there is, like in all Berger's work (as in all direct cinema, as Comolli argues in the quote that opens this chapter), a discernibly political element here, and this is a big part of its influence on Tanner's film. It is not simply that both *A Fortunate Man* and *Docteur B., médecin de campagne* are about country doctors; both are about the larger political meaning of rural existence, and use the life of a doctor as a way of gaining access to that meaning. About halfway through *Docteur B., médecin de campagne*, there is a medium-long shot of men working in the snowy forest, and on the voice-over is the Doctor explaining how the people in this region are still basically peasants, and as such tend to be very timid. About halfway through *A Fortunate Man*, Berger explains the community he has been portraying like this:

> The area as a whole is economically depressed. There are only a few large farms and no large-scale industries. Fewer than half the men work on the land. Most earn their living in small workshops, quarries, a wood-processing factory, a jam factory, a brickworks. They form neither a proletariat nor a traditional rural community. They belong to the Forest and in the surrounding districts they are invariably known as "the foresters." They are suspicious, independent, tough, poorly educated, low church. They have something of the character once associated with wandering traders like tinkers. (83)

This is, in many ways, the world that Tanner is evoking as well. This becomes clear not only because of the Doctor's explicit classification of his community as a peasant one, but also because the film is filled with sequences where we see that his patients are if not suspicious then definitely taciturn, perhaps not poorly educated but defined mostly by menial work, and, in the francophone-protestant Canton Vaud, are a Swiss equivalent of low church. This is a world that by the 1960s was beginning to disappear. As Berger's career went on he became more and more committed to it, eventually moving to a small alpine village in France and writing his "Into Their Labours" trilogy about peasant life in Europe, the first of which was 1979's *Pig Earth*. Tanner's interest in this world of tough, alienated peasantry was more fleeting; in *Docteur B., médecin de campagne* it serves more as a means to explore the nature of commitment and rootedness. It is a world that seems made for a man like the Doctor, a world that allows him to indulge in what Berger (speaking of John Sassell, the doctor at the centre of his book) calls "the part of the gentleman allotted him" (83) when Tanner shows us a shot of him eating fondue, smoking pipes and talking shop with two fellow doctors, but which also allows him to cut an old man's fingernails with a love and commitment similar to what he brings to cutting his son's birthday cake (to summarize a montage sequence that comes at the end of the film).

Docteur B., médecin de campagne's visuals are also strongly influenced by the photographs of *A Fortunate Man*. This is especially true of the images of the doctor's car. Photographs like the one of Sassell talking to an old man as he sits in the driver's seat, stopped along the road (67), have no literal equivalent in *Docteur B., médecin de campagne* but they do give a sense, as do the numerous images of the Doctor driving that Tanner shot from the same passenger's seat POV, that a country doctor spends an inordinate about of time, and mental energy, in the car. Mohr's image of Sassell's land-rover in the evening winding its way down an impossibly narrow country path (76) is a genuine icon of a country doctor's life and everyday struggles. That image is very close to the film's concluding image, a long shot of the doctor's car driving though the snowy Jura night which turns into a slow zoom that moves towards the car's headlights. Looking at that image of the VW Bug next to the Mohr photo of Sassell's land-rover would almost make you think that Tanner had plucked that still photograph right out of the book and dropped it into his film. Such close correspondence is not surprising, for *A Fortunate Man* is a remarkably cinematic book. This is especially true of photo sequences like those of a town hall meeting (97–101), where five photographs move the viewer gently through a space and smoothly across an unspecified period of time in a way that is completely consistent with the logic of cinematic découpage. It is also true of a series of four photographs of the same man which get gradually closer, and whose depth of field becomes discernibly narrower, as though we were zooming in on him, only to finish with a "rack focus" (actually two images) onto the woman sitting next to the man (107–11). Berger, Mohr, and Tanner are all speaking a very similar language here, on that crosses the boundaries of film, literature, and still photography. They share some of the political possibility that Comolli invests in vérité, but to say that both *Docteur B., médecin de campagne* and *A Fortunate Man* are simply different manifestations of "le direct" doesn't seem quite right. This is not to minimize the degree to which the form of *A Fortunate Man* is influenced by contemporary developments in documentary cinema; that influence is considerable. But really, both *Docteur B., médecin de campagne* and *A Fortunate Man* are examples of a formal pattern consistent with the realism that Berger hoped for in *Permanent Red*, which he tries to define by contrast: "What do the rules of the new art forbid? The answer is staggering: any precise hopeful reference to the objective world. And so the Realist must look at the modern world, which has so unnerved the Formalist, and come to terms with it" (208–9). Looking hopefully at this objective world and coming to terms with it through the aesthetics of cinema, still photography, or written language, is precisely what *A Fortunate Man* and *Docteur B., médecin de campagne* are trying to do.

One question that such an approach inevitably poses is who these works are for. It is clear that, even though both *Docteur B., médecin de campagne* and *A Fortunate Man* are works about tightly knit communities, they are not simply records of those communities made for internal consumption only. Berger spends a lot of time writing in *A Fortunate Man* about the degree to which Sassell is a kind of record-keeper for his community. "With the 'foresters,'" Berger writes, "he seems like a foreigner who has become, by their request, the clerk of their own records" (83). Elsewhere Berger writes that "He is their own representative. His records will never be offered to any higher judge. He keeps their records so that, from time to time, they can consult them themselves" (103). It is easy to ascribe this sense of Sassell to an autobiographical impulse on Berger's part, and this is exactly what Geoff

Dyer does in his study of Berger's work. "Sassell in his work is what Berger will become in his," he writes, by way of explaining that very passage from *A Fortunate Man*. "More exactly, Sassell's relationship with his patients prefigures, in some ways, Berger's relationship with the peasants who are to become the subjects of *Pig Earth*" (67). I don't doubt that this was part of Berger's frame of mind when writing his "Into Their Labours" trilogy. But *A Fortunate Man* is about someone who is a clerk of the community's records; it is not itself an example of such record-keeping. This is where we can reverse the hermeneutical flow a bit and allow *Docteur B., médecin de campagne* to clarify *A Fortunate Man*. *Docteur B.* is very much about Swiss society; the village here contains restless young people, neglected old people, alienated immigrants, and comfortable burghers. Tanner presents the Doctor's commitment to the village not as an exercise in parochialism or elder-worship but as evidence of critical engagement with that society; this is why Tanner also not only shows us the Doctor driving in the car with a voice-over that discusses how important it is to help people die well (which is a recurring topic in *A Fortunate Man*) but also shows us the Doctor talking about Third World under-development to earnest-looking Boy Scouts. By allowing the Doctor to speak at such length (usually on the voice-over) Tanner is, in some ways, speaking as "nous," as he believes a documentarian should. But he is speaking as "nous" to a general audience, not simply to "nous autres." Indeed, these worlds as made by Tanner and Berger/Mohr are worlds that they make *for* their protagonists, the Doctor and John Sassell. They are, obviously, not simply given and returned to the viewer untouched. But nor are they records that only the participants will consult themselves; they are being offered, if not exactly to a higher judge, then at least to a distant one in the form of an unknown (and unknowable) viewer. Ivan Maffezzini hits this nail right on the head in his essay on another Berger/Mohr collaboration, the 1982 photo-book *Another Way of Telling*. He writes of those images:

> The photos of the life of the woodcutter have the same effect on me as those of Marcel's peasant life. The forest is not a woodcutter's forest. It's a forest made for the woodcutter. An artistic, photographic forest. The photos resemble sequences in a film and not sequences from life – and, anyway, do such sequences even exist in life? (149)[23]

These photos in *A Fortunate Man* also resemble sequences in a film: *Docteur B., médecin de campagne*. They resemble that film because both works are possessed of a deeply committed realist aesthetic. That aesthetic, as Berger was at pains to point out in this period, comes with a lot of radical possibility. But it is an *aesthetic*. They are works that speak as "nous," but they also speak in a subjective and ultimately artificial way. Both are great works of art. They are not great works of record-keeping.

Indeed, one of the ways that the film's and the book's aesthetic qualities are made manifest are through their common use of a certain kind of montage aesthetic, one that is fully compatible with the use of realist techniques. In that collective text on "Montage" published in the March 1969 *Cahiers*, Sylvie Pierre tried to define several different kinds of films that used montage. Her second definition is particularly germane, both to *Docteur B.* and *A Fortunate Man*:

> Films that don't seem connected to montage as creative work, in which montage is absent as a sovereign effect, but which, when you look at them, the apparent absence of montage at the creative stage turns out to have been hiding various workings of montage: these include the maximally efficient use of a small number of connections between long takes, or the displacement – through means of cinematic technique other than montage as such – of the gestures of montage (such as *découpage*, as in Straub, or by an articulation from within a shot, as in Mizoguchi or Renoir) (20–21)[24]

A good example of this sort of montage comes about ten minutes into *Docteur B.*, in a sequence that cuts between the consultation room and the waiting area. Following Pierre, the sequence seems to be defined by a découpage that is hiding some montage effects. A medium-long shot where an older man pops off his sweater so the Doctor can listen to his heartbeat has both synch sound and a lot of camera movement, and the shot eventually zooms into a close-up of the Doctor as he puts the stethoscope on the man's back and then pans right, to frame the patient in close-up. There is also a very brief close-up of the Doctor tapping the man's back. These shots have over them a voice-over of the Doctor explaining why he chose to practice in the countryside, and that voice-over bridges this sequence with the images in the waiting room. These images are not long takes at all, although there is plenty of hand-held camera movement, as in the two images in the consultation room. This sequence begins with a man opening the door and walking into the waiting room. The images get gradually closer on the people in the room, until we have series of close-ups of hands: going through a magazine, rubbing fingers nervously, knitting. Finally the sequence closes with the man from the first shot walking through the door into the consultation room. The visual grammar at work here is very close to a sequence of photos of Sassell doing consultations in *A Fortunate Man* (the whole sequence is 42–47). This begins with a shot of Sassell in a dispensary; this is a *very* crowded image, with the camera close to Sassell, who is surrounded by files and peering at a woman through a small window. The photo on the next page is of a man walking through a waiting room door, visible head to toe and slightly blurred as he moves; it was probably taken with a very slow shutter speed. This in turn is followed by a two-page spread of Sassell, cut off at the knees, working with two large metal instruments over a patient on a table; again the slow shutter speed has the effect of blurring Sassell as he moves. The two images that follow this one, though, are very different: a perfectly clear two-shot of Sassell cutting off a cast, and a very close shot of Sassell peering through a lupe and removing something with a tiny needle; that last image is shot with a telephoto lens, and thus has practically no depth of field. As in *Docteur B.*, there is a very real way that this, like other sequences in the book, works on the level of découpage, moving the viewer slowly through a space. But as with the varied camera positions and and always-mobile camera of *Docteur B.*, these photographs are different enough in composition and degree of implied movement so as to make them feel more like individual fragments than part of a smooth whole. The sense of the doctor's office as a place where countless individual stories come together without fully meshing is realized in both works via a form of montage that is, basically, being hidden behind a cloak of continuity.

The sequences in both works also have a montage-inflected text-image relationship. Just as there is a voice-over in *Docteur B.* that joins these images but is not simply an explanation of them, this sequence in *A Fortunate Man* has Berger's text explaining some of the aspects of the consultation rooms that we do see ("The consulting rooms do not seem clinical. They seem lived-in and cozy" [46]) but also some aspects that we don't ("Once he was putting a syringe deep into a man's chest: there was little question of pain but it made the man feel bad" [46]). The effect in both cases is to invoke important aspects of a doctor's life – why one chooses to practice in a given place, how one deals with the odd emotions that accompany bodily violations like needles through chests – seem connected to the spaces in which they work. But the fact that there is a slight disconnect here, the fact that we are not actually seeing the things about which the text speaks, also makes it clear that such problems go beyond what happens in the doctor's office, go beyond what can be accomplished through the everyday routines of the profession. That this is being communicated not through what is said in any image or piece of text but in the *conflict* between image and text is indicative not only of Berger and Tanner's shared Marxist sensibilities (for montage, based in dialectics as it is, has impeccable Marxist credentials), but also of their shared belief in the fundamental complexity of the ways that people interact with their communities. Sassell and the Doctor are both presented representatives of medicine, as exemplary of a form of committed professionalism. But sequences like these remind the viewer that there is just as much meaning in the gaps or divergences in representation, just as much to be gained by understanding how Sassell and the Doctor are not directly presented in the film. Montage may be more or less absent as a "sovereign effect" in these works (although there are a few montage sequences in *Docteur B.*), but that spirit of critical inquiry into both presence and absence that so characterizes the relationship that montage cultivates with its reader is a central aspect of both *A Fortunate Man* and *Docteur B.*

For all the idealism, both political and formal, that these works contain, the story of each has something of an unhappy ending, one that is linked to some of the sociological significance of cinéma vérité. Dyer writes that "*As if* overwhelmed by the shadows cast by the urgent imperatives by which he lived his life, *as if* tormented by the uncertainties of Berger's closing pages, Sassell killed himself" (70). Dyer links this to the only passage in *A Fortunate Man* where Berger acknowledges his presence explicitly, where he recalls how "when he was unaware of my presence, I saw him weep, walking across a field away from a house where a young patient was dying" (112). Tanner identified a very similar ethical dilemma at the core of *Docteur B., médecin de campagne*. His first feature film, *Charles mort ou vif,* tells the story of a rich industrialist who, after being interviewed for a television program, has something of an existential crisis and abandons his life for the bohemian instability of the Jura mountains. In an interview with the *Cahiers du cinéma*'s Michel Delahaye and two other writers upon the release of that film, Tanner had the following exchange about the series that *Docteur B., médecin de campagne* was made for, "Aujourd'hui":

> *Cahiers:* Does that exist, a TV series like the one you show in *Charles mort ou vif?*
> *Tanner:* It exists, but it's not exactly the same thing. I've already made four portraits for that series. As for the rest, the idea, the starting place for the film – inasmuch as the rest of it is very different – it's a real experience. One of the portraits was of a country doctor: television arrived in the guy's life, and the fact was that he thought of himself in some ways as a sort of a spokesman for the medical profession. We stayed with him for a fortnight, and we spoke at great length. That was sort of a breaking point in his life. He sort of rethought things, and having done the show marked him profoundly. Afterwards he fell into a fairly serious nervous depression. (29)[25]

Both of these extra-cinematic misfortunes speak to one of the best known quandaries of early vérité filmmaking: the effect that a filmmaker's presence has on the lives of "civilians," people otherwise not involved in filmmaking and not likely to be fully aware of its power. Now, Sassell and the Doctor were grown-ups when they got involved with Berger and Tanner, and no doubt that they knew more or less what they were getting themselves into. But both projects remain haunted by the extra-textual reality of the affect that the process of filmmaking – the technology of realism, basically – had on what Berger calls "the objective world."

For a pre-history of the collaboration

Although he doesn't use the words "objective world," Roland Barthes has written about a realist aesthetic in ways that are close to Berger's writings on realism and, more important for our purposes here, close to the way in which these Berger and Tanner documentaries approach the task of realist aesthetics. Writing in his short text *Leçon*, Barthes could very well be explaining the way that cinéma vérité, at its best moments, respects the look and feel of the material world at the same time that it presents itself as fully cinematic, fully aestheticized. Invoking the great French food writer Curnonsky, Barthes recalls his famous maxim that "in cooking 'things must taste like what they are.' In the regime of knowledge, for things to become what they are, we need that ingredient, that salt of words. It's the taste of words that makes for deep, fecund knowledge" (21).[26] Giving images and words their taste is, for Berger and Tanner, not simply a matter of serving experience up raw. But nor is this a matter of smothering representation with formal embellishment. Rather, their works present things for what they are because of the aesthetic and thematic ingredients they add: cultural mixture, political idealism, iconicity, montage. This may seem the opposite of what a de-naturalizing, Brechtian aesthetic would call for, but of course it's not at all. Barthes, like Brecht before him, respected art that tried to present the world for what is was. But he respected *art* that did that, and understood, just as Barthes did, that art has formal elements that can be of a lot of use in helping the viewer see the world as it is. All of Berger and Tanner's work should be via this Barthesian/Brechtian approach to realism: together they made films about the material realities of their societies, but they made those films using aesthetic patterns that, like the gentle application of some spices or the tactful placement of a Kurt Weill song, lead the viewer to a knowledge whose emotional resonance makes it truly deep, truly fecund. This aestheticization/realist tension is more *explicitly* present in these documentaries than in any other films they made together.

So although this early work may seem minor in comparison to the three features that Berger and Tanner did together, it contains a great deal that makes it both important in its own right and significant as a predictor of the concerns of *La Salamandre*, *Le Milieu du monde*, and *Jonas qui aura 25 ans en l'an 2000*. The search for new sound-image relationships; the difficulty of reconciling science, education, and political activism; the relationship between landscape, community, and commitment: these are central issues for all three features Berger and Tanner made together and they are dealt with in these three early works in ways that are admirably rigorous and, as befitting a curious, searching sensibility, basically unresolved. It would be easy to see the films as curiosities on the basis of their length or their pedigrees as commissioned works. But film history tends to be overly exclusionary on bases like this; too much criticism is written on the implicit assumption that the only real filmmaking is when someone sets to making ninety-minute fiction film. *Une Ville à Chandigarh, Mike et l'usage de la science*, and *Docteur B., médecin de campagne* are important contributions both to documentary cinema during a time of aesthetic transition and hybridity and should be seen as important both for Berger and Tanner's work together and for European political art of the 1960s.

Notes

1 "Conditions de travail et pressions font que le direct est en situation politique, même si la plupart des films qui le pratiquent ne se veulent pas, ou ne sont pas au premier chef des films politiques."

2 "Un journaliste parle même de Marcel Bezençon, alors directeur de la SSR, comme du « huitième Conseiller fédéral »". Although Switzerland has a president, her role is largely ceremonial; technically she is "Président du conseil fédéral," a seven-member body that is drawn from the coalition of the ruling parties, and which exercises actual executive power.

3 "Les programmes diffusés par la SSR doivent défendre et développer les valeurs culturelles du pays et contribuer à la formation spirituelle, morale, religieuse civique et artistique des auditeurs et téléspectateurs…. Les programmes doivent servir l'intérêt du pays, renforcer l'union et la concorde nationales et contribuer à la compréhension internationale."

4 "En Suisse romande, les deux grands navires amiraux de l'information que sont CONTINENTS SANS VISA, puis TEMPS PRÉSENT rendent compte de réalités internationales mal connues tout en sensibilisant l'opinion à la brutalité des rapports Nord-Sud. CONTINENTS SANS VISA aborde également certains sujets chauds avec une émission sur le secret bancaire en 1964, ainsi qu'un « Dossier », réalisé par Alain Tanner, consacré à « L'ouvrier suisse » (19 mai 1966). Une émission, au caractère militant affirmé, qui, au vu des vagues suscitées, sera suivie par un programme similaire sur « Le paysan suisse », puis, une année après, sur « Le patron suisse »."

5 "… l'amour impossible entre un cinéaste qui avait besoin de créer des images en liberté, pas forcément du documentaire, et une institution qui en produisait mais qui subissait les lois de la rationalisation, donc de la bureaucratisation."

6 "Phases. Il y a eu trois phases dans le développement de la télévision et trois façons de la regarder. La première, c'était une époque de créativité, de travail et d'un peu de croyance. La seconde, c'était la découverte de ce qu'est vraiment la télévision, accompagnée d'une boulimie perverse et d'une jouissance au troisième degré, jusqu'à la connaissance – et rapide épuisement de cette connaissance – des codes et des signes. La troisième c'est maintenant : le meuble, avec un peu de football et quelques films anciens le soir."

7 "Je n'avais pas tourné un film documentaire depuis une trentaine d'années. Dans la fiction, on dit « je » et cela vous donne un plus grand espace de liberté. En disant « je », on n'a de comptes à rendre qu'à soi-même et aux spectateurs. Dans le documentaire, on dit « eux » et on a des comptes à leur rendre à eux, on n'est pas libre de se servir d'eux, sans leur accord et leur participation. Mais il ne faut pas faire le film sur eux, cela vous place au-dessus et ce n'est pas la bonne position. Il faut être avec eux, et que ce « eux » se transforme en « nous ». Ça, c'est la bonne place pour travailler le documentaire."

8 "La télévision, c'était le début de l'expérience du son synchrone, de la camera à la main, en filigrane des premières expériences de Jean Rouch, par exemple. La fiction ne m'attirait pas et les dramatiques ne m'intéressait pas de tout." An excellent English-language introduction to Rouch's work can be found in Joram ten Brink, ed., *Building Bridges: The Cinema of Jean Rouch* (London: Wallflower Press, 2007). Rouch's own writings on cinema and ethnography have been translated and collected as Jean Rouch, *Ciné-Ethnography*, Steven Field, ed. and trans. (Minneapolis: University of Minnesota Press, 2003). In French, an excellent introduction can be found in *CinémAction* 17 (1981), a special issue edited by René Prédal called "Jean Rouch, un griot gaulois."

9 "En France, celui que je préfère aujourd'hui : Jean Rouch, il est á la pointe des recherches pour un langage nouveau et la découverte de la vérité."

10 "La division traditionnelle entre « action à filmer » et « action de filmer » se résout en « action filmée »."

11 "On a beau vouloir respecter ce document, on ne peut pas éviter de le **fabriquer.** Il ne préexiste pas au reportage, mais en est le produit."

12 "Nous avons tourné *Les Apprentis* d'une façon tout à fait anachronique (mais ces techniques [du direct] n'existaient pas chez nous) avec une grosse caméra blimp 35mm alors que c'était le sujet idéal pour une technique léger."

13 "Inspiré par expérience anglaise du « Free Cinema » et le film de Brandt *Quand nous étions petits enfants*,

nous avons mis sur pied un projet d'une série de moyens métrages documentaires sur des sujets qui mordaient un peu dans la vie sociale du pays."

14 "Par la suite le cinéaste n'a cessé d'importance et je crois qu'il est le premier réalisateur romand qui soit parvenue à faire comprendre à un large public l'importance et les pouvoirs du cinéma dans la vie moderne. La présence des films de Henri Brandt à l'Exposition nationale fut un véritable événment."

15 The United Arab Republic was a relatively short-lived union between Egypt and Syria; its capital was Cairo and its only president was Gamal Abdel-Nasser. It lasted from 1958 to 1961, although Egypt kept the name even after Syria had left the union. It was a classic Nasser-era endeavour, inasmuch as it was an explicitly pan-Arab project that had a shifting relationship with the USSR and made the United States and British governments exceedingly nervous.

16 "Pendant tout le film, nous retrouvons ce rapport, formel et sémantique, entre éléments européens et éléments indiens. La ville est construite par les Indiens et pour eux, mais les étudiants portent des habits européens. Les ruppies [*sic*] sont convertis en francs. L'architecture est occidentale, mais la musique et les sons indigènes. Le côté optimiste de Le Corbusier est partagé par Tanner : c'est surtout la recherche de la joie de vivre, l'aspiration à vivre dans une cité radieuse, qui comptait."

17 "... entre les cinéastes qui « font » le film essentiellement au tournage (et à la préparation de ce tournage : par exemple, donc, Ford et Renoir), et

ceux qui pour ce travail de l'écriture, ou de la *stratégie*, et de la prise de vues n'est que l'accumulation d'une « matière » (d'un matériel), qui est ensuite toute remise en cause, et ne prend son ordre et son sens que dans la salle de montage (c'est aussi bien Rouch et Perrault que Godard et Eisenstein). »

18 « On y sent l'influence très forte de John Berger qui a collaboré au scénario…. Mike et son esprit se retrouvent, probablement dédoublés, dans plusieurs personnages de *Jonas*. »

19 « Si enfin la télé est notre prose (et on ne parlera jamais assez bien), le cinéma n'a plus de chance que dans la poésie. »

20 « La télévision est un art de la bouche, et ça n'est pas toujours ragoûtant. »

21 « La télé relevait de l'écologie parce qu'elle touchait en nous le citoyen responsable, c'est-à-dire l'adulte. »

22 « Pour un goût d'entrer dans les vies des gens et de les voir chez eux. »

23 « Les photos de la vie du bûcheron me font le même effet que celles de la vie paysanne de Marcel. La forêt n'est pas la forêt d'un bûcheron. C'est une forêt faite pour le bûcheron. Une forêt artistique, photographique. Les photos ressemblent aux séquences d'un film et pas à celles d'une vie – et, d'ailleurs, est-ce qu'il existe quelque chose comme des séquences de la vie ? »

24 « Les films qui ne semblent pas se situer par rapport au montage comme travail créateur, dans lesquels le montage est absent comme effet souverain, mais où, on l'a vu, l'absence apparente du montage au stade créateur peut cacher diverses manœuvres de montage : soit l'utilisation, au maximum de leur efficacité, d'un petit nombre de liaisons entre les plans longs, soit le déplacement sur d'autres charnières de la combinatoire filmique que celles du montage proprement dit, des gestes du montage (par le découpage – voir Straub —, par l'articulation à l'intérieur même du plan – voir Mizoguchi or Renoir). »

25 « *Cahiers :* Ca existe, une série TV comme celle que vos montrez dans « Charles » ?

Tanner : Ça existe, mais ce n'est pas tout à fait la même chose. J'ai fait déjà quatre portraits dans cette série. Et du reste, l'idée, le point de départ du film – bien que tout le reste soit très différent – c'est une expérience réelle, un de ces portraits qui était celui d'un médecin de campagne : il y a eu l'arrivée de la télévision dans la vie de cette homme, et le fait qu'il s'est estimé à certains égards un peu comme le porte-parole du corps médical. Nous sommes restés quinze jours chez lui, nous avons parlé très longuement. Cela a fait comme une sorte de cassure dans sa vie. Il s'est repensé en quelque sorte, et le fait de faire l'émission l'a marqué très profondément. Par la suite il a fait une dépression nerveuse assez grave. »

26 « Curnonski disait qu'en cuisine il faut que « les choses aient le goût de ce qu'elles sont ». Dans l'ordre du savoir, pour que les choses deviennent ce qu'elles sont, ce qu'elles été, il y faut cet ingrédient, le sel des mots. C'est ce goût des mots qui fait le savoir profond, fécond. »

CHAPTER TWO

LA SALAMANDRE

"Pangloss taught metaphysical-theologico-cosmologo-nigo-logy. He proved incontesibly that there is no effect without a cause, and that in this best of all possible worlds, his lordship's country seat was the most beautiful of mansions and her ladyship the best of all possible ladyships" – *Candide* (20)[1]

"All history is contemporary history: not in the ordinary sense of the word, where contemporary history means the history of the comparatively recent past, but in the strict sense: the consciousness of one's own activity as one actually performs it. History is thus the self-knowledge of the living mind. For even when the events which the historian studies are events that happened in the distant past, the condition of their being historically known is that they should vibrate in the historian's mind." – John Berger, *G* (54)

In a classic example of Parisian parochialism, Gérard Legrand's basically positive review of *La Salamandre* that appeared in the French film magazine *Positif* (the arch-rival of the *Cahiers du cinéma* and strongly critical of the French New Wave) stated that "What bothered me about this film from the start is that it (already) had the scent of the anachronistic. Alain Tanner has remade a for sure better version of the 'New Wave'" (26).[2] It's not hard to see what elements of the film would lead a critic in this direction; not only is it shot, using lots of handheld cameras and long takes, on location in the metropolis of Geneva, but it even stars Bulle Ogier, who had just a few years earlier made a huge splash in Jacques Rivette's *L'amour fou* (1969). But I would argue that the film shares relatively little with the New Wave of the 1960s, and that this goes well beyond what Legrand patronizingly refers to as "une « romanité » locale" or "a local 'French-Swiss-ness'" (26). Instead, *La Salamandre* is an essay on the difficulty of communication, be it on the level of interpersonal relations, mass media representations, or cinematic constructions. In this way it is a seminally modern film; it is about the same thing that forms it, which is the encroachment of technology and manipulation into everyday life. It is ostensibly a story about Rosemonde, who two young writers, the freelance journalist Pierre and the more bohemian Paul, are trying to understand so they can write a television script about her having shot her petit-bourgeois uncle with his own army rifle. But as in Yeats's formulation, things quickly fall apart; the centres of stable knowledge and clear communication do not hold. Tanner and Berger render this "falling apart" in both narrative and formal terms, using devices such as complex and unresolved narrative elements, sequence shots, disembodied voice-over, and so on. This goes well beyond anything that was going on *chez* Truffaut or Rohmer, and brings us a lot closer to what was going on in the late 1960s and early 1970s Godard. That is a period of his work that saw Godard turning very clearly away from the legacy of the New Wave (a turning that was signalled, in no small part, by his moving first to the French border town of Grenoble and eventually settling in Rolle, Switzerland) and towards a use of film language that was both explicitly political and highly self-aware. I alluded to this in the previous chapter, somewhat dismissively mentioning his "Groupe Dziga Vertov" films, which I do indeed see as not terribly successful (despite my great admiration for the post-new wave work of Godard, especially his collaborations with Anne-Marie Miéville). This is the context in which *La Salamandre* belongs, and in this light it can be seen not only as cutting-edge but also as very rigorously conceived.

Tanner has defined modernity in art more or less in terms of self-conscious form, something that was also quite important to Berger during this period. He wrote in *Ciné-mélanges* that

> I'm recalling from memory Octavio Paz, who had defined what
> modernity is in art very well. For him, modernity was first of

all at the interior of a work; in the way it works and its very tissues, it launched a critique of its own means of expression, be it literature, painting or cinema, and this critical position would transform both the texture and the finished product. From Paz, it's clear that you can only move towards Brecht. (74)[3]

I believe Tanner has in mind here Paz's 1990 Nobel Prize address, wherein he said that "Modernity is the spearhead of historical movement, the incarnation of evolution or revolution, the two faces of progress." Paz went on in that speech to say that "I returned to the source and discovered that modernity is not outside but within us. It is today and the most ancient antiquity; it is tomorrow and the beginning of the world; it is a thousand years old and yet newborn."[4] This view of modernity as something that is the product of a deep dialectic between present and past, a dialectic that is, as Paz says, *adentro de nosotros*, brings us to Brecht inasmuch as both writers see progress as something that engages with and is inseparably linked to history, not something that moves away from it (hence Brecht's attachment to, say, dance-hall musicals). This movement towards Brecht is testament to the importance that Tanner gives to a form that is self-aware; something very similar was going on in Berger's work at this time. When I spoke to him on the phone on 20 October 2009, Berger was at pains to point out that at the time he began collaborating with Tanner, he was working on his 1972 novel *G.* This was probably his most experimental novel up to that point (and it remains one of his more formally eccentric works), a point that Berger himself made to Richard Appignanesi when he explained why he and Tanner didn't work together any more: "Several years previously [to the end of their collaboration after 1976's *Jonas*], I had written the novel *G*, which is an experimental work in terms of its narrative. But after *G*, the next fiction work I wrote, *Pig Earth*, was about peasants, and in writing this I found it necessary to return to a much more traditional form of narrative" (306). With *Pig Earth* Berger was, in many ways, moving away from modernity, and felt a parallel need to move away from self-critical form; starting at Paz, Berger moved *away* from Brecht, and towards Ramuz. For Tanner, though, the Brechtian imperative remained central and offered a way to redeem two of his films that felt dated to him. He wrote in *Ciné-mélanges* that "I have, for a long time, put certain films out of my mind, because I find them too discursive, head to toe connected to the present. I'm thinking of *La Salamandre* or *Jonas Who Will Be 25 in the Year 2000*. I'd bet that if they resurface, it'll be above all because they are completely anchored in modernity" (75).[5] This is much more true of *La Salamandre* than it is of *Jonas*, for it is this earlier film that has, *dans son fonctionnement et son tissue même*, the sense that communication is an inherently thorny process and is being made all the more so by the evolution of bourgeois, capitalist societies like that of Switzerland's. *La Salamandre* is significant for the Berger-Tanner collaboration not only because it is their first narrative-feature film, but also because it lays out certain thematic and, just as importantly, formal characteristics that mark it as a critique of modernity that is unmistakably launched from the inside. It is not a nostalgic lament against modernity, nor a bohemian jam session that tries to stand apart from it. Rather, it is an alternative vision of that cultural condition, a vision that is both deeply critical of the state of western capitalist societies but is also often lyrically optimistic about what resistance to those societies can look like.

These formal patterns to which I allude are not as fully, meticulously executed as they are in *Le Milieu du monde*, and *Jonas qui aura 25 ans en l'an 2000*, but they are present. Early on, *La Salamandre* introduces an off-screen commentator, who is not exactly a narrator but whose voice is completely non-diegetic. This voice first appears when Paul is riding his mo-ped from his house in the country down to Geneva to begin work on his profile of Rosemonde. It explains a bit about Paul's life and motivations, gives some economic details of his existence, and specifies the setting of the film. But it doesn't do this in a cold, factual way; the setting, for example, is explained this way: "Here we are at the extreme west of the country, two steps to the border, and Switzerland seems far behind. We turn our backs on her" (*L'Avant-scène cinéma*, 10).[6] This is an echo of the kind of narrative interruptions that Berger would insert into *G*, but in that novel this extra-diegetic voice is not disembodied; it is clearly Berger's own, and it is frequently about the problems he is having writing the novel, set in late-nineteenth and early-twentieth-century Europe. "I cannot continue this account of the eleven-year-old boy in Milan in 6 May 1898," he writes by way of concluding a depiction of the rioting that presaged the failed Milanese revolution of the turn of the century. "From this point on, everything I write will either converge on a final full stop or else disperse so widely that it will become incoherent" (77). Following a passage depicting, in a prose-poem kind of way, a sexual encounter, he recalls coming out of a Paris laundromat in the morning: "Every personal desire, preference or hope has become an inconvenience. I wait at the bus stop. The waving red indicator of the Paris bus, as it turns the corner, is like a brand taken from a fire. At this moment I begin to doubt the value of poems about sex" (110). The narrator of Berger's novel *G* is a character: an autobiographical one, but a character nevertheless, and one who makes the borders between diegetic and non-diegetic basically meaningless.

That's not quite what's going on with the narrator in Berger's scenario *La Salamandre*. The grain of the narrator's voice, to borrow Roland Barthes' famous image, is nowhere near as pronounced, and her tone is nowhere near as sceptical. And yet, there is some crucial information in this commentary, and the narrator's tone is often an ironic one. This is most evident midway though the film, when the narrator explains why Paul thinks of Rosemonde as "La salamandre": "Paul wrote in his pad: 'The Salamander is a pretty little animal, part of the lizard family. It's black with yellow-orange spots. The Salamander is venemous. It's not afraid of fire and can walk right through the flames without getting burned'" (*L'Avant-scène cinéma*, 31).[7] The extra-diegetic material helps to break the illusion of narrative in a way that is comparable to *G*, but the spirit of criticism and scepticism that such breaking is supposed to inspire is left to the viewer, rather than contained in the text itself. Arguably this is actually the more progressive, non-manipulative strategy, since the viewer of *La Salamandre* is essentially being given a lot of detail and some hints at a world-view (such as the sense that to go out into the border country is to turn your back on Switzerland, or that Rosemonde's brashness is like someone who walks though fire without getting burned), whereas the reader of *G* is being given actual criticism, explicit scepticism about the contours of specific passages in the novel. The extra-diegetic voice-overs in Berger and Tanner's later films will become a bit more aggressive about positing a specific analysis of the film ideological project (that's most true of *Le Milieu du monde*, although it's true of *Jonas* too), but they will still not be quite the same as what is going on in *G*. In all of this work, though, the narrative is frequently interrupted in a way that insists that narrative and spectacle be understood for what they are. Michael Tarantino has a similar sense of Berger's interest in self-reflexive forms, writing that "His point of view attempts to close the distance between the writer as observer/audience and the writer as the object of perception, the source of the original text. When translated into fictional/narrative terms, the result is an increased perception in the role of narration itself" ("The Voice Off-Screen," 35). This strategy of disjuncture between the visual and aural fields in the name of synthesizing something new, and to do so in a way that forces the viewer to do some work is dear to the heart of theorists of montage. This was also quite visible in *Une Ville à Chandigarh*, and Tarantino also notes this as being important to the films they would go on to do together: "Ultimately the film [*Une Ville à Chandigarh*] resides on the suspicion of that which is apparent, a suspicion which is used to expose certain underlying ramifications. In this case, the methods of the documentary would foreshadow the approach to the fictional narrative" ("The Voice Off-Screen," 34). This is certainly true of the sound-image relationship of *La Salamandre*, and the commentary is playful about this from the beginning. As Paul rolls into Geneva on his mo-ped, that voice-over says "Despite certain appearances, in which you must never trust, Paul was neither a house painter nor a singer, but a writer" (*L'Avant-scène cinéma*, 10).[8]

But as Jim Leach notes, this engagement with this ethic of montage via an aesthetic of disparate fragments coming together does not mean that Tanner accepts the inherent conflict between montage and sequence shots. Something very similar to the way *La Salamandre* uses extra-diegetic voice-over is true of the film's use of long takes. I mentioned in the introduction the degree to which Tanner seems to be in a kind of argument with André Bazin over the meaning and possibilities of the long take and their relationship with montage and découpage. The editing patterns of *La Salamandre* echo these arguments, although as with the use of extra-diegetic voice-over, this self-conscious aesthetic gesture is present here in a fairly gentle, almost introductory way, and will become a lot more rigorous in later films. Tanner explained his sense of the duality of the long-take aesthetic to Lenny Rubenstein, saying that:

> What we have tried to do, by not cutting within a sequence, is to give back to a scene its reality. There is a paradox in this, since if you don't cut, instead of it being more real which it should be, in fact you are getting unreal because of the traditions in the eye of

the spectator. The basis of the language of my films is the theory of alienation, and by giving a shot its full value, strength and importance, an alienation effect is caused. If you don't cut, you see everything differently. (99)

This is very close to Roland Barthes' sense of the paradox of realist aesthetics, which he spelled out in his 1968 essay "L'Effet de réel": "realist literature is, no doubt, narrative, but this is because the realism in it is only marginal, erratic, confined to the 'details,' and because the most realist story that you could imagine would develop along non-realist lines" (88).[9] We can very clearly see this in sequence shots like the one where Pierre takes Rosemonde to a café. They come in, find a table, Rosemonde goes over to the jukebox and drops in coin, listens for a moment, rejoins Pierre at the table, and lets him order for her. The shot lasts about a minute and a half; Rosemonde is at some point framed first in a medium-long shot, then medium close-up, and then medium shot. The effect is definitely one of time stretching out, and of the viewer becoming highly aware of the small space of the café and the way that Rosemonde moves through it. Moreover, the sound-image relationship is very eccentric; the music isn't clearly diegetic or non-diegetic, since it is on the soundtrack before Rosemonde goes over to put her coin in the jukebox. Despite these eccentricities, though, the sequence is bookended by sequences that use découpage of one form or another to move around a space: it is preceded by a sequence in Pierre's car that alternates close-ups of them both as they talk, and it is followed by a sequence in Pierre's apartment which begins with a fairly long take but shifts to shot/reverse-shot as Pierre photographs her. Tanner uses long takes throughout *La Salamandre*, and he always uses them to expressive effect. But they are one element of the cinematic toolbox; they do not predominate, and indeed set the critical-ideological tone, to quite the degree that they do in *Le Milieu du monde* or even *Jonas*.

In addition to frequently drawing on a self-consciously slow and deliberate pattern of long takes, *La Salamandre* is also quite self-conscious at the level of subject matter; it is a film about the impossibility of knowing someone and as a film it has narrative situations that constantly reinforce the constructed, subjective quality of all knowledge. The first time Paul and Pierre meet to discuss how they will approach the writing of the television script about Rosemonde's life, Paul spins an elaborate tale about her being from a giant family, deep in the country, and suffering various deprivations. Pierre and Paul then have the following exchange:

> *Paul:* Not bad, that story. I'll stick around. What do you think?
> *Pierre:* It's not bad, but there's a little problem all the same.
> *Paul:* Which is?
> *Pierre:* What's all that got to do with reality?
> *Paul:* Hey, I've been talking to you about reality for the last five minutes. Except for maybe a few details, I feel like I've already put in a good day's work.
> *Pierre:* Sure, you've put in a good day's work, but it's also quite possible that you've been dreaming. I don't really see why we need to first go with your imagination when the story really happened. The girl exists, and the uncle too. They're here, in some way. It's reality that interests me... (*insistent*) ... things! You have to start from there, and understand,.... touch what you can touch. (*Paul tries to interrupt.*) No, you mess around afterwards. You have to start with an inquiry.
> *Paul (gruffly):* I'm not a cop.
> *Pierre:* A journalistic inquiry, bonehead!
> *Paul (same tone):* I'm not a journalist.
> (*L'Avant-scène cinéma*, 12)[10]

One of the most telling of the little jokes in this sequence is Paul's easy equation of being a cop with being a journalist. Both, in his view, exercise an authority (which he likely sees as illegitimate) largely by insisting on the existence of, and more importantly our access to, a single vision of events. Tarantino argues that this is the way Berger sees history in *G*, saying that for Berger, "To write as if all words were a priori facts is to adopt a coercive stance towards one's audience" ("The Voice Off-Screen," 37). *La Salamandre* is practically militant in its rejection of this sort of coercion. This is not a matter of a simple-minded relativism; it is important to distinguish between a rejection of the existence of physical reality and an insistence that we do not have pure, unfiltered access to that reality. This, really, is what Berger and Tanner are making clear in *La Salamandre*. The girl exists: her uncle too. Berger and Tanner show them to be *there*, and thus they exert some control on what Pierre and Paul can do with them. We see them exerting this control throughout the film: when Pierre interviews the uncle shortly after this exchange, but more importantly, when Rosemonde manipulates and confuses Pierre and Paul throughout the film. Pierre and Paul are trying to be the authors of Rosemonde's life, and as authors they are not only free to act creatively on that text but they really can't do anything else. But what they discover is what all writers eventually discover: before too long, that text starts acting on them. Rosemonde exerts some control on what can be done with her.

I allude here to the 1981 debate between Stanley Fish and Wolfgang Iser in the pages of *Diacritics*. "The object is not purely perceived, but it is *there*," Iser wrote, in response to Fish's criticism of his approach to interpretation (specifically his 1978 book *The Act of Reading*). "And because it is there it exerts some control on what we can do with it" (87, italics his). *La Salamandre* is, basically, about Pierre and Paul's attempt to interpret Rosemonde; the research they do is mostly a matter of interviews with Rosemonde (the text) and her family and friends (who are a kind of paratext, as Voltaire's celebrated volumes of correspondence are for someone writing a television script based on *Candide*). Coming to grips with her is difficult, and there are times in the film when it seems that Pierre and Paul will never even be able to settle whether Rosemonde really shot her uncle, let alone understand what really makes her tick. But the film ends with some basic facts established, some skeleton to the text. In a medium shot of Pierre, Paul, and Rosemonde, Paul asks her, simply, "Was it you, Rosemonde, who shot your uncle?" She replies, just as simply, "Oui, c'est moi." And she goes on to say:

> But I didn't really want to, I don't know.... It just happened like that, in a fit of rage. I couldn't take him, the old jerk... he never stopped bugging me. He always wanted me to work ... even when there was nothing to do. Like in the army *(silence)*. He never stopped his moaning, his lecturing. I was always afraid of getting carried away, of doing something stupid. I don't know what to do.... (*L'Avant-scène cinema*, 36)[11]

La Salamandre (Alain Tanner, 1971). SVO Cine. Pictured: Bulle Ogier and Jean-Luc Bideau. Photo from The Kobal Collection/ Art Resource, NY.

This is where the matter of interpretation enters into the picture, and the film makes no bones about its completely indeterminate nature. Why Rosemonde did what she did, and what it means for her own life or for the life in a place where life is often defined like life in the army, remains a matter for ongoing debate and is fundamentally unclear, even for the ostensible author of these events, Rosemonde herself. But there is, finally, some basis of fact. She shot her uncle. Oui, c'est moi.

Rosemonde as an active force in the writing of her own life is a key part of the film's narrative and has strong ties to Berger's work elsewhere. During the 1960s and 70s especially Berger wrote frequently about issues of sexual representation. The signature works of criticism there are *The Success and Failure of Picasso* (1965) and *Ways of Seeing* (1972), both of which deal extensively with the ways that changes in the ideology and technology of painting led to the rise of an aesthetic where artists presented women as a proxy for property. (In *Ways of Seeing* Berger argues that the rise of oil painting is particularly important for this ideological shift; in *Success and Failure of Picasso* it is the twentieth-century emergence of art as pure investment that Berger focuses on.) The signature work of fiction on this front, though, is *G* (published in 1972, the year after the release of *La Salamandre*), and there is a great deal there that connects with Rosemonde's place in the narrative as someone who is desired precisely because she cannot be represented. Shifting into a didactic voice, Berger writes of nineteenth-century European women:

> Men surveyed them before treating them. Consequently how a woman appeared to a man might determine how she would be treated. To acquire some control over this process, women had to contain it, and so they interiorized it. That part of a woman's self which was the surveyor treated the part which was the surveyed, so as to demonstrate to others how her whole self should be treated. And this exemplary treatment of herself by herself constituted her presence. Every one of her actions, whatever its direct purpose, was also simultaneously an indication of how she should be treated. (150)

The above quoted passage from *G* appears almost verbatim in *Ways of Seeing* (on page 46), during a discussion of how "The social presence of women has developed as a result of their ingenuity in living under such tutelage within such a limited space. But this has been at the cost of a woman's self being split into two. A woman must continuously watch herself. She is almost continually accompanied by her own image of herself.... From earliest childhood she has been taught and persuaded to survey herself continually" (46). That passage is in turn reproduced almost verbatim in *G*, on page 149. Containing the process of being surveyed by interiorizing it is a very precise way of describing what Rosemonde is doing throughout the film; demonstrating the ingenuity that she has developed as a result of being socialized, probably from childhood, into such self-surveillance, is a big part of the narrative. It's not that Rosemonde rejects the process of being surveyed by Pierre and Paul; she basically cooperates with what they want to do. But the film makes it clear that she has interiorized this process of being surveyed by acting very differently when she is with men than when she is alone.

Late in the film, this contrast is so marked that it rises to the quality of the semi-abstract, or perhaps iconic. Late in the film there is a sequence where Rosemonde sits alone on her bed, naked, in a medium-long shot; her voice-over on the soundtrack describes her body, as though through an interior monologue: "I'm twenty-three years old. If I was born six days later, I'd have been named Héliodore. I have small breasts. I like the shape of my legs. I have blonde hair." Then there is a reverse-shot, so that the camera is facing Rosemonde in a medium close-up. In the background her roommate Suzanne enters, they have a brief exchange about how she can get her a job at a shoe store, she withdraws, and Rosemonde's interior monologue continues: "People hate my independence and are always trying to break me. They say that I'm soft, wild, hysterical" (*L'Avant-scène cinéma*, 33).[12] She is echoing here what Paul has actually said about her origins (he believes that because she came from such a big family her parents eventually started naming their new kids after the saint day that was closest to their birthdays) as well as what Paul is probably thinking about her (she has small breasts). But she also assumes control over the surveying: *she likes* the shape of her legs, she recognizes her independence as something under threat, her free spirit as something that she is all too aware that others disapprove of. And most importantly, she is alone as she chews all this over, sitting in her room naked, completely herself; her introspection can only resume when her roommate leaves. These two shots constitute a moving statement of the situation that she finds herself in, and together become a truly cinematic icon whose image- and soundtrack come together to evoke the process by which someone regains some control over their own image. The sequences that follow make very clear the spare eloquence of her interior voice and the beauty of it coming together with her naked body next to a window. We first see her in a medium-long shot as she tries to sell shoes; the film then cuts to a low-angle medium shot of her standing on a ladder as she sorts boxes, and is saying, over and over, "Godasses! Godasses! Godasses!" (a slangy word for shoes) as a co-worker hands her shoeboxes. The film cuts to a two-shot of a middle-aged woman asking her son why he persists in hiring "des jolies petites mômes qui ne savant rien faire" [pretty little chicks who can't do anything], and he replies that "old grannies don't sell anything these days" ["les vieilles mémères, ça ne fait pas vendre aujourd'hui"]. This is followed by a two-shot of Rosemonde and the owner's son trying to get her to go out with him. The next sequence has her sitting in Pierre's apartment, being interviewed yet again by the two guys. Paul asks her how she felt when she left her family at the age of twelve, and she replies with babble: "When I was twelve?.... When I was twelve.... I had pretty, cute little.... feet. One day, I put on my cute little feet... One day, I got into my pumpkin. I met the son of the king who had such nice feet... huge.... with big toes. Nicer than your guys'!" (*L'Avant-scène cinéma*, 34).[13] The camera tilts down slightly as she gets down on her knees and starts talking about the guys' feet. Both scenes play, at first, as childish innocence; Rosemonde seems almost touched, or simple so to speak. But this isn't simple at all. Rosemonde rebels not through taking action or refusing to participate in these processes of the control of her image – using her to sell shoes, using her as grist for a TV script. Instead, she replies by deforming *language*, by deforming the process of signification, the process through which control over her is being exercised by men. That icon of her on her bed describing her body is an elegant statement of just how in control of language and representation Rosemonde is capable of being, and it is also an elegant statement of how in control of her own body she really is, despite the way that she is, in the next scene, ogled by male customers at the shoe store where she works or, in previous scenes, seen to be employed in the alienatingly repetitive and exhausting work of sausage stuffing. Frédéric Bas sees the importance of the body as central in Tanner's cinema, especially in *La Salamandre*. Linking his films with those of Phillipe Garrel and Chantal Akerman, he writes that "We can see Tanner's films as a succession of bodily states. *La Salamandre*, for example, where the truth about Rosemonde comes through her body more than through her words. At the beginning, moreover, we only know Rosemonde through the poses of her body: on the assembly line (working), at the pool (resting), at her house dancing, to say nothing of the walking body that opens and closes the film" (180–81).[14] Seeing the narrative as a succession of Rosemonde's bodily poses places this sequence by the window at the very centre of the film, which is indeed where it belongs. It is the point in the film where Rosemonde internalizes all the tensions of the film's narrative, and does so in a way that makes them fully her own because they are part of her body and only part of her body, naked in that scene as she is.

This sequence is, in Berger's formulation an exemplary treatment of herself by herself that allows her to constitute her presence, to keep her from drifting into becoming a non-person who is used by other people, represented by other people, for their own ends. Once cast back into the external world of clothes and shoes and television programs, she understands that she is no longer able to exert the kind of control over the image she presents to the world that she was able to when she was only internalizing it, and so she defends herself on the plane of signification itself. It is this placing together of these three sequences (the first of which is a pure sequence shot and the other two of which are a series of long-ish takes) that expresses this; the realization of Rosemonde's sophistication about the use and abuse of signification is made clear not in any of the sequences alone but by the way they come together. This is, in Tanner's phrase, *montage entre les scènes*, and it is important to note that this supremely expressive montage synthesizes sequences that are, more or less, Bazinian long takes (the sequence with Rosemonde is two shots; the sequence in the shoe store is five; the sequence in Pierre's apartment is a single shot).

This is very similar to a sequence slightly earlier in the film, where Rosemonde is being interviewed by Paul and Pierre. This sequence is made up of three shots but the majority of it is a single, still medium close-up of Rosemonde, directly facing the camera (although ostensibly talking into Pierre's tape recorder) as she recalls holidays in the south of France with her boyfriend Albert, how her uncle had called the cops when she went with him, how her uncle preferred to vacation at a terrible mountain hotel in the canton of Valais (which is Swiss wine country), etc. The monologue concludes with her saying "Now ... I feel old. It's more like before (*a pause*). I ask myself what I will become. Before, it was all the same to me. And it didn't really mean anything.... (*bothered*). I've messed up your stuff. Shall we stop?" (*L'Avant-scène cinéma*, 21).[15] Aesthetically this is more Brechtian than the scene on the bed; the meat of the sequence is a very long take that features Rosemonde in a position that is practically a direct address to the viewer; no extra-diegetic voice-over is necessary. Furthermore, we are made extra-aware of the cinematic apparatus by the presence of the tape recorder, which is the camera's stand-in; when Rosemonde asks Pierre if he wants to stop, she could just as well be talking to Tanner. In terms of what she is saying, we are close to what Berger had in mind in *G* when he talked about nineteenth-century women taking control of the process of men surveying them by interiorizing it. She doesn't stop her surveying of herself, of the choices that she's made in her life and the direction that it is presently taking, but she does stop broadcasting it. She thus demonstrates to Pierre and Paul how she wishes to be treated: as someone who has led an interesting, sometimes wild life, but who doesn't want their help in facing her most serious misgivings about what her choices have meant.

There are comparably iconic moments between Pierre and Paul as well, although they tend to have a more comic tone. The most oft-cited of these is the sequence on a Geneva tram where Paul pretends to be a Turk drumming on a large case and singing, while Pierre pretends to be a reactionarily outraged passenger, trying to rile up his fellow riders – "Italians and Spaniards, you don't care about them, eh? That's OK with you! And now we've got Turks! Arabs! In Geneva! It's impossible. I'm telling you, if it keeps on like this, we'll have Negroes in our trams, with their dances, their boobs in the air, the tam-tams, the drums – incredible!" (*L'Avant-scène-cinema*, 34).[16] This sequence on the tram is certainly expressive of the degree to which Pierre and Paul are a countercultural couple, rejecting the mainstream values of that most respectable Swiss city of Geneva but doing so in a playful, clowning way. Their work as writers, and writers who challenge mainstream Swiss values, here takes on the form of clowning, a well-worn tradition among left intellectuals. The ideology of their performance here, while more explicit than any of the work they had done together so far, is consistent with what we've seen them do together: work collaboratively to confront social convention. But despite this sense of challenge through performance, the sequence mostly draws upon semi-classical découpage or something like it; most of the compositions are medium shots, and there are a few cuts to medium close-ups of Pierre as he bellows. Formally speaking (although not in terms of its subject matter), it is a fairly straightforward piece of comedy.

A more formally adventurous example of their politically loaded tom-foolery comes when they are walking through the forest during a visit to Rosemonde's family in the country. Pierre loudly laments that they are out here doing nothing and then puts out his arms and yells, "Ah, happiness is close! I feel it coming. You feel it? Ah, happiness is close! Ah happiness is faraway! And prehistory is long!" Paul responds "And we're walking bit by bit towards death," and this seems to really set Pierre off. "Before it bursts, capitalism, in its fundamental perversity, and bureaucracy, in its obtuse dogmatism, will keep crapping on the world!" (*L'Avant-scène cinéma*, 33). Paul continues to chant: "Ah, happiness is close!... Ah, happiness is faraway." They are both dancing by that point.[17] This sequence unfolds in a single shot, with both Pierre and Paul in long shot and the camera moving slightly to follow them. This is comparable to the icon of Rosemonde on the bed, partially because its editing is so minimalist (more so that the sequence with Rosemonde, really). Like the scene with Rosemonde by the window that shortly follows this, though, there is a kind of interiority at work. Pierre and Paul wandering through this empty forest are as removed from the world as Rosemonde was sitting in her spare room; as Rosemonde was only talking to herself, they are only talking to each other. This combination of visual minimalism and interiority combine to render the image iconic rather than indexical, a semi-abstract but still representational embodiment of lyricism and political discontent. This is close to the way that Berger talked about the film to Richard Appignanesi; when Appignanesi asked him if he shared Tanner's interest in absurd or "clownish behaviour," Berger replied:

In *La Salamandre*, for example, that scene in the forest when the two friends suddenly break into an absurd kind of song and dance is a very obvious scene of the type you must be referring to. But I'm not sure that the function of that scene is simply to show the absurdity of human behavior. It seems to me that it is actually a lyrical moment. It is a lyrical moment about hope, but also about disappointment, and I think hope and disappointment can exist together perfectly without adding up to absurdity. (302)

The coexistence of absurdity and hope is a good way to define the politics of both characters; they are both vaguely leftist and, as the scene on the tram shows, critical of the hypocrisy of their surroundings. But neither one is able to accomplish much in terms of concrete political action. They have hopes for a better world, but their lives as they lead them are defined more by quiet disappointments, like what we see in the film's opening sequences: Pierre negotiating a fee for the bland travel article on Brazil he's written for a Parisian magazine, and Paul working at his day job as a house painter. Charles Sanders Peirce writes of icons that they "convey ideas of the things they represent simply by imitating them" (88). These sequences become icons not only because, as in Tanner's formulation, if you don't cut, you see everything differently, but because they are conveying *ideas* about the characters by imitating them, not by trying to point to their place in physical reality, as an indexical sign would do. The scene by the window coveys the idea of Rosemonde as someone heavily invested in interiority and self-surveillance; this scene in the forest conveys the idea of the guys as part of a left that is both jovial and slightly defeatist. This is an approach to film language, and to narrative as well, that does not jettison realism for the abstraction of the symbol. But sequences like this also reject an indexical or realist strategy for a pattern that is more imitative that representational. Describing his hopes for an Epic Theatre, one that could rise to the task of illuminating a culture for a truly engaged audience in the way classical epic had, Brecht said (in the dialogue with Friedrich Wolf that I mentioned in the introduction) that "It by no means renounces emotion, least of all the sense of justice, the urge to freedom, the righteous anger; it is so far from renouncing these that it does not even assume their presence, but tries to arouse or reinforce them" (227).[18] Rosemonde by the window; the guys pulling the tram stunt; the guys in the forest: these are sequences full of emotion, sequences that arouse and reinforce the viewer's anger at the way women must deal with the regime of self-surveillance that defines their lives, scenes that arouse the viewer's love of freedom though an anarchic, anti-capitalist song and dance, iconic images that appeal to the viewer's sense of justice.

Small wonder that this "lyrical moment about hope, but also about disappointment" happens in the forest of Rosemonde's home village; that village is, of course, in the Jura. The Jura mountains divide France and Switzerland, and in the 1970s the Bernese Jura was in the middle of considerable political upheaval. Tanner had already made a fiction film that used the Jura as his setting: his debut 1969 feature *Charles Mort ou vif*, where a wealthy industrialist reconnects with the counter-cultural sensibility of his ancestors, one of whom had been part of nineteenth-century anarchist commune in the Jura mountains, by hooking up with a bohemian couple living amidst those very peaks. Tanner had also already made a film about the politics of Jura "separatism," the effort of the majority-francophone parts of Canton Berne (which is majority German-speaking) to secede and form their own Canton Jura: *L'Indépendance au loin* (1965). At the time of *La Salamandre*'s production, 1971, there was still no canton of Jura (the first referendum to separate from Berne came in 1974 and was followed by several municipal referenda and a final federal one in 1978), but in the late 1960s and 70s, the very word "Jura" conjured, in the imagination of most Swiss, the spectre of intense political unrest (at least by Swiss standards). Berger's aforementioned essay about the French painter Courbet, described the French Jura in a 1978 essay as "a region which is both lawless and irreducibly real" (*About Looking*, 137–38). But this Jura "separatism" began as a kind of conservative semi-nationalism, one that drew upon not only a sense of linguistic oppression but also the region's vigorous traditions of Swiss patriotism and overwhelmingly Catholic culture. Pro-Jura rhetoric also often drew on the contrast between the semi-metropolitan culture of Berne, the federal capital, and the mostly rural culture of the Jura. Its imagery was thus very similar to that employed by a lot of early-twentieth-century Irish nationalism. And Paul, in that early sequence when he is describing how he imagines Rosemonde's upbringing from Pierre's Geneva apartment, could just as well be talking about metropolitan Dublin's perception of County Donegal as the storied Jura village of Saint-Ursanne: "So: big family, a real brood, eh! And you say big family, you say countryside. In the city, it's impossible with the real-estate racket. So: countryside, but not just any countryside. It's Catholic, still a little wild … contraception unknown…. kids named after saints, everyone exhausted. The dad's kind of thick. Education's not very good" (*L'Avant-scene cinéma*, 12).[19] *La Salamandre* presents the Jura[20] as a sort of (presumably priest-ridden) backwater that is consistent with a lot of mainstream Swiss imaginings of the place. At one point a young hoodlum tries to grope Rosemonde, and she pushes him away yelling "con de paysan!," or "peasant asshole!" Furthermore, Rosemonde's petty-bourgeois uncle, who is particularly unhappy about being shot with his own army rifle because after serving with it in the army for thirty years, "it becomes more than just a gun…. It's more the symbol of our liberty" (*L'Avant-scène cinema*, 17),[21] is entirely consistent with popular perceptions of Jura culture as being superpatriotic and attached to the military. Tanner and Berger are thus visualizing the life of the *montagnards* as a border culture, part of an interstitial zone where one is equally likely to meet nonconformist radicals dancing in the forest as you are a mother slaving over a hot stove as she tries to prepare supper for her giant family (as we see Rosemonde's mother doing when she brings Paul home to meet her). This vision of the mountains as an unstable, unpredictable space where nonconformist visions of both tradition and modernity collide into each other is, as I argued in the introduction, utterly Swiss, very much a product of the country's history (a history not limited to Jura) of small alpine communities struggling for autonomy against all manner of centralizing forces.

This is, of course, a supremely optimistic view of the world of the mountain community, and it is just that spirit that brings Tanner and Berger into the frame of the Enlightenment tradition. Bas tries to connect Tanner's work to *Candide*, partially by noting that this was one of Brecht's favourite books. In addition to the work's irony leading Brecht (and Tanner) to an interest in distanciation, Bas points out that all of this work is defined by a key tension: "on one hand, the innocence and optimism of the characters; on the other, the horrors of the world" (170).[22] The visions of horror in *La Salamandre* come mostly in the form of images of disaffection, and the most vivid such image is definitely the shot of Rosemonde working in a sausage factory. We first see this in a sequence that directly follows Pierre and Paul meeting for the first time and Paul sketching out his semi-fictional view of Rosemonde's background. The sequence is two shots, although most of that is a single shot of Rosemonde, framed from the waist up, working at the nozzle that spits out sausage innards into casings. The camera doesn't move, there is no sound except for some industrial sounds and some music, and the shot lasts about ninety seconds; it is followed by a very brief shot, set slightly further back, of Rosemonde with two co-workers. (There is a similar sequence, also two shots, a bit later in the film; that one is mostly made up of a very long take of a close-up of the phallic-looking innards dispenser itself.) The contrast between this existence and Pierre and Paul's goofy, slightly intellectualized vision of who she is and how they can write about her is harsh. Part of the sharpness here is at the formal level. The sequence in which Pierre and Paul chatter about big families and kids named after saints is edited following a basically recognizable shot/reverse-shot pattern. It feels a bit slow, but is still relatively easily consumed. It feels "real." The very long take of Rosemonde working that inescapably phallic-looking sausage machine, on the other hand, takes on a discernibly artificial feel, just as Tanner said he felt that long takes can do. The shot that follows it, with Rosemonde at the sausage machine, is slow, still, and clearly signifies the repetitive, meaningless labour that defines a large portion of her day. This is not exactly a moment of Brechtian distanciation, but it is just as clearly not a moment of illusionist narrative. Because Tanner doesn't cut, he causes us to see things differently. Rather than a semi-indexical moment of narrative clarity, this is another icon, as powerful in its way as the one of Rosemonde on the bed: an icon of modern, industrial-strength estrangement. Just as Pierre and Paul, as pleasantly gadfly-ish bohemians, are clearly the best possible writers to try to capture this mysterious woman, Rosemonde is the best possible alienated labourer in this best of all possible worlds.

So while it is not a fully realized critique of a violent, bloody world (as *Candide* is), *La Salamandre* is quite a considered critique of representation, of the ways in which people's lives are re-written and presented as re-tellings of reality rather than as fully artificial constructions. The degree to which this is a function of the mass-media increasing omnipresence is much more central to *La Salamandre*'s 1995 "remake," *Fourbi*, which I will discuss in Chapter 5. The critique that is being launched here is a more philosophical one; Berger and Tanner are mainly concerned with the impossibility of re-telling anyone's life, at any level: to a mass audience through a television script, from one friend to another as they chat amicably, or to yourself as you sit completely alone, trying to come to grips with your subjectivity. Part of this scepticism has to do with Tanner's interest in what he calls alienation effects (which he clearly means in a Brechtian sense, as in the audience becoming alienated from or at a distance to the spectacle of the narrative). But Tanner and Berger are more interested in the ways in which the complexity of everyday life is simply incompatible with clear, unambiguous narrative. In some ways this has fairly obvious Wellesian overtones; the name of the main character could certainly be read as a wink to the famous cry "Rosebud!" that comes at the beginning of *Citizen Kane* (1939). But really, the better analogy is with Berger's own towering masterpiece, *G*. To speak in the terms of the epigraph from *G* that opens this chapter, the biography of Rosemonde, the story of whether or not she shot her uncle, emerges here as the self-knowledge of the living minds of Pierre, Paul, and Rosemonde herself. The emergence of this kind of self-knowledge is at the heart of the film. Tarantino writes that "the emphasis in *La Salamandre* is on ways of seeing in themselves, the very existence of different types of knowledge, and therefore, means of obtaining it" ("The Voice Off-Screen," 39). This kind of diversity at times feels deep and fecund, following the Roland Barthes formulation with which I concluded the last chapter. That's true of the sequences when Pierre and Paul are with each other and hatching schemes about how to better get at the story. It's also true of sequences with Paul and Rosemonde, many of which have a very gentle intimacy about them; that's most true of the sequence where the two walk through the wintry Jura landscape, chatting aimlessly about Rosemonde's childhood and eventually breaking into song. Paul sings "There once was a Swedish countess / So pretty and so pale / Oh lumberjack, Oh lumberjack / My suspenders fell to my tail / To my tail, to my tail / Lumberjack, to your knees / And fix them up, don't you mind" (it doesn't rhyme much better in French) (*L'avant-scène cinéma* 32).[23] That entire sequence is only two shots; it is made up of a very long-lasting tracking shot where they are facing the camera which is moving backwards to follow them (and which cuts them off at the waist) and is followed by a briefer reverse-shot, which cuts them off at the knees and also follows them as they walk down the road. The fact that both images are two-shots helps establish some intimacy, or at least some connection between the two, and the slow, leisurely pace both of the characters who walk, combined with the camera that moves with them, all gives the sequence a sense of gentle flow into the snowy landscape. It is an artificial moment, a sequence whose long takes both give back some reality to the viewer and give an effect of the slightly unreal, the slightly abstract. There are other places in the film where this kind of uncertainty feels more alienating and challenging, and this is most true of the film's pre-credit sequence, which is a jagged montage of close-ups and extreme close-ups, all shot in slow motion and all of which seem to depict Rosemonde shooting her uncle, although we never actually see her with the gun. In the interview that accompanied that *Positif* review that I mentioned at the beginning of this chapter, Laurent Bonnard asked Tanner point-blank, "What, finally, is the point of *La Salamandre*?" Tanner replied that "Contacts with the public have to be made on many levels" (34).[24] This is echoed in the ways that Pierre, Paul, and Rosemonde all try to make sense of the history that is constantly evading their grasp: interviews with friends, family, and witnesses; introspection; fictionalization. As all of these ways of knowing collide with one another, we can feel them, in the words from *G* that open this chapter, vibrating in the minds of all three.

It should be no surprise that *La Salamandre* deals with anxiety around the meaning of history and does so through the story of a rebellious young woman, for it was made at a time when Switzerland was undergoing serious changes in its historical understanding of itself, especially when it came to women's roles in society. The film was released in 1971, the same year that a national referendum (held on 7 February 1971) giving women the vote at the federal level was, finally, passed. This followed a previous referendum in 1959, which had been defeated fairly soundly. By 1971 women had already achieved the right to vote in many, although certainly not all, of Switzerland's cantons, and that cantonal process had begun amazingly late; the canton of Basel-Stadt was the first to pass a referendum that allowed for universal suffrage at the cantonal level, in 1966. The last holdout was Appenzell Innerrhoden, which rejected referendum after referendum, only to be ordered by Switzerland's supreme court to give women the vote at the cantonal level in 1990. This is all to say that the figure of an independent, rebellious woman who refuses to let herself be easily known by outsiders has a special significance in Switzerland of 1971. Freddy Buache sees Rosemonde's power largely in terms of how she indicts the illusions of capitalist culture, writing that "Rosemonde is touching because she confusingly resents (more so than [*Charles mort ou vif*'s] Charles Dé) an oppression that is exactly that which capitalism visits upon any individual who refuses the mirages of an eased conscience" (*Le cinéma suisse*, 149).[25] But Rosemonde is also refusing the mirages of tranquility that a society defined by gender inequality offers, especially to women. *Kinder, Kirche und Kuche* is the old way of referring to women's roles in traditional Switzerland: children, church and kitchen. That this formulation is in German is no minor matter; it was mostly German-speaking cantons that were the last holdouts against universal suffrage (Appenzell Innerrhoden was only the most extreme example). Rosemonde is indifferent to or in conflict with all three (especially the first; one of the minor plot points is the discovery that she has had a child that she gave up for adoption), and so as a figure of a new Swiss woman she is startling. That she emerges in 1971 of all years makes her a kind of icon of a resistance to tradition and a headlong rush into an uncertain modernity.

Less than a jazzy, anachronistically New-Wave-style romp through the bohemian environs of Geneva, then, *La Salamandre* is a meditation on knowledge and the ability to communicate that knowledge in a Switzerland whose relationship with modernity, was, in the 1970s, highly fluid. Although it is a lot less experimental in its narrative structure than Berger's *G*, it is very close to that novel's thematic concerns. *G*, in addition to being engaged with the ways that knowledge and modes of communication always exist in multiple and sometimes conflicting forms, is also obsessed with the contours of European history, moving us through a number of that continent's failed revolutions (from workers' uprisings in Milan of the 1890s to early attempts to fly across the alps, and ending in Trieste as the Austro-Hungarian empire breaks apart and that city's Italian and Slavic populations assert themselves in violent opposition). *La Salamandre*, although it has none of the historical detail of Berger's novel, is still also very much engaged with the politics of European insurgency. The film's characters are all restless and aimless, and it's hard not to see that as being a product of the post-68 era, a period in Europe characterized by the failure of revolutionary moments (Paris's days of May, the Prague Spring) and the gradual onset of a sense of powerlessness and disconnection that seemed to be the distinguishing quality of emergent 1970s. That sense solidifies into "normalization" in Berger and Tanner's next film, *Le Milieu du monde*, a work that presents a European experience marked by a near-complete neutralization of political idealism. *La Salamandre* presents that experience in its nascent form, and through the story of a slightly harried journalist, his shaggy poet friend, and the genuinely mysterious woman whose essence they fail to capture, hints both at some ways that it can be resisted and at the pitfalls of such resistance. It is a deceptively complex film; hiding beneath its eccentric story of shambling young people trying to make their way through the world is a portrait of the culture of western capitalism stuck in a kind of holding pattern. Revolution could be everywhere, but it doesn't ever quite come together. Voltaire's best of all possible worlds is out there somewhere, but this doesn't seem to be it. *Ah, que le bonheur est proche ! Ah que le bonheur est lointain ! Et que la préhistoire est longe !*

Notes

1 "Pangloss enseignait la métaphysico-théologo-cosmolonigolie. Il prouvait admirablement qu'il n'y a point d'effet sans cause, et que, dans ce meilleur des mondes possibles, le château de monseigneur le baron était le plus beau des châteaux et madame la meilleure de baronnes possibles" (138).

2 "Ce qui m'a frappé d'abord dans ce film, c'est un (déjà) parfum d'archaïsme. Alain Tanner refait en mieux certain « Nouvelle Vague »."

3 "Je cite de mémoire Octavio Paz, qui a très bien défini ce qu'est la modernité en art. Pour lui, la modernité, c'est lorsque, à l'intérieur de l'œuvre, dans son fonctionnement et son tissu même, il apparaît une critique de son propre moyen d'expression, quel qu'il soit, littérature, peinture ou cinéma, et cette position critique vient en transformer à la fois la texture et a finalité. À partir de Paz, il est évident qu'on ne peut que déboucher sur Brecht."

4 The English text is taken from the Nobel website: http://nobelprize. org/nobel prizes/literature/laure-ates/1990/paz-lecture-e.html (6 May 2010). The Spanish text is as follows: "La modernidad es la punto del movimiento histórico, la encarnación de la evolución o de la revolución, las dos caras del progreso" (55–56) …. "Volví a mi origen y descubrí que la modernidad no está afuera sino adentro de nosotros. Es hoy y es la antigüedad mas antigua, es mañana y es el comienzo del mundo, tiene mil años y acaba de nacer" (63).

5 "J'ai longtemps sorti de mon esprit certains de mes films, parce que je les trouvais trop discursifs, pieds et poings liés au présent. Je pense à *La Salamandre* ou à *Jonas qui aura vingt-cinq ans en l'an 2000*. Je m'aperçois aujourd'hui que s'ils refont surface, c'est avant tout parce qu'ils étaient complètement ancrés dans la modernité."

6 "Ici, nous étions à l'extrémité ouest du pays, à deux pas de la frontière, et la Suisse semblait déjà lointaine. Nous lui tournions le dos."

7 "Paul écrivait dans son carnet : « La Salamandre est un joli petit animal de la famille des lézards. Elle est noire avec des taches jaune-oranges. La Salamandre est vénimeuse. Elle ne craint pas le feu et peut traverser les flammes sans se brûler. »"

8 "En dépit de certaines apparences, auxquelles il ne faut jamais se fier, Paul n'était pas peintre en bâtiment ou chanteur, mais écrivain."

9 "… la littérature réaliste est, certes, narrative, mais c'est parce que le réalisme est en elle seulement parcellaire, erratique, confiné aux « détails » et que le récit le plus réaliste qu'on puisse imaginer se développe selon des voies irréalistes."

10 "PAUL. C'est pas mal, cette histoire! Je vais rester. Qu'est-ce que tu penses ?

PIERRE. C'est pas mal, mais il y a tout de même un petit problème.

PAUL. Lequel ?

PIERRE. Qu'est-ce que tu fais de la réalité dans tout ça ?

PAUL. Eh bien, ça fait cinq minutes que je t'en parle de la réalité !... Mis à part peut-être quelques détails, j'ai l'impression d'avoir déjà bien gagné ma journée.

PIERRE. Bon. Tu as bien gagné ta journée, mais il est aussi très possible que tu aies rêvé. Je ne vois pas très bien pourquoi on aurait du prime abord recours à ton imagination alors que l'histoire s'est réellement passée. La fille existe, l'oncle aussi. Ils sont ici, quelque part. C'est la réalité qui m'intéresse,... (*insistant*) ... les choses ! Il faut partir de là et connaître ... toucher ce qui peut se toucher. (*Paul veut intervenir.*) Non, tu gambergeras après. Il faut d'abord faire une enquête.

PAUL (*bourru*). J'suis pas un flic.

PIERRE. Une enquête journalistique, tête de lard !

PAUL (*même ton*). J'suis pas journaliste."

11 "Mais j'ai pas vraiment voulu, je sais pas.... ça s'est passé comme ça, sur un coup de colère. Je pouvais plus le supporter, ce vieux connard,... il arrêtait pas de m'emmerder. Il voulait toujours que je travaille,... même quand il y avait rien du tout à faire. Comme à l'armée (*un silence*). Il arrêtait pas de râler, de me faire la morale. Depuis, j'ai toujours peur de m'emballer, de faire une connerie. Je sais pas quoi faire...."

12 "J'ai 25 ans. Si j'étais née six jours plus tard, je m'appellerais Héliodore. J'ai des petits seins. J'aime bien la forme de mes jambes. J'ai les cheveux blondes.... Les gens détestent mon indépendance et essaient toujours de me briser. Ils disent de moi que je suis paresseuse, sauvage, hystérique." The published scenario says twenty-five years old; the dialogue in the film says twenty-three.

13 "Quand j'avais douze ans?.... Quand j'avais douze ans.... j'avais de jolis petits pieds,... mignons. Un jour, j'ai mis mes jolis petits pieds,... mignons. Un jour, j'ai mis mes citrouille [*sic*]. J'ai rencontré le fils du roi qui avait de si beaux pieds,... immenses,... avec des grands orteils. Plus beaux que les vôtres!"

14 "On peut d'ailleurs raconter bien des films de Tanner comme une succession d'états du corps. *La Salamandre*, par exemple, où la vérité de Rosemonde passe par son corps davantage que par ses mots. Au début, on ne connaît d'ailleurs Rosemonde que par des postures de son corps : à la chaîne (au travail), à la piscine (au repos), chez elle en train de danser, sans oublier son corps marchant qui ouvre et conclut le film."

15 "Maintenant ... (*elle hésite*). Je me trouve vieille. C'est plus comme avant (*un temps*). Je me demande ce que je vais devenir. Avant, ça m'était égal. Puis, ça ne fait rien ... (*énervée*). J'en ai marre de votre truc. On arrête?"

16 "Les Italiens et les Espagnols, ça vous intéresse pas,... hein? Ça vous suffit, d'ailleurs. Et voilà les Turcs maintenant!... Les Arabes!... A Genève!... Pas possible ça. Moi, je vous le dis, hein Monsieur, Mademoiselle aussi, si ça continue comme ça, on aura des nègres dans nos tramways, avec leur danses (*il mime*) avec les lolos en l'air, des tams-tams, des batteries,... incroyable!" This sequence takes on an extra edge in retrospect; I am writing this in December 2009, less than a

week after 59% of Switzerland voted to ban the construction of minarets (although I am writing it from the staunchly Catholic city of Fribourg, where the initiative got only 39% of the vote).

17   "PIERRE. Ah, que le bonheur est proche ! (*il respire.*) Je le sens venir. Tu le sens?… (*gueulant presque.*) Ah, que le bonheur est proche ! Ah que le bonheur est lointain ! Et que la préhistoire est longue !… (*il rit.*)

PAUL. (riant et déclamant). Et nous marchons à petits pas vers la mort.

PIERRE. Avant de crever, le capitalisme, dans sa perversité fondamentale, et la bureaucratie, dans son dogmatisme obtu [*sic*], feront chier encore pas mal de monde !

PAUL (déclamant). Ah que le bonheur est proche !… Ah, que le bonheur est lointain !"

18   "Es verzichtet in keiner Weise auf Emotionen. Schon gar nicht auf das Gerechtigkeitsgefühl, den Freiheitsdrang und den gerechten Zorn: es verzichtet so wenig darauf, daß es sich sogar nicht auf ihr Vorhandensein verläßt, sondern sie zu verstärken oder zu schaffen sucht" ("Formprobleme des Theaters," 254).

19   "Donc : famille nombreuse,… la vraie marmaille, quoi ! Et qui dit famille nombreuse dit campagne. En ville, c'est impossible avec le racket immobilier. Donc : campagne, mais pas n'importe laquelle, campagne catholique, encore un peu broussailleuse,… contraception inconnue,… saints du calandrer, tout le fourbi. Le père a un peu de plomb dans l'aile. L'éducation souffre de quelques imperfections."

20   The word "Jura" is not spoken in any of the dialogues of *La Salamandre*, although the published screenplay specifies that when Rosemonde, Pierre, and Paul go to visit Rosemonde's family, they are driving to "Quelque part dans le Jura" (26). More importantly, though, Rosemonde recalls how for a brief period during her childhood, "on habitait de l'autre côté de le frontière, en France" (*L'Avant-scène cinéma*, 32).

21   "Ça devient plus qu'un simple mousqueton; c'est un peu le symbole de nos libertés, à nous autres."

22   "… d'un côté, l'innocence et l'optimisme du personnage; de l'autre, les horreurs du monde."

23   "Il y avait une fois une comtesse suédoise / Elle était très belle et très pâle / Monsieur le forestier, Monsieur le forestier / Ma jarretelle a sauté / Elle a sauté, elle a sauté / Forestier, vite à genoux / Et rajustez-la sans peur."

24   "— Et quel est, en définitive, le propos de La Salamandre? — Les contacts avec le public doivent se faire à plusieurs niveaux."

25   "Rosemonde touche juste parce qu'elle ressent confusément (plus confusément encore que Charles Dé) une oppression qui est exactement celle que le capitalisme opulent fait peser sur chaque individu refusant … les mirages de la conscience tranquille et la veulerie."

CHAPTER THREE

LE MILIEU DU MONDE

"The soul of 'le milieu du monde' is in the reflection of running water; in the apple shed – shutters drawn – of an old house. It's in the peasant's gestures and in the turning of the mill-wheel; in the smiles of yesterday's and today's grandmas and aunties, who keep house, and thanks to whom we have fresh bread in the oven. It's in the smallest flower and in every seed; in the school-bell and the graveyard's slope. It's the soul of a living country, rich in markings and rich in beauty." – Georges Duplain, introduction to Pierre Deslandes' and Fred Schmid's 1943 photo book *Milieu du Monde* (39)[1]

"It was very clear from the beginning, for example, that we would use very long shots, that the film was built as a series of a hundred little short films each done in one take – and this of course is directly influenced by Brecht's epic theatre. This is, in a sense, epic cinema." – Alain Tanner, on the film *Le Milieu du monde* (Monaco 33)

Perhaps it was simply a stroke of dumb luck that the day after I watched Berger and Tanner's second feature-length film *Le Milieu du monde* (1974) at the Bibliothèque cantonale et universitaire Fribourg, the Cinémathèque Suisse, just down the line in Lausanne, was showing new films by Jean-Marie Straub and the recently deceased Danièle Huillet, with Straub in attendance. First on the docket was *Itinéraire de Jean Bricard* (2008), the last film that the couple had made together; the other two films were the first works Straub had made by himself in thirty-five years: *Il Ginocchio di Artemide* (2007) and *Le Streghe* (2009). Of these three, the most rigorous, and the most pleasurable to watch, was definitely *Itinéraire de Jean Bricard*, a richly visual study of the landscape of the Loire valley. Shot mostly from a riverboat, the film is made up largely of movements around a small, forested island, over and over again; midway through there is a slight digression, with a complexly composed sequence shot: a few people climb aboard a boat at dusk, with a small town and a bridge visible in the extreme background; the boatman looks directly at the camera, and starts the motor; the boat putters away, the motor still audible long after the boat itself has left the frame. In addition to completely still long takes such as these, though, the film is also filled with jump cuts to slightly different angles of more or less the same landscape formation, 180-degree pans across fields and brushy forests, and slight re-framings that bring out important elements of graphically striking elements of either the scenery or the things built on it (fences, ramshackle sheds, etc.). It is entirely typical of the work the pair did together, and wonderfully so: it is a lush, highly demanding meditation on a landscape, one that is never taken as some sort of unspoiled arcadia but is instead, as good Marxist-materialists would demand, marked by the cultures and economies that have existed as part of the landscape and continue to mark it. The Cinémathèque Suisse's new director Frédéric Maire gave an introduction that spoke of the institution's great affection for Straub and Huillet's work, and he's certainly not the only Swiss to speak in those terms. In his history of the "Nouveau cinéma suisse," Martin Schaub writes that "It's no surprise that Jean-Marie Straub[2] has exercised a particularly profound influence on Swiss cinema. Straub has stripped from his films (*Not Reconciled, Chronicle of Anna Magdelana Bach, History Lessons, Moses and Aaron*, etc.) all the myths and clichés of a cinema of consumption, to find a language that is lucid and perfectly intelligible" (15).[3] Renato Berto, the cinematographer on all three of the films that Berger and Tanner made together, has recalled in the texts that accompanied the film's published screenplay that "After *Charles mort ou vif*, the most enriching experience for me was Straub's *Othon*, for which I was an assistant-cameraman" (Boujut, 148).[4] In that same book, the actress who stars as Olympia in *Le Milieu du monde* recalls that she had played Camille in *Othon* (139). Responding in a 1976 interview to James Monaco question about the influence of Jacques

Rivette, Tanner himself said that "Politically I would be much closer to Godard or Straub" (33).

In another stroke of basically dumb luck, while browsing the shambling stacks of the Fribourg used bookstore Le Book'in as I procrastinated writing this very chapter, I happened upon a 1943 photo book called *Milieu du Monde*, by Pierre Deslandes and Fred Schmid. In some ways it is close to the sorts of books that Berger did with Jean Mohr from the 1960s to the 80s, and which I discussed in Chapter 1 or will discuss in Chapter 4: *A Fortunate Man* (1967), *A Seventh Man* (1975), and *Another Way of Telling* (1982). Like those books, which were first published for the members of Writers and Readers Publishing Cooperative, *Milieu du monde*'s back leaf states that this is an "Edition hors commerce réservée aux members de la Guilde du Livre." It is a mixture of text and photographic image, with the text basically talking around the images rather than directly explaining them. There is a simple explanation for this; the text was originally published as a series of letters by Delandes in *Le Gazette de Lausanne*; the book itself, along with Schmid's photos, was only published after Delandes had died. Those newspaper columns were titled "Lettres du milieu du monde," and took as their subject the landscapes and cultural practices of the same place where Berger and Tanner set their film: that part of the canton of Vaud at the foot of the Jura mountains known as La plaine de Moruz but also known as Le Milieu du Monde, which, as the extra-diegetic voice-over in the opening scene tells us, "marks the watershed-divide between the south and the north of a continent" (Boujut 46).[5] There are a few of Schmid's photos – a close-up of a man staring off (38), an awkwardly composed and shadowy shot of a woman working in her kitchen (59), a shot of a dense forest at dusk with a shaft of light, seemingly from a headlight, filling the middle of the frame (136) – that have a Mohr-esque quality to them. But overall the tone both the text and the images is nostalgic and sentimentally pastoral.

One way to understand *Le Milieu du monde* is as an attempt to steer between these two poles, between the spare intensity of Straub-Huillet and the sentimental nostalgia of writers like Pierre Deslandes. On one hand, the film is unmistakeably a work of Brechtian-influenced counter-cinema, of epic cinema, to follow Tanner's formulation. But the film's first images, including the credit sequence, are landscape shots that, in a way, strongly recall the photos of the book *Milieu du monde*: the film's very first image, of fog rolling over a field, looks a lot like that book's photo of a field next to a wood (124), and the film's second image, of a small bridge over a creek, looks a lot like Schmid's photo of a creek that runs between a few trees (18). But the shots that follow this credit sequence could not be further away from those of the book *Milieu du monde*. They are of a film crew working on *Le Milieu du monde* itself (you can see that they are shooting an image of the two lead characters, Paul and Adriana, walking across a bridge), and an extra-diegetic female voice explaining some of the practical and ideological conditions under which the film was made: "A film's narrative is in large part dependent on where and when the film is made and under what circumstances. This film was shot in a place called Le Milieu du Monde.... This film was shot in 1974, in a time of normalization. Normalization means that between nations, classes, and even between theoretically opposed political systems, everything can be exchanged on the condition that nothing changes the nature of things" (Boujut 46).[6] This matter of normalization is at the centre of the film overall and will return again and again. But even this sequence is a mixed bag; it opens with shots of the snowy Jura, images that are possessed of a lovely melancholy that is typical of the way that the film moves throughout. The film never fully distances its viewer from its characters, or its landscapes; both are, at least partially, bearers of aesthetic pleasure, spectacles. Writing about the film in the French magazine *Écran*, Noël Simsolo brought in Straub as well: "Getting past the leftist simplicity of Tanner's cinema, isn't it time to look for something more *essential*, that which even Brecht, like Straub, has reclaimed: an articulation between theory and spectacle permitting the viewer to question himself in relation to a representation that deconstructs bourgeois cinema" (47, emphasis his).[7] Tanner himself voiced that desire to get at something fundamental in this film, something, following the title, at the very centre of film aesthetics, when he tried, in that interview with James Monaco, to distinguish his work from Godard's militantly anti-spectacle work of the early 1970s (both during and after the Dziga Vertov period that I discussed in the introduction). He told Monaco that "I would be completely incapable of doing what Godard does. What he is doing is filming *theory*. What I want to do is to use theory to film *things*" (32, emphases in the original). *Le Milieu du monde* is very much about things, about the material and emotional world of electoral politics, landscapes, migration, sex, economics, and friendship.

But it presents these things in a way that is clearly, unmistakeably inflected by theory, by work dealing with ideology, representation, and cinematic classicism.

I want to explain the significance of *Le Milieu du monde* along two lines. The first is largely theoretical: more than any of the films that Berger and Tanner made together, this is the one that tries to both integrate and critique key issues of 1970s French film theory. The second, following from the first, has to do with pleasure and spectacle: the main critique of these theoretical positions that the film offers is, to paraphrase the 1969 text on "Montage" that I have been citing throughout this book, that the inability to escape reason is itself oppressive. *Le Milieu du monde* offers such an escape through moments of rather pure emotional affect; rather than a simple "escapism," though, these moments are thoroughly linked to the film's overall critique of "normalization," for it is moments such as these that cannot be contained by reason, cannot be normalized.

The film's narrative is very different from that of either *La Salamandre* or *Jonas qui aura 25 ans en l'an 2000*, both of which are defined by a veritable rogues' gallery of appealingly eccentric left-wing goofballs. *Le Milieu du monde* is about an affair between Paul – a successful engineer, married with a small child, who is gearing up for a run at political office – and Adriana – an Italian woman working as a waitress in a café near "Le milieu du monde." The film details the intensity of the affair, all the while making it clear that neither one can fully commit to the other and thus submit to the instability and unknown possibilities that uncontrolled passion promises. But in addition to being a "love story," a narrative about erotic love – as was Berger's novel *G*, completed two years before *Le Milieu du monde* was finished – it is also a narrative about migrant European labour. Berger told Richard Appignanesi "that film began with Alain saying to me, 'Can we make a film about an Italian waitress' – there are thousands of them working in Swiss cafes, at least in French-speaking Switzerland – 'and a Swiss man, who has an affair with her?' I think he added that the Swiss man should, in some way or another, be involved (in a career sense) with Swiss politics. That was all, at the beginning" (304). The perilous existence of migrant labourers in Europe was also the subject of Berger and Jean Mohr's photo-book *A Seventh Man*, published the year after *Le Milieu du monde* was completed; his subjects there are mostly emigrating to "rich Europe" (the

UK, France, Germany, Switzerland) from "poor Europe" (Italy, Portugal, Yugoslavia, Turkey). Like *Le Milieu du monde*, *A Seventh Man* engages with "normalization" and the way it undergirds the society of the capitalist west. Berger writes in that photo book that:

> It is difficult to grasp a "normal," familiar situation as a whole: rather, one reacts with a series of habitual responses which, although they are reactions, really belong to that situation. History, political theory, sociology can all help one to understand that 'the normal' is only normative. Unfortunately these disciplines are usually used to do the opposite: to serve tradition by asking questions in such a way that the answers sanctify the norms as absolutes. Every tradition forbids the asking of certain questions about what has really happened to you. (100)

The critique of normalization unfolds along different lines in *Le Milieu du monde*, whose stand-in for the ravages of bourgeois tradition is not social science but mainstream, technocratic politics. But the overall thrust of the narrative is similar: what the proliferation of migrant labour shows us is that capitalism requires systems of support that are alienating on many levels. In *A Seventh Man* a lot of this has to do with the toll such working conditions takes on the bodies of migrant labourers; in *Le Milieu du monde* it is more a matter of how the experience of migration leads to emotional and political isolation. In both works, the migrant labourer is the bleeding wound of Europe, the signifier of the failure to create a just, emotionally and politically nourishing social framework.

Theory

What are the theories that Tanner, and Berger along with him, use to film things? By and large they have to do with the desire to expose the hidden ideologies at work in classical form, a desire that is a central part of the post-'68 *Cahiers du cinéma*, of which Tanner was a habitual reader (references to this material do not come up in Berger's writing and interviews the way they do in Tanner's). Realist form, sometimes called invisible form or classical form, was by and large the enemy among these theoreticians. As I mentioned in the introduction, Jean-Louis Comolli and Jean Narboni's seminal 1969 essay "Cinéma/idéologie/critique" contained the statement "the tools and techniques of filmmaking are a part of 'reality' themselves, and furthermore 'reality' is nothing but an expression of the prevailing ideology. In this sense, the theory of 'transparency' (cinematic classicism) is eminently reactionary" ("Cinema/Ideology/Criticism" [translation modified], 25).[8] Rigorously anti-spectacle filmmakers like Straub/Huillet and Godard/Miéville[9] were emerging as the heroes/heroines of this theoretical school. In a similar fashion as these filmmakers' work, *Le Milieu du monde* uses a variety of techniques to disrupt the spectacle that defined classical form, a number of techniques that refuse to present the world created by the film as "reality" and thus refuse to take part in the reactionary project that Comolli and Narboni decry. The most important of these is camera movement and duration, which brings us back to a key component of the theoretical paradox at the core of Berger and Tanner's work: the reconciliation of Bazin and Brecht, of long takes and montage. These techniques also encompass, however, the film's overall narrative structure, along with occasional gestures within the storyline towards filmmaking itself.

The tension between montage and long takes emerges very early in the film. The first sequence to establish the connection between the film's two main characters, Paul and Adriana, is a good example. This is a montage sequence that alternates between shots of a boisterous meeting of a party executive whose members are debating whether to put Paul forward as a candidate and shots of Adriana walking through a small town with her suitcase, having just gotten off the train from Italy. Both sequences use different setups, but throughout both there is a marked use of both camera movement and stillness. These are, basically, two complete spaces, two tableaux – both assembled along the lines of a slow-paced découpage – that are being juxtaposed by way of creating a connection, and meaning, not present in either one alone. It is a merger of the sensibilities of Brecht and Eisenstein, along just the lines that Roland Barthes lays out in his essay "Diderot, Brecht, Eisenstein," published in 1973, the year before the release of *Le Milieu du monde*. Barthes writes there that "Brecht indicated that in epic theatre (which proceeds by successive tableaux) all the burden of meaning and pleasure bears on each scene, not on the whole.... The same is true in Eisenstein: the film is a contiguity of episodes, each one absolutely meaningful, aesthetically perfect, and the result is a cinema by vocation anthological, itself holding out to the fetishist, with dotted lines, the piece for him to cut out and take away to enjoy" (*Image-Music-Text*, 72).[10] I wouldn't go so far as to say this sequence (or others like it) is holding anything out to the fetishist, but otherwise it is operating in precisely this Brechto-Eisensteinian manner. These tableaux are very precisely conceived from an aesthetic standpoint, and as such are fully autonomous objects capable of bearing considerable burdens of meaning and pleasure. The harshly lit, smoke-filled room is a striking icon of the banality of mainstream politics, even more so because of the way in which everyone talks over each other, creating plenty of sound and fury that, in terms of fully-thought-out political positions, signifies little. Furthermore, the camera movement in that room is mostly circular and (like most of the movements in the films Tanner and Berger made together) not simply a matter of tracking in on whomever is speaking; this has the effect of pulling the viewer out of the spectacle slightly rather than simply making him or her feel like s/he is in the room with the bosses. This tableau also makes sharp use of montage within the scene. Early on there is a montage of the faces of the bosses: the camera is still, the editing is rhythmic, and there is a sense of relentless constancy here, a sense that this is a regularized ceremony whose outcome is fixed. The tableau of Adriana in the city is just as precisely conceived, and uses camera movements whose motion is independent of that of the characters in the frame. The first shot of this entire montage sequence is of Adriana in extreme long shot and in the centre of the frame walking up stairs and towards the camera; as she gets closer and closer, the camera tracks right to left, and this means that she moves out of the centre of the image towards its edges, slowly transforming a very classically composed image into something more awkward and striking. The next time we see Adriana (which follows a slow track circling around the table where the bosses are sitting), she is just as far from the camera as before but is now walking down the stairs, with the camera moving in the opposite direction, again moving her slowly to the edge of the frame. These sequences both draw upon a self-consciously visual strategy to show us something about their own words: the circular, sterile sameness of the party meeting, the slow onset of feelings of alienation and marginalization as someone moves through a strange city for the first time. Their form is self-conscious, and as tableau they are relatively self-contained. But in good Eisensteinian fashion, there is a new meaning when they are put together; the film argues, in short, that the marginalized loneliness of the migrant worker is part and parcel of mainstream politics in a capitalist system. They are woven into the same ideological fabric, and this becomes clear through the act of weaving these two (fully-realized, aesthetically-autonomous) tableaux together into a single piece of cinematic fabric, a fabric whose edges (as both Brecht and Eisenstein would demand) are always showing, whose borders are never smoothed out.

Another key theoretical concept that *Le Milieu du monde* is wrestling with is that of "Suture." This is the title of Jean-Pierre Oudart's two-part, 1969 article in *Cahiers du cinéma*, which explained the illusion of all holes in a narrative, diegetic world being sutured closed by the workings of classical film language; shot/reverse-shot editing, as the veritable backbone of that language system, is particularly responsible for this effect (the verbosity of his explanation precludes a quote; see "Cinema and Suture," 37 / "La Suture" part 1, 37–38). One way that *Le Milieu du monde* is engaging this concept is through its renunciation or radical changing of that editing pattern. This was also true of *La Salamandre*, which sometimes used variations of the form, such as volleys of opposing medium shots rather than close-ups during a few dialogue sequences. One sequence about twenty-five minutes into *Le Milieu du monde*, where Paul comes to Adriana's apartment for the first time, is illustrative of the way that this later film tweaks this most important visual convention of narrative cinema. This begins in Paul's car, in a medium shot of the back of his head, taken from the back seat. The film then cuts to a close-up of a door, which opens to reveal Adriana's face in a medium close-up. Within this single shot there is a fair bit of dialogue between Paul and Adriana – "what do you want?"; "to talk"; "now?" – and the shot lasts about twenty seconds. There is then a cut to a reverse-shot of Paul, where again *both* of them are talking; this shot lasts almost thirty seconds. Then it's back to original medium close-up of Adriana, and the conversation concludes with her closing the door after, once again, *both* of them have exchanged several lines within a single shot; that shot lasts about twenty seconds. This is shot/reverse-shot, strictly speaking; it is an editing pattern that moves between two close-ups of people talking. But what is missing is the rather crucial element of an editing rhythm that is linked to the exchange of dialogue, a rhythm that demands a cut to whoever is speaking. I don't want to get into whether *Le Milieu du monde*'s rhythmic alteration of the schema does or doesn't invoke the "absent one," the abstracted subjective agent who Oudart feels reigns over a shot/reverse-shot sequence, controlling the spectator's ideologically inflected perceptions, while remaining hidden behind an invisible form, all as part of what Oudart calls "the suture (the abolition of the Absent One and its resurrection in someone)" (37).[11] Suffice it to say that shot/reverse-shot is a fundamental element of classical form, a form whose rhythmic smoothness helps to naturalize, or normalize, a film's artificiality, and its ideological assumptions along with it.

Tanner was explicit in his writing on *Le Milieu du monde* about his desire to move beyond this conventional editing pattern. Describing the editing pattern of the film, and the compromises that a real spirit of montage demanded he make with the radical form he was seeking, he wrote that:

> In the whole film, there are not more than ten "correct" match cuts – that is to say match cuts within a single scene and maintaining a temporal continuity – whereas a "normal" film would no doubt have quite a few. It is a matter of deconstruction to work on this traditional language, but obviously it's not enough to simply obliterate everything. Montage, if it seeks oppositions and ruptures, only makes sense if between the fractures, there exists some connections. ("Le pourquoi dire," 17)[12]

This is quite consistent with the workings of all of the films that he made with Berger, and for that matter it is consistent with the work the two have done on their own. Furthermore, it is fully consistent with Robin Wood's analysis of Brecht's aesthetic practice which I discussed in the introduction. Indeed, Wood describes Brecht's insistence on leaving some elements of realist form in place using language very close to Tanner's in the passage I just quoted. Where Tanner writes that "il ne suffit évidemment pas de simplement tout *bouleverser*," Wood recalls how Brecht's sense of critique of identification uses "operates to counter this without *obliterating* it" (13, italics mine). This is, of course, very typical of modernism generally, which is marked by a self-conscious manipulation of formal conventions rather than an all-out rejection of them. *Le Milieu du monde*, like *La Salamandre* and *Jonas*, but I would say more so than those two, illustrates the basic definition of modernism offered by Douwe Fokkema and Elrud Ibsch, that "the syntactic code of Modernism is no more than a one-sided emphasis on particular syntagmatic options – a particular selection from among the many syntagmatic possibilities, which in general are provided by the linguistic system and only rarely are newly invented" (34). Neither the sequence shots upon which the film's aesthetic is based nor the slowed-down shot/reverse-shot upon which it occasionally draws are newly invented; both forms basically exist within the realm of narrative cinema. The change is in emphasis; the regularized, rhythmic aspect of découpage, so important to classical cinematic form, is almost completely absent here. *Le Milieu du monde* tweaks these conventions rather than rejecting them, thus putting them into expressive opposition.

But *Le Milieu du monde* also addresses the concept by occasional calls back to a formal pattern that more fully eschews classical film language, and suture along with it, by adopting a kind of pre-Griffith, and I daresay a pre-Porter grammar. Oudart writes about "a stage, which can be ignored now, in which the image was not perceived as a filmic field, but more like an animated photograph." He describes this kind of film language as being "a hypothetical and purely mythic period, when the cinema alone reigned, enjoyed by the spectator in a dyadic relationship." During this period, he writes, "space was still a pure expanse of *jouissance*, and the spectator was offered objects literally without anything coming between them as a screen and thus prohibiting the capture of the objects" (41–42).[13] Is this not what is happening in a sequence (about halfway through the film) in Adriana's one-room apartment, when she sits at a table by the window, at first naked and then wrapped in her overcoat, drinking coffee? This is a single shot, without any camera movement at all, lasting just over a minute.[14] It could be a Lumière *actualité*. Of course, it is not: it is a part of a narrative film. But it is a part of a narrative film where dominant narrative film language can find no purchase whatsoever. It is strongly reminiscent of the scene in *La Salamandre* of Rosemonde sitting on the bed describing herself, which I discussed in the last chapter. But despite that sequence's iconicity, even there we had a reverse-shot to reveal the entry of Rosemonde's roommate, with whom she has a brief exchange. But in this *Milieu du monde* shot, there is no découpage, no dialogue, no advancement of a plot. There is only a body, in a space, in motion. Despite this fully pared-down grammar, though, this is a fully legible part of the narrative; it does not stand outside the diegesis in the way that the opening shots of the camera crew working do. Suture as a formal pattern is fully absent; what remains is the basics of narrative cinema: representation.

There is a better analogy for the use of film language in this sequence than Edwin S. Porter or the Lumière brothers: Straub and Huillet. "He may construct his films from the most realistic materials," Richard Roud writes of Straub (seeming to mean Straub-Huillet), "and yet the result is a musical structure which transcends realism – but without rejecting it" (*Straub*, 11). What is going on in *Le Milieu du monde* is the similar emergence of a structure that rejects the limitations that realist form places on form itself, places on matters such as duration, stillness, and expressive mise-en-scène. This is not a moment of full-on artifice along the lines of what defines most of Straub-Huillet; where they usually have their actors delivering lines in completely flat tones, and oftentimes directly facing the camera, *Le Milieu du monde* maintains throughout (and this is very true of this scene as well) a toned-down realism that nevertheless maintains the integrity of the diegetic world. In his article "L'effet d'étrangeté," published in *Cahiers du cinéma* a few months after *Le Milieu du monde* was released, Pascal Kané uses Rossellini and Pasolini to distinguish between two kinds of self-aware gestures:

> With Rossellini, the signified identifies itself exactly with the referent of the (supposedly complete) fiction, without even constituting an autonomous production. With Pasolini, all discourse is only a discourse on the narrative itself, only a tangible referent (the historical referent is emptied of any role). (81)[15]

Much the same could be said of Tanner-Berger and Straub-Huillet. In films such as *Le Milieu du monde*, the self-conscious gestures always refer back to the fiction itself. This is true even of the opening image of the camera crew working; this is a sort of autonomous production, in that it is about stepping back from the diegetic world, but Tanner and Berger only do this through an image of that world being produced. That's not true of filmmakers like Straub-Huillet, where all of their discourse – the acting styles, the way voice-over narration is used, the highly structured and often repetitious camera movement – is a discourse *on* their narrative (which is always adopted from some other source – literature, drama, opera) rather than something that creates that narrative. Tanner and Berger cannot do away with realist form altogether, nor are they satisfied by the limits that it imposes on the expression of complexity (be that complexity ideological, emotional, or some combination of the two). This is a moment in a cinematic, and in some ways realist-illusionist narrative; this is the *character* of Adriana, not the actress Olimpia Carlisi, that the viewer is being asked to see. But the shot nevertheless demands an engagement on the part of the viewer, and it presents itself as an undisguised example of representation; it becomes "more than real" precisely because of the access to reality that very long and thus eccentric-and-artificial-feeling take promises to provide, a paradox that was dear to Tanner's heart. What we see in this image is an emergence of a structure that transcends realism – but without rejecting it.

What we can also see in this pared-down vision of Adriana alone in her room are the traces of sexual love, and that is what connects this sequence, and the film overall, not only to suture and Tanner's interest in allied theoretical work, but also to Berger's work of this period. This sequence with Adriana drinking coffee naked, although it eschews all of the elements of dominant film language that Oudart indicts, leaves one aspect of cinematic representation solidly intact: eroticism. As I mentioned in the introduction, Oudart argued that there was a profoundly erotic quality to suture, writing, in an afterword he says was meant to "corriger quelque peu cet extrémisme," that when it comes to reading a film, "something is said which can only be discussed in erotic terms, and which is itself given as the closest representation of the actual process of eroticism" ("Cinema and Suture, 47").[16] What he had in mind here, I think, is that the experience of two bodies coming into contact – the body of the spectator and the bodies of the on-screen representations – created not only meaning but also emotional and visceral sensation through that sense of bodily contact, an experience whose connections to eroticism are not so hard to understand. This kind of pure, bodily experience is surely at the heart of this scene in *Le Milieu du monde*; it is a moment of cinematic purity, and also a moment of bodily purity, being made up entirely of a naked woman moving through space.

Le Milieu du monde
(Alain Tanner, 1974).
Citel / Action Films.
Pictured: Phillipe
Léotard and Olimpia
Carlisi. Photo from The
Kobal Collection/Art
Resource, NY.

Reading such bodily representation in visual art (mostly in painting, but in photography and cinema as well) has long been a central part of Berger's work as a critic, and this interest reached a kind of apex at just the moment *Le Milieu du monde* was coming out. This is most visible in the two works that I discussed in the last chapter, two works that came out in 1972, just a year after *La Salamandre* was released and two years before *Le Milieu du monde* was: the novel *G* and the critical work *Ways of Seeing*. It is in *Ways of Seeing* where Berger holds forth at length on the legacy of naked women in painting and photography, and there that we find a description of the "exceptional nude" that fits this image of Adriana, distinguishing it in many ways from the comparable scene in *La Salamandre*. Writing about post-Renaissance oil painting's tendency to use nudity as a means to signify a basically economic power that belonged entirely to men, Berger states:

> There are a few exceptional nudes on the European tradition of oil painting to which very little of what has been said above applies. Indeed they are no longer nudes – they break with the norm of the art-form; they are paintings of loved women, more or less naked. Among the hundreds of thousands of nudes which make up the tradition there are perhaps a hundred of these exceptions. In each case the painter's personal vision of the particular women he is painting is so strong that it makes no allowance for the spectator. The painter's vision binds the woman to him so that they become as inseparable as couples in stone. The spectator can witness their relationship, but he can do no more: he is forced to recognise himself as the outsider he is. He cannot deceive himself into believing that she is naked for him. He cannot turn her into a nude. The way the painter has painted her includes her will and her intentions in the very structure of the image, in the very expression of her body and face. (57–58)

I would not argue that Adriana is being bound to Berger and Tanner in the fashion of a model sitting for the sort of painting that Berger is evoking here. But describing the image of Adriana as that of a loved woman, more or less naked, seems quite correct, given that this image comes at a point in the narrative shortly after she and Paul have made love for the first time and where Paul's obsessive love is becoming fully central to the film's narrative (as their affair progresses the story of his running for political office seems to fall away, only to return again after his relationship with Adriana has fractured). Furthermore, it is clear that, in this tableau of Adriana in her room, the viewer is, in Berger's formulation, "forced to recognise himself as the outsider he is. He cannot deceive himself into believing that she is naked for him. He cannot turn her into a nude." This is due, really, to the radical rupture with dominant film grammar. At this point the film makes no allowance at all for the spectator; far from being sutured via shot/reverse-shot, or découpage of any kind, into a perfectly fully conceived duplication of reality, the viewer is held at a distance via the use of a still camera, a complete lack of editing, and a dense and evocative mise-en-scène. The spectator can witness this image of Adriana alone in her room, but s/he can do no more. S/he is not invited in.

This refusal of dominant film language also emerges at the level of the storyline as well. As the film moves forward and their affair starts to disintegrate, Paul gives Adriana a home movie camera. She is as annoyed with this gift as she is with his earlier suggestion that she go with him on a trip to New York, an exchange where she tells Paul that "tu ne me vois pas; tu vois une autre": you don't see me, you see someone else (Boujut 92).

> *Adriana.* – What am I going to film?
> *Paul.* – Beats me; whatever you want.
> *Adriana.* – But what?
> *Paul* . – I don't know. There's lots of stuff to film.
> *Adriana (almost angry).* – What stuff? The customers at the café? Or the widow Schmidt washing the glasses? Or dogs peeing in the street? Or maybe me, like this (*She stretches out her arm and points the lens at her face*), in my room, that'd make a nice film. A nice shitty film! I'd show you the film, and you'd never even see me. (Boujut 94)[17]

Here, then, is a sort of rejection of the analysis of the non-dominant film language that I was celebrating earlier. Just a shot of a woman in a room? Some shitty film that would be! Most importantly, though what is being rejected here is that a simple, utterly non-institutional cinematic image (like that of a home movie) would somehow bind Adriana and Paul together through the purity of the vision that it enabled. For Adriana, the opposite is true; Paul is incapable of seeing her no matter what, even if he watches a film made up entirely of her face. Small wonder, then, that Paul is *absent* from the tableau of Adriana in her room. This is an image of self-discovery, of the projection of *Adriana*'s self, not a projection of Adriana and Paul as a couple. It is clear by this point in the narrative that a home movie camera wouldn't make Paul see Adriana any more clearly. The idealism of that image of her in her room is, in this exchange between Paul and Adriana about the possibilities of non-dominant film language, melancholically clarified. Adriana may have been, in that tableau, a loved woman, more or less naked. But Paul, like the spectator, can no longer deceive himself into believing that she is naked for him. He cannot turn her into a nude. Like the spectator, he is forced to recognize himself as the outsider he is, love her though he may.

Another way that the film distances the viewer is though its self-consciously linear narrative structure. The film takes place over 112 days, which the viewer knows because it opens with a title card that says "6 décembre" (this is the first image after the scenes of the film crew and landscape shots that follow them, and thus marks the opening of the film's narrative) and episodes are broken up with other title cards that give the date; the last one says "28 mars." Jim Leach has written of this device that:

> The titles giving the date before each sequence (as well as the apparently arbitrary omission of certain dates) and the difficulty of accounting for the order of the seasons changes work against any sense of natural continuity and make us aware that our experience of time in watching the film is part of a cinematic process. A tension is set up between a detached "structuralist" perspective and the sensuous immediacy of the "realist" treatment of nature and sexual passion. (119)

This tension between sensuality and detachment strongly recalls the tension created by these films' use of long takes. As I mentioned in the last chapter, Tanner told Lenny Rubenstein of the paradox he saw in using long takes, that "if you don't cut, instead of it being more real which it should be, in

fact you are getting unreal because of the traditions in the eye of the spectator" (79). These title cards giving the dates, and the complete and explicit
linearity that this creates, give *Le Milieu du monde* a similar kind of "unreal"
quality. As Leach notes, we are aware that watching the film is a cinematic
process, an awareness that is equally central in sequences like the ostensible
"zero-degree" tableau of Adriana in her room, an image that, like the device
of title cards, calls attention to itself because of the way that it refuses to
consolidate either space or time into a more easily consumable form. This
refusal is the defining formal element of *Le Milieu du monde*, and this is a
project that clearly engaged with (although never pedantically imitative of)
the theoretical debates of the era in which it was made.

Pleasure and Spectacle

That is not to say that all of *Le Milieu du monde* is self-consciously theoretical or distancing. I very much disagree with Todd Gitlin's assessment of
the film as a failure because it is too engaged along these lines: he writes of
Le Milieu du monde that "When a film of theirs [Berger and Tanner's] fails
it is because the characters have gone abstract and joyless, and so has the
style" (37). In actual fact, these characters are richly fleshed out (the result
of a long process on the part of Berger himself, who wrote long letters to
both of the lead actors), and the spectator is often invited into the spectacle
of the narrative. It would be all too easy to make a political film that holds
the viewer at a distance, insisting on a cold didacticism that makes the filmmakers' ideological assumptions completely explicit (and which, echoing
Pauline Kael, would be a didactic pain). I mentioned in the introduction
how Brecht had rejected the idea that his epic theatre "proclaims the slogan: 'Reason this side, Emotion (feeling) that'" (227). To organize aesthetics in such a neat way would, after all, be the essence of normalization, a
strategy that seeks to maintain received notions such as the incompatibility
of reason and emotion. Berger was quite explicit about his desire to resist
normalization on a cultural/aesthetic level as well as on an economic one; in
a 1976 interview accompanying the release of *A Seventh Man*, he told Pierre
Henri Zoller, of the leftist Swiss newspaper *Construire*, that "I believe that
the division of culture into categories is one of the means that underpins

current culture, that is to say our current society, where everyone keeps to themselves, sticks to their domain, their speciality, their category" (7).[18] *Le Milieu du monde* contains a great deal that evokes very raw emotions, emotions that spill outside of categories like "melodrama" or "political art," and this is part and parcel of its overall critique of normalization. Its argument, which Berger and Tanner are making in equal part on the levels of storyline, visual form, and narrative structure, is that a world defined by the cold technocracy of capitalism is, at its core, anti-human.

One way into the charged emotional content of the film is via a para-text that is attached to *Le Milieu du monde* without really being part of it: the letters that John Berger wrote to the two lead actors. These were written before work on the script had even begun; Berger recalled to Richard Appignanesi that "The first thing I wrote was not a scenario at all, but two letters" (304). They were written in English[19] about a year before the shooting of the film commenced; the letter to Olimpia Carlisi (who played Adriana, although the letter refers to her character as "M.") is dated 27 February 1973, and the letter to Phillipe Léotard (who played Paul, although the letter refers to him as "François") is simply dated "Geneva, 1973" (the diary that accompanies the published screenplay states that shooting began on 16 January 1974; Boujut, 103). Berger ends his letter to Carlisi by saying "Dear Olympia – there's almost nothing of the story in this" (26), and that's true of the letter to Léotard as well. But there are nevertheless moments where important parts of the film are contextualized, and then re-appear in the film itself quite closely to the way they are evoked in the letter. This is most true of the scene where Adriana tells Paul about how she was burned in a house fire and feared she would be disfigured as a result. Strongly echoing what he has to say about women's self-surveillance in *G* and *Ways of Seeing*, Berger's letter talks about how, following this accident, "She [M./Adriana] then had to come to terms with the space between how she would always appear to most people and how she *was* for herself. Or, to put this another way, her responsibility for her own life became *interiorised*; it no longer depended on visible roles" (25). Fairly early in *Le Milieu du monde*, there is a sequence (a single medium shot that pans between Paul and Adriana as they talk to each other) where she explains this experience:

You see this? (*she shows him her scar*) There was a fire in our house. I was burned. It's still there. But I stayed in the hospital for two months. I couldn't see anything for a month, because my eyes were always bandaged. All alone at night.... So I changed. Other people changed too, because I thought that all that would happen afterwards would be different. I saw myself one way, and other people saw me differently. You're always performing for other people, you're putting on a mask for them. But I couldn't do that anymore, with a disfigured face.... (*She makes a gesture that imitates going into herself*) E verso di se stesso.... towards yourself. Responsibility for yourself. Finally it wasn't so bad; I still had a face. But that changed me. (Boujut, 63–64)[20]

This kind of close correspondence to the film itself is the exception for these letters, though. For the most part they are about fleshing out details and interior states of the characters. He tells Carlisi that "In some respects she belongs to the 19th century rather than to the 20th American century. She is still, to a degree, outside the controls of the managerial consumer society" (23). He tells Léotard that "When he is entirely concentrating upon and astounded by, her physical existence, he loses himself completely in the immediate, and the delight he finds in it. This delight – and his ways of expressing it – are childlike (That is not to say innocent: but spontaneous and single-minded)" (20).

Berger also writes at some length about the relationship between passion and the social world; this is actually most of the substance of the letter to Léotard. The letter to Carlisi connects her character's traits to political concerns, such as the matter of being beyond the control of a managerial society, or how "She is *not* a political being, but she has a consciousness of class and a familiarity with certain Marxist categories" (23). But for the most part anything political is contained within a description of the character's "deep background." The letter to Léotard, on the other hand, holds forth at some length on the ways in which worldly, materialist concerns interact with love. "Lovers love one another *with* the world," he writes to him. "(As one might say *with* their hearts or *with* caresses)" (19). He also asserts that "Passion aspires to include the world in the act of love. To want to make love in the sea, flying through the sky, in this city, in that field, on sand, with leaves, with salt, with oil, with fruit, in the snow, etc., is not to seek new stimuli, but to express a truth which is inseparable from passion" (18).

This connection between the forces of passion and the material of the everyday – salt, oil, fields, cities, and, this being Switzerland, endless acres of snow – is at the core of *Le Milieu du monde*'s critique of normalization. The problems for Paul's political career begin, not when he starts to have an affair with Adriana, but when he cannot keep the affair a discrete part of his life, safely bracketed off from the rest of his existence. He can't do this, of course, because he is genuinely passionate about her; passion isn't amenable to being managed, to being neatly shunted to one side in a way that prevents its mixing with other parts of life. Thus it is not sex or even infidelity that is the threat to a bourgeois, managerial, normalized existence; it is *passion*. It is not the sensual, but the uncontrollable that is the real threat. The last third of the film has a number of party members talking about the affair, either between themselves or with Paul, and this culminates with a meeting that is shot using a constantly moving camera, which circles around the table, framing various party members in close-up as they complain about the trouble this affair is causing them. One member says hey, he loves her, let him be. This annoys the chairman of the meeting, who says "Everyone's talking about this. You create the image of a serious family man, a town councillor, technical director, worker, honest guy, and you find that you've got a dumb-shit who chases Italian waitresses! [The subtitles translate this as 'a dopey skirt-chaser'] Everywhere where I could get a little feedback, I got the same reaction. You'll see when this wipes out our ticket. It's not going to work if this continues" (Boujut, 87).[21] This tendency to see the world in neat, bifurcated segments – one is either an essentially ersatz version of a respectable burger or "un connard qui court des serveuses de café italiennes" – is a desperately impoverished view of human nature, but it does allow for a more efficient management of political campaigns, being so reliant on sudden shifts in public opinion (which functionaries such as these insist are knowable by "sonder l'opinion des gens," however that's supposed to be accomplished). This is obviously not an ethical problem for these politicos, or even a real political problem. The problems created by obsessive sexual passion are entirely managerial.

Denis de Rougemont has argued that Switzerland's politics are unusually managerial in nature, something whose broader implications are visualized throughout *Le Milieu du monde*. To a certain extent, this is a matter of the sort of leadership that it takes to hold together a particularly complex country, one made up not only of four language groups (German, French, Italian, and Romansh), but more importantly of twenty-six cantons, each having a great deal of sovereignty over matters of everyday governance, some of which overlaps with the jurisdiction of communes. But de Rougemont focuses specially on Switzerland's Conseil fédéral, which is the body that wields executive power at the national level; it is made up of only seven members, even though it is always composed of members from each of the four parties that form the government, and as a result it is an ongoing exercise in compromise. De Rougemont writes how attempts to enlarge the council to nine members have been repeatedly defeated by popular referenda, stating that proponents of such proposals "are basically trying to politicize the executive, and the great majority of Swiss people refuse to do this. The Conseil fédéral must remain above partisan disputes, inasmuch as it constitutes the chief of state; it must remain a team of 'sages' as well as of 'managers' inasmuch as it administers federal affairs" (129–30).[22] This illusion of a "non-political," technocratic politics is a recurring image in *Le Milieu du monde*. At Paul's first campaign rally, his introducer says this: "As you can see today more than ever, the time of ideologies, of extreme positions, and of pretty speeches, has passed, and so what we need are competent people, organizers and technicians capable of mastering the complex problems of industrial society, and not just loudmouths hawking the latest hot idea at the top of their lungs" (Boujut, 58).[23] Paul is running for the Action Démocratique pour le Progrès, a fictional party whose main rival seems to be the Parti démocrate-chrétien (PDC), a Christian-Democratic party which is traditionally centrist to progressive on economic issues and relatively conservative socially. (The PDC is never mentioned by name in the film, but there are frequent jokes about how if Paul loses it means that the church will win.) This vision of Swiss politics basically matches that of de Rougemont; the difference is that for Berger and Tanner, this is symptomatic of a society whose need for "techniciens capables de maîtriser les problèmes complexes de la société industrielle" has conscribed passion, and all comparable forms of human messiness (such as ideology) to the dustbin of the inefficient. Just as if someone is not a manufactured family man he must be a dopey skirt-chaser, if something is not managerial and efficient, then it can only be some form of extremism.

Clear examples of *Le Milieu du monde*'s rejection of this kind of simple-minded managerialism can be found in the film's sex scenes. A sequence where Paul and Adriana have sex in a tub is particularly instructive; it's two shots, both a few seconds long, with their intertwined bodies first in a medium-long shot and then in a medium close-up. There is nothing on the soundtrack except for the dripping of a faucet into the tub. There is a kind of rawness to the scene, which its brevity only enhances. Furthermore, it is brightly lit and the only colours are flesh tones (the actual flesh of the actors against a tannish-orange wall), in contrast to the shot immediately preceding it, where Paul kisses Adriana in their warmly lit hotel room. The scene is almost edgy, although there is also a pronounced sensuality at work here. This play between tension and intimacy is disquieting rather than voyeuristically appealing, and the combination is one way that the film evokes the truly overwhelming, uncertain quality of the feelings that Paul and Adriana are experiencing. This overwhelming quality may be part of the reason that it so often comes up in criticism of the film as exemplary of some sort of larger aesthetic failure. Panning the film for *Journal de Genève*, Christian Zeender writes that "As series of one little deception after another, *Le Milieu du monde* seems most of all to break certain promises…. Further to this, let's quickly forget the 'erotic' scene in the film: it is so ungainly as to become almost shocking."[24] Even Swiss cinema's *éminence gris*, Freddy Buache (at this time a bit less *gris*) had a problem with this scene, writing in his review of the published screenplay that "The stylistic coherence in maintained from one end of the extreme to the other, except during sequences of intimate eroticism, which the filmmaker hasn't mastered and which disrupt the tension of the work because of their naturalist character" ("*Le Milieu du monde*," 14).[25] This sequence, though, uses this sort of naturalist harshness to disrupt the spectacle in a way that is different from but still consistent with the film's overall tendency to distanciation. Nobody should be shocked (shocked!) to see this kind of sharp austerity in a film like this.

There is a similar duality to the scene that directly follows the one where Paul gives Adriana the home movie camera. This is almost a jump cut; Paul is in more or less the same place as he was in the previous shot, but a change in lighting seems to signify that time has passed. Furthermore, Adriana has taken her skirt off; the camera pans and tracks from its medium shot of Paul to a medium shot of her on the bed, smoking and naked from the waist down. They argue harshly about whether to make love; Paul asks her to undress, she insists she's cold and they can do it like this, Paul responds that this is how whores do it. But the next shot is of a close-up of their entangled bodies making love. This is also a single shot lasting about twenty seconds and ends with Paul playfully pretending he is dead; again, there is nothing on the soundtrack except for ambient sounds, this time of their breathing and rolling around. Tension and intimacy were packed into the same shot in the first sex scene I mentioned (harsh lighting and complete silence, save for dripping combined with intense bodily passion): montage within a shot. This time it is a matter of montage between shots: a raw, hurtful argument about sex in a gradually moving medium shot first, followed by a completely still shot of two bodies intertwined in gestures of profound intimacy. This is all slightly difficult to watch, but also intensely expressive. None of it is clean or neat or easily managed.

The transplantation of a political critique into the realm of sexuality should in no way be seen as a retreat from the political. Tanner has repeatedly expressed misgivings about how easy it was for him to make a film with explicitly political characters and situations like *La Salamandre*, and how uncomfortable he was with the kind of easy pleasure that seemed to bring audiences. In his text accompanying the published screenplay of *Le Milieu du monde*, he recalls that "After *La Salamandre*, I became a bit dubious with regard to humour, which invited agreement a bit too easily and especially contained a sort of admission of weakness" ("Le pourquoi dire," 22).[26] He recalled something similar to Lenny Rubenstein in an interview that accompanied the release of *Le Milieu du monde*, saying that "I was very much surprised when I saw audiences in Paris and Geneva watching *La Salamandre*. They were laughing in the right places, but far too much, far too much. I realized the oral satisfaction they had when they picked up on those lines, and I didn't like it. I realized this facility had to be wiped out from this film, which is more austere and colder" (101). Now, I'm not sure I entirely accept this definition of *Le Milieu du monde*, which seems to play into the hands of critics like Todd Gitlin, who, lacking the (oral? I'm not so sure about that either) pleasure of a film like *La Salamandre* (or *Jonas*, which is what he was actually reviewing when he wrote his dismissal of the film), would unsurprisingly classify it as "abstract and joyless." What I've tried to show here is that the film is anything but cold, anything but joyless. It overflows with emotion in places, even if in other places it is possessed of a harsher aesthetic. I am thus echoing assessments like Guy Braucourt's, who (himself echoing Brecht) wrote in *Les Nouvelles Littéraires* that "By this ideological reading of a love story, Tanner succeeds in reconciling two fundamental notions of auteur cinema: on the one hand an element of reflection of society and the connections with which we live every day, and on the other a sense of spectacle, of telling a story which connects the audience to characters, to a narrative. The first quality does nothing without the support of the second" (8).[27]

The film's real contribution is to show just this point: not only can these elements co-exist, but they are always connected, and this sort of elemental reality is a big part of what makes technocratic, managerial capitalism such an inhuman system. Thus *Le Milieu du monde* is quite a bit more political than *La Salamandre*, and I dare say it's also more political than *Jonas*, which, for all its accomplishment, definitely uses humour as an admission of weakness. There really is a different kind of filmmaking at work here, one that radically transforms the language system of narrative cinema without abandoning it altogether, one that puts a story about the dialectic between passion and control into a secondary dialectic of illusionist and didactic modes of address. Furthermore, it does this mostly on the level of *form*. While I wouldn't say that the film's storyline is banal, certain fairly conventional elements of the love story are clearly present. Suffice it to say that, simply as narrative, it is only political in passing; its ideological and political interventions are occurring at the level of cinema, not story. "El contenido de la obra de arte está en su forma," Tanner said to *El País*'s Fernando Trueba and Carlos S. Boyero in 1978. As I hope is emerging throughout this book, this is one of his maxims, and it is an ideal that defines John Berger's work across fiction and criticism as well. No film demonstrates it more clearly than *Le Milieu du monde*. It is totally amazing to me that this is the least-discussed of the three features that Berger and Tanner made together, and the one most frequently dismissed as dull or somehow lacking. Even Berger himself admitted to Richard Appignanesi that he was unhappy with the film, telling him of "my initial disappointment in that film," although he also recalls that after speaking to people who had seen it, he came to see his disappointment as unfounded (305). He also recalled to Appiganesi that "the one film which differs from how I had visualized it is *The Middle of the World*." But however Berger may have initially visualized it, *Le Milieu du monde* is, in its actual realization, an unprecedented combination of theoretical sophistication, political insight, and emotional power. I know of no European film of its era quite like it.

Notes

1 "L'âme du Milieu du Monde, elle est dans ce reflet de l'eau qui court; dans la chambre aux pommes – violets tirés – d'une ancienne demeure. Elle est dans le geste du paysan et dans le ronronnement du moulin ; dans le sourire des grands'mères et des bonnes tantes, celles d'hier et celles d'aujourd'hui, qui maintiennent la maison, et grâce auxquelles on fait de nouveau du pain dans notre four. Elle est dans la moindre fleur et dans chaque graine ; dans la cloche de l'école et sur la pente du cimetière. C'est l'âme d'un pays vivant, riche de signes et riche de beauté."

2 I am working hard here to resist the temptation to correct every instance of "Straub" with "Straub and Huillet"; it is only French's brutalizing rules around the inflection for the plural that are holding me back. Although Richard Roud's path-breaking book on their films is just called *Straub*, it was, until Danièle Huillet's death in 2008, more typical to refer to the films they made together as being "Straub-Huillet" films (or, less frequently, films made by "the Straubs"). The fact that "Straub-Huillet" was also the name of their production company made this even more natural. Jonathan Rosenbaum has explored these issues in his article "The Place(s) of Danièle." Detailing the ambiguity around Straub and Huillet's co-authorship, he writes that "Danièle only began to be credited as coauteur belatedly, after their first few films. But was this because she gradually became more active as a filmmaker or because the two of them began to place a higher value on

her participation? Again, I have no idea." This October 2009 screening at the Cinémathèque Suisse made her importance very clear; the film they made together, *Itinéraire de Jean Bricard*, was a lush and fully realized study in landscape, whereas the two films Straub had made by himself and finished after Huillet's death, *Il Ginocchio di Artemide* (2007) and *Le Streghe* (2009), struck me as more airless and academic.

3 "Il n'est pas étonnant que Jean-Marie Straub ait exercé une influence particulièrement profonde sur le cinéma suisse. Straub a dépouillé ses films (*Non réconcilié, Chronique d'Anna Magdalena Bach, Leçon d'histoire, Moïse et Aaron*, etc.) de tous les clichés et de tous les mythes du cinéma de consommation, pour retrouver un langage limpide, parfaitement intelligible."

4 "Après « Charles », l'expérience la plus enrichissante, ce fut « Othon » de Straub, auquel j'ai participais comme assistant-caméraman."

5 "Ce lieu marque l'endroit de la séparation des eaux entre le sud et le nord d'un continent."

6 "Le récit et la forme d'un film dépendent dans une large mesure d'où et quand ce film est fait, et dans quelles circonstances. Ce film a été tourné en un lieu appelé Le Milieu du Monde…. Ce film a été tourné en 1974, en un temps de normalisation. La normalisation signifie qu'entre les nations, les classes et même entre des systèmes politiques théoriquement opposés, tout peut être échangé à

condition que rien ne change la nature des choses."

7   "Sous la simplicité gauchisante du cinéma de Tanner, ne serait-il pas temps de chercher quelque chose de plus **essentiel**, cela même dont Brecht comme Straub se réclament : une articulation entre théorie et spectacle permettant au spectateur de s'interroger sur lui-même par rapport à une représentation déconstruisant le cinéma bourgeois."

8   "Mais cette « réalité » susceptible d'être reproduite fidèlement, reflétée par des instruments et techniques qui, d'ailleurs font partie d'elle, on voit bien qu'elle est idéologique tout entière. En ce sens, la théorie de la « transparence » (le classicisme cinématographique) est éminemment réactionnaire" ("Cinéma/idéologie/critique," p.1, 12). As I also mentioned in the introduction (note 21), Susan Bennett's very strange translation of this passage renders that second sentence as "Seen in this light, the classic theory of cinema that the camera is an impartial instrument which grasps, or rather is impregnated by, the world in its 'concrete reality' is an eminently reactionary one." I have modified that here.

9   Godard started making films with his partner Anne-Marie Miéville in the early 1970s; the first work in which she has a credit is *Numéro Deux* (1975). The following year, the two made the twelve-part series *Six fois deux : sur et sous la communication* for French television; the *Cahiers* had Gilles Deleuze write on the series for issue number 271 (1976). While both Godard and Miéville also made films

separately, they continued making work together until 2002.

10   "Brecht a bien indiqué que, dans le théâtre épique (qui procède par tableaux successifs) toute la charge, signifiante et plaisante, porte sur chaque scène, non sur l'ensemble.... Même chose chez Eisenstein : le film est une contiguïté d'épisodes, dont chacun est absolument signifiant, esthétiquement parfait : c'est un cinéma à vocation anthologique, il tend lui-même, en pointillés, au fétichiste, le morceau que celui-ci doit découper et emporter pour en jouir" (187).

11   "... la suture (l'abolition de l'Absent et sa résurrection en quelqu'un)" ("La Suture," 38).

12   "Il n'y a, dans tout le film, pas plus d'une dizaine de raccords « justes » − c'est-à-dire de raccords à l'intérieur d'une même scène et en continuité temporelle − alors qu'un film « normal » en compte au minimum plusieurs centaines. Il y a un travail de déconstruction à opérer sur le langage traditionnel, mais il ne suffit évidemment pas de simplement tout bouleverser. Le montage, s'il veut oppositions et ruptures n'a de sens que si entre les fractions existe un rapport."

13   "... une étape que nous négligerons désormais : celle où l'image n'était pas appréhendée comme un champ filmique, mais, disons, comme une photographie animée.... Posons un temps, purement mythique, où règne le cinéma seul, où le spectateur en jouit dans une relation dyadique. L'espace n'y est encore qu'une pure étendue de jouissance, les objets s'offrent à lui sans qu'à la lettre aucune

présence fasse écran entre eux et lui et interdise leur capture" ("La Suture, Deuxième partie," 50).

14 There is a very similar sequence towards the end of the film, where Adriana is in her room, drinking coffee and getting dressed. This, however, is comprised of two shots, the first of which (just over a minute in length) also includes a track to the right and slightly in as she goes to her mirror to brush her hair, and then a cut to a close-up of her as she brushes her hair (which lasts about five seconds). There is thus a flash of découpage editing here (via both editing and camera movement), which is completely absent in the earlier sequence.

15 "Chez Rossellini, le signifé s'identife-ra exactement au référent de la fiction (réputé plein) sans jamais constituer une production autonome. Chez Pasolini, tout discours n'est qu'un discours sur la narration elle-même, seul référent tangible, seule butée du sens (le référent historique est vidé de tout rôle)."

16 "… quelque chose se dit, dans le procès même de ce qui est à la fois la jouissance et la « lecture » du film … dont on ne peut parler qu'en termes d'érotisme, et qui se donne lui-même comme la représentation la plus approchante du procès même de l'érotisme" ("La Suture, Deuxième partie," 55).

17 "*Adriana*. – Mais je vais filmer quoi ?

Paul. – Eh bien, je sais pas… Tout ce que tu veux.

Adriana. – Mais quoi ?

Paul. – Je sais pas. Il y a des tas de choses à filmer.

Adriana (Presque fâchée). – Quoi des tas de choses? Les clients du bistrot? Ou la veuve Schmidt qui lave les verres ? Ou les chiens dans la rue, qui font pipi ? Ou alors moi, comme ça (*Elle tend le bras et braque l'objectif contres on visage*) dans ma chambre, ça fera un beau film. Un bel film di merda ! Je te montrerai le film, tu ne me vois jamais."

18 "Je crois que la division de la culture en catégories est un des moyens qui soutiennent la culture actuelle, c'est-à-dire la société actuelle, où chacun se replie sur soi, s'enferme dans son domaine, sa spécialité, sa catégorie."

19 These were also translated into French and published in the 1974 edition of the Zurich film magazine *Cinema*. The English-language versions were published in the first issue of the Montreal film journal *Ciné-Tracts* (which was an English-language review), which came out in 1977.

20 "Vous voyez ça ? (elle montre sa cicatrice). Il y a eu le feu dans notre maison. J'ai été brûlée. Il me reste ça. Mais je suis restée deux mois à l'hôpital. Pendant un mois je voyais plus, j'avais toujours un bandage sur les yeux. La nuit, toute seule…. Les autres aussi ils ont changé, parce que j'ai pensé que tout ce qui se passerait après serait différent. Moi je me voyais comme ça, et les autres me verraient autrement. On joue toujours la comédie pour les autres, on se fait une tête affreuse, C'est tout pour eux. Et mois je pourrai plus le faire, avec une tête affreuse…. (*Elle fait un geste qui mime l'interiorisation*) E verso di se stesso … vers soi-même."

La responsabilité vers soi-même. Et finalement c'était pas si grave. J'ai encore une tête. Mais j'ai changé à cause de ça."

21 "Tout le monde parle de ça. Vous fabriquez l'image d'un personnage père de famille, sérieux, conseiller municipal, directeur technique, travailleur, honnête, et vous vous retrouvez avec un connard qui court des serveuses de café italiennes ! Partout j'ai pu un peu sonder l'opinion des gens, c'est la même réaction. Vous verrez qu'on le biffera des listes. Il ne passera pas si ça continue."

22 "Elles visaient en effet à *politiser* l'exécutif, et la très grand majorité des Suisses s'y refuse. Le Conseil fédéral doit rester au-dessus des luttes partisans, en tant qu'il constitue le chef de l'État; il doit rester une équipe de « sages » autant que de « managers » en tant qu'il administre les affaires fédérales."

23 "Car qui ne voit pas non plus qu'aujourd'hui le temps des idéologies, des extrémismes et des beaux discours est passé et que ce dont nous avons besoin c'est de gens compétents, d'organisateurs et de techniciens capables de maîtriser les problèmes complexes de la société industrielle, et non pas d'hurluberlus qui colportent aux quatre vents les idées les plus fumeuses…"

24 "Succession de multiples petites deceptions, **Le milieu du monde** nous semble surtout ne pas tenir certaines promesses…. A ce propos, oublions vite la scène « érotique » du film : maladroite, elle en devient presque choquante."

25 "La cohérence du style est maintenue d'un bout à l'autre, sauf au cours des passages d'érotisme intimiste que le cinéaste n'a pas su maîtriser et qui rompent la tension de l'ouvrage par leur caractère naturaliste."

26 "Après « La Salamandre », je suis devenu un peu méfiant à l'égard de l'humour, qui sollicite un peu facilement l'adhésion et qui surtout contient un sorte d'aveu de faiblesse."

27 "Par cette lecture idéologique d'une histoire d'amour, Tanner réussit à concilier ces deux notions fondamentales pour un cinéma d'auteur : une dimension de réflexion sur la société et les rapports que nous vivons quotidiennement, et le sens du spectacle, de l'histoire à raconter qui attache le public à des personnages, à un récit. La première qualité ne servant à rien si elle n'est pas soutenue par la seconde."

FOUR.

JONAS QUI AURA 25 ANS EN L'AN 2000

"'There is a chain of events in this best of all possible worlds; for if you had not been turned out of a beautiful mansion at the popint of a jackboot for the love of Lady Cunégonde, and if you had not been involved in the Inquisition, and had not wandered over America on foot, and had not struck the Baron with your sword, and lost all of those sheep you brought from Eldorado, you would not be here eating candied fruit and pistachios.'

'That's true enough,' said Candide; 'but we must go and work in the garden.'" – *Candide* (144)[1]

"When we talked about *Jonah*,[2] before the script was written, we described it to ourselves as a film written about individual dreams of transforming the world. The image we used was that we would try to show this dream like a large colored square of silk on the ground, and then air would come in under the silk and blow it up, so it became almost like a tent or a canopy. Then, we said, we must take that tent down, bring it back to earth, at its four corners. In a way, that is the movement, the melody of that film. We continually are seeing a colored hope rise, and then pinned back onto the earth – the earth here functions as a kind of reality principle. This melody, this counterpoint of hope and realism, is what the film is about, but I don't think that quite adds up to disillusionment." – John Berger, to Richard Appignanesi (301)

It would be very easy to make both French and American analogies for *Jonas qui aura 25 ans en l'an 2000*, by far the most famous film that Berger and Tanner made together. It's like *The Big Chill*, but in French! It's like an Éric Rohmer talkfest, but with odd accents! It's like *Return of the Secaucus Seven*, but funnier! Such analogies would not be entirely misplaced; like these American films I invoke, *Jonas* is preoccupied with political events of the 1960s that did serve as a generational touchstone across linguistic and national borders. And like Rohmer's films, it reads these sorts of external events mostly through a series of intertwined narratives about friendship, love, failed dreams, and only occasionally addresses politics directly. But I would argue that the film is really better understood in terms of Berger and Tanner's work specifically. Berger told Richard Appignanesi that "in those three films there is a kind of development. It's not easy for me to define that development in very precise terms, but I think that from each film we learned something which we tried to apply to the next. I think the development reached a peak with *Jonah*" (306). Part of what Berger was trying to enunciate there is that all three films hold the interpersonal in a delicate balance with the political. *La Salamandre* was a kind of warm-up for this project, a film that alternated between political and personal engagements quite unpredictably. *Le Milieu du monde* was a studied, rigorous film whose backbone was a narrative about mostly personal issues: it was a complex political meditation submerged beneath a love story. *Jonas* is just the inverse: it is a film about childhood and its relationship to maturity, submerged beneath a story about the aftermath of 1968. *Le Milieu du monde* looks like a drama about sexual passion but it's really a discourse on the ideology of normalization; *Jonas* looks like a discourse on the ideology of revolution but it's really about the evolution of childhood enthusiasm and optimism. This is not to say that one is really a political film and the other really isn't. The real contribution that Berger and Tanner's films have made – right back to *Une Ville à Chandigarh* – is to blur such distinctions, to insist on the interconnected nature of harvest dances and modernist architecture (take *that*, Frank Zappa), a doctor's life as a father and a part of his peasant community, the work of a scientist in nuclear physics and anti-apartheid activism, two cheerfully bohemian writers and their genuinely marginalized subject, an alienated Italian waitress and a politically ambitious Swiss engineer. It can serve as a model for political filmmaking, even though it is missing the sort of didacticism and ideological purity that so many 70s advocates of political filmmaking – particularly in the United States – believed to be indispensible. Some of the criticism of *Jonas* from the American left seemed to be using something like Saul Landau's *Rules for Radicals* as a starting point and found *Jonas* coming up short. This is a mistake. Rather, the film's antecedents are found, as I have argued is true of Berger and Tanner's work as a whole, in the Enlightenment. Forget Landau. *Jonas*'s roots are in *Candide, ou, l'optimisme*, and in Jean-Jacques Rousseau's *Émile, ou, de l'éducation*.

The latter is obvious to anyone who has seen the film. *Jonas*'s second sequence is a slow, low-angle tracking shot around the statue of Rousseau in Geneva's old city, with the following lines on the soundtrack: "All of our wisdom consists in servile prejudices. All our practices are only subjugation, impediment, and constraint. Civil man is born, lives, and dies in slavery. At birth he is in swaddling clothes; at his death he is nailed in a coffin. So long as he keeps his human shape, he is enchained by our institutions" (43).[3] This is from the first book of *Émile*, a point in the text where Rousseau is holding forth on the virtues that need to be instilled into a child in order to make a fully formed person. This is where Rousseau offers his maxims about action as the essence of life that opens this chapter. It is also where he writes about stoicism and adaptability: a few paragraphs earlier he insists, in a fully pan-European mode, that a child must be able "to brave opulence and poverty, to live, if he has to, in freezing Iceland or on Malta's burning rocks" (42).[4] These sorts of virtues are the real meat of *Émile*. It is about education in the same way that *Jonas* is about politics; each one is a means to enter into a series of meditations on the fate of individuality in a society that demands conformism. Both *Émile* and *Jonas* are thus in keeping with a broad, humanist project at the same time that they are both sharp works of social criticism. They can both serve as rebukes to criticisms of humanism as somehow evasive or apolitical. Tanner and Berger use *Émile* to indict a capitalist society that stifles the virtues of childhood and adulthood alike, a culture that imposes a bland view of subjectivity that is stripped of all possibilities for both growth and dignified death, for both rationalism and passion. Its vision of society that is thus very close to that of *Le Milieu du monde*, even though its means of address is through humour and satire rather than drama.

Its narrative, though, bears little resemblance to the form of *Émile*, which combines philosophical rumination and imaginary dialogue. In many ways, it is closer to *Candide* and almost feels like a sequel to that work: here's what *Candide*'s characters look like a few years later, after they have decided to tend to their gardens. On one level this is a literal matter. At the centre of *Jonas*'s narrative is an organic farm. In some ways this setting seems to anticipate Berger's "Into Their Labours" trilogy of novels (1979–90), which is set in the peasant farming communities of the French Alps. But there are important differences as well; the most important is that the characters here are not the taciturn, marginalized *paysans* of those later works, but a motley assortment of bohemians and nonconformists, most of them more urban than rural. The farm is owned by the eccentrically environmentalist couple Marguerite (who also has sex with the migrant workers who live in the barracks down the road, charging them twenty francs [Swiss francs and Canadian dollars are roughly equivalent], she says in order to keep things simple) and Marcel (who is slightly obsessed with whales). This is the place that Mathieu, a typesetter who was fired because as a union militant he was at the top of the redundancy list, finds work as a farmhand, and eventually creates a short-lived alternative primary school. It is the place that Marco, a history teacher who is eventually fired because of his unconventional methods, buys his cabbages. It is the site that Max, a disillusioned '68-er who now gets most fulfillment from gambling, decides will be the beachhead in his fight against Geneva-led land speculation and suburbanization. All of these characters are, in the scene with the big dinner at the end of the film, joined by the female characters: Madeleine (a secretary who tips Max off to the speculation deals, who likes to travel through the far east in search of sensual pleasure and who becomes romantically involved with Max), Marie (a supermarket clerk who as a French national must sleep on the other side of the Swiss border and who is eventually imprisoned for intentionally undercharging elderly customers, just after becoming romantically involved with Marco), and Mathilde (married to Mathieu, who works in a factory and announces, at the film's climax, that she is pregnant with a child she is sure is a boy, and who everyone agrees, after the whale-loving Marcel's suggestion, should be named Jonas). On another level, though, *Jonas* is consistent with *Candide*'s more metaphorically expressed interest in the relationship between philosophy and lived experience. Voltaire's novel is about a young man who, enraptured by ideas like Professor Pangloss's metaphysical-theo-logical cosmology, goes out into the wide world to try to engage with those ideas (*Candide* is a remarkably globalized work, wherein its main charac-ter moves, as he recalls at one point, "from Surinam to Bordeaux, from Bordeaux to Paris, from Paris to Dieppe, and from Dieppe to Portsmouth. I have sailed down the coasts of Spain and Portugal. I have crossed the Mediterranean, and have spent several months at Venice" [112][5]). Candide is the prototypical soixante-huitard, someone with a passion for esoteric theorizing who, given the chance to join theory and practice, ends up facing some fairly serious setbacks (the Baron and the Inquisition for Candide, the union-busting factory-owners, and the Gaullists for the '68-ers). What to do once such problems have completely derailed your efforts to live out in-tellectual engagement in Surinam (or Congo), Venice (or Prague), or Paris? Cultivate your garden, as Candide says in the novel's famous last line. Grow organic cabbages on the outskirts of Geneva.

Gardening is also quite an important metaphor in *Émile*. Expounding on his desire to respect the natural evolution of the human spirit, Rousseau could be explaining the reason for Jonas's countryside setting when he writes, midway through the second book, that "I want to raise Emile in the country far from the rabble of valets – who are, after their masters, the lowest of men – far from the black morals of cities which are covered with a veneer seductive and contagious for childen, unlike peasants' vices which, unadorned and in all their coarseness, are more fit to repel than to seduce when there is no advantage in imitating them" (95).[6] These dark morals include, as we see in *Jonas*, gambling, land speculation, and political apathy. Early in the first book, Rousseau also writes that "Plants are shaped by cul-tivation, men by education" (38).[7] This is clearly what Berger and Tanner are eluding to when Mathieu decides to start his alternative school in a green-house; he is trying to cultivate these kids, to allow them to grow on their own. In a slightly more playful tone, Rousseau also writes how "Peasant women eat less meat and more vegetables than city women. This vegetable diet appears to be more beneficial than injurious to them and their chil-dren" (64),[8] and in an imaginary discussion (also in the second book) about respecting the property and labour of others, he has his interlocutor Robert remind both himself and Emile to "remember that I will go and plough up your beans if you touch my melons" (99).[9] These passages strongly recall the goofy hymn that Mathieu sings to the onion, which goes: "The onion is a superb and democratic vegetable. It grows everywhere. It has a tough skin to protect it from the cold." He goes on to say (in a non-sing-song-y tone) that "It flavours everything. It lasts. You can eat it raw or cooked. It's sweet and a little bitter too. It kills germs. It's cheap." Marco then declares himself aligned to cabbages ("Moi, c'est le chou"). Max, in a dubious tone, echoes the Rousseau readers everywhere when he replies "All manner of virtue in vegetables. Eat your vegetables! And you're going retire to an old people's home? And become a kind of leek?" (132)[10]

It's not hard to see why Enlightenment types found the garden metaphor useful; its value to the European left is a trickier matter. Rousseau's ideas about human beings living most purely when they are closest to the state of nature is a well-worn element of European philosophy: "the closer to his natural condition man has stayed, the smaller is the difference between the faculties and his desires, and consequently the less removed he is from being happy," Rousseau writes in *Émile* (81).[11] A child munching on freshly grown vegetables would seem to be the very essence of the human uncorrupted by any trace of civilization, be it the technology to butcher animals or to butcher entire populations. No doubt the appeal of the image of the garden for the post-'68 left is similar; it is certainly readable as being driven by a desire to withdraw from the ravages of consumerist capitalism once the struggles to overthrow it have failed. But Jim Leach writes that "Although neither *Émile* nor *Jonah* advocates a simple return to nature to escape from social constraints, they are both concerned with the way in which 'our institutions' organise our experiences of life from birth to old age" (127), and this is an important point to bear in mind. None of *Jonas*'s characters are fully withdrawn from that society; the machine continues to invade the garden. Marcel and Marguerite may run an organic farm, but Marguerite is always talking about market day and is always concerned with economics. This concern leads her to fire Mathieu because his school takes away too much time from his work on the farm; he winds up working in the city again. Marie's immigration problems are never solved. The film's closing image may be a long shot of Jonas in 1980 (as a title card tells us) painting on the farm's mural, but the shot that directly precedes it is of Max going into a newsstand to buy cigarettes and complaining about inflation, an image that duplicates almost exactly the film's first sequence (the camera setup is identical; in the first scene Max complains that cigarettes are 1.90, at the end he complains that they are 2.30). This is followed by a shot that clarifies both the film's and Rousseau's vision of the garden metaphor: another slow, low-angle track around the Rousseau statue, with the following on the soundtrack: "needs change according to the situation of men. There is a great difference between the natural man living in the state of nature and the natural man living in a state of society. Emile is not a savage to be relegated to the desert. He is a savage man made to inhabit cities" (205).[12] This, really, is the world of *Jonas*: Geneva. The countryside outside of its pale is part of this larger metropolitan existence, finally inseparable from it, regardless of whether people like Max succeed in derailing land speculation scams. The film is showing us here that Rousseau is really a harbinger of this modern consciousness, less an Arcadian poet with a fetish for primitivism than a thinker who was all too aware of the interconnectedness of wilderness and civilization.

The emergence of this sort of consciousness is at the centre of Raymond Williams's book *The Country and the City*, published in 1973, the year before the release of *Le Milieu du monde*. Evoking the seismic shifts that marked late eighteenth- and early nineteenth-century England, Williams writes there that:

> The essential connections between town and country, which had been evident throughout, reached a new, more explicit and finally critical stage. It was characteristic of rural England, before and during the Industrial Revolution, that it was exposed to increasing penetration by capitalist social relations and the dominance of the market, just because these had been powerfully evolving within its own structures. By the late eighteenth century we can properly speak of an organised capitalist society, in which what happened to the market, anywhere, whether in industrial or agricultural production, worked its way through to town and country alike, as parts of a single crisis. (98)

Criticizing *Jonas* in the pages of the American film journal *Jump Cut*, Linda Greene, John Hess, and Robin Lakes denounced what they saw as the film's tendency to sublimate political, theorize-able issues into personal dramas and transformations: "Tanner crucifies revolutionary theory on the altar of the heart, thus eliminating most political work and class struggle. Rousseau has triumphed over Marx" (9). I quite agree with that last statement: it is Rousseau, and not Marx, that gives the film its philosophical backbone. Part of this does have to do with the use of personal development as a metaphor for political enlightenment; classrooms and farms here take the place of factories. But it is a metaphor, not a replacement. It does not mean the end of politics; very much the opposite is the case. Rousseau has triumphed in the film because *Jonas* is defined by a vision of modernity that realizes the foolishness of conscribing to the desert the naturally formed subject (Bloom's "savage" and Rousseau's "sauvage," which is not quite the same thing[13]). That vision understands the inevitability that such a young person will, in some way, become part of a system which works its way through town and country alike. This becoming part does not mean that the young person will be assimilated into the system, but it does mean that some compromises with it are essential. Following Jim Leach, neither *Émile* nor *Jonas* are simply about a withdrawal from society. In that second passage from *Émile* that the film ends with, Rousseau goes on to say of Emile's status as a savage/sauvage made to live in the cities (and this is not in the film) that "He has to know how to find his necessities in them, to take advantage of their inhabitants, and to live, if not like them, then at least with them" (205).[14] This is far from an apolitical, personal-development-led analysis; Rousseau is evincing a very keen awareness of the power dynamic at work in this social experiment of his, a dynamic with obvious links to France's imperial legacy. It's just that it doesn't conform precisely to the contours of an orthodox-Marxist critique of western capitalism.

Something similar is happening on the level of form, despite Tanner's own joking about how his use of sequence shots in the films was "dogmatic." He made that crack in a 1977 interview with François Albera for the French Marxist review *La Nouvelle Critique*,[15] where he explained *Jonas*'s approach to the long take this way:

> The first principle is the choice of the sequence-shot. In an almost mechanical way, there is a refusal to cut within a scene. There are 150 shots in the film, or around 170 with the shots in black and white. All of the scenes are in sequence-shot or in

two shots maximum.... The sequence-shot implies and allows a completely different kind of camera work, especially camera movements that are apparently "incongruous." In the scene at the beginning, for example, where Rufus [the actor playing Mathieu, whose real name is Jacques Narcy] enters the farm's kitchen, there is a sequence-shot of around four and a half minutes. The camera cuts the scene like you would with scissors, inasmuch as it films first one character, then a second, a third, then two, then three, then it moves past them following the text, coming back then and finishing in "total." You've thus got découpage without scissors. But the viewer's first impression is that the functioning of the découpage is completely different: normally, you have to change shots, axes, or focal points for a close-up. Here, there is already a distancing effect because it pulls you along but there are holes, moments where the camera isn't on anything, where it's between characters and it continues to move at the same speed, autonomously. (47)[16]

This sequence moves very smoothly through the space of the kitchen (it is a series of tracking shots and pans) and also imitates découpage inasmuch as it frames each of the three characters (Mathieu, Mathilde, and Marcel) in medium shots or medium close-ups; a shot/reverse-shot pattern tends to have a single person in the frame and this sequence is comprised mostly of two-shots, but that's the major difference in terms of mise-en-scène. The movement of the camera, however, is not tightly linked to the rhythms of the character's exchanges the way that shot/reverse-shot rigorously synchronizes its cutting to focus on whoever is talking. At times the camera moves to frame whoever is talking. Early in the shot, Mathilde is explaining to Mathieu how rich in nutrients horse manure is, and the camera tracks and pans around a two-shot of them; but it slowly moves to the left, and just as she says that at last those useless horses do something right and gestures towards Marcel, the camera continues its slow movement to get him into the frame, just as he exclaims "they shit!" From the standpoint of smooth, "découpage sans ciseaux," it's an impressive piece of choreography. But the camera continues to move, finally re-framing a two-shot of Mathieu and Marcel, even though Marcel isn't talking anymore (he is intently plucking a chicken) and Mathilde continues to talk to Mathieu about his work on the farm and elsewhere; she is still talking, but her questions about why he was fired from the printer's where he was a union militant are now coming from off-screen. Moments ago, and within the same shot, she was sutured into this perfect little narrative world; now she is unseen, distant, precisely because the camera has continued to move, at the same speed, slowly away from her. This distancing effect is very real, and the film is constantly making its viewer aware that is an artifice, that the camera very literally has a mind of its own, and it not simply linked to the minds of these characters. But this distancing effect does not completely preclude identification with those characters, does not fully obscure that linear narrative. The basics of realist visual form are here. It's just that these visual patterns are a sort of starting place for the film, a base point from which visual experimentation (especially with camera movement) can take place. Tanner connected his approach to editing with his agnostic relationship to classical narrative cinema overall in a 1977 *Cahiers du cinéma* interview, stating that "I call on certain relevant elements from the 'classical' code of representation: a feeling for the real, for example recognizable characters. But these elements only appear within the strict limits assigned to them – in the guise of reference points for the audience. They are precisely circumscribed within the little 'pieces' of the film, inside the scenes, but they never operate on the level of total structure" (66).[17]

This is also true of the film's narrative structure, which follows certain conventions of linear storytelling but uses that set of conventions as a starting point from which the film expands. Marcel Schüpbach takes up the matter of narrative structure in his piece on the film for *Journal de Genève*'s "Samedi littéraire," writing that "*Jonas* marks a new stage in the evolution of Tanner's cinema. Previously, from *Charles mort ou vif* to *Milieu du monde*, right through *La Salamandre* and *Le Retour d'Afrique*, the filmmaker, through the study of one, two or three people's behaviour, shored up solid connections between them… Now, enlarging the story through numerous main characters, he literally bursts the narration apart, privileging numerous moments and cementing them together without necessarily forming a story in the traditional sense of the term" (1).[18] This is the narrative structure of montage. *Jonas* tells a single story but one that is made up of many fragments, in many "morceaux" to use the word that is invoked in that *Cahiers* interview. Those "morceaux" come together to create something that isn't present in any one them on their own, but that coming together isn't a process of melting them into one big narrative blob. Their edges show; they are still visible, and still understandable, as distinctive elements. To return again to the bit from Barthes' essay "Brecht, Diderot, Eisenstein" that I invoked in the last chapter, "all the burden of meaning and pleasure bears on each scene, not on the whole.... The same is true in Eisenstein: the film is a contiguity of episodes, each one absolutely meaningful, aesthetically perfect" (*Image-Music-Text*, 72).[19] All of these small stories are fully realized (if not, perhaps, aesthetically perfect); they are autonomous narrative objects that take on new meaning when they are put together. This insistence on evoking the political struggles of the 1960s as necessarily decentred is not only in keeping with leftist idealism about collective action and the importance of understanding historical forces above individual achievement, but is also quite consistent with the leftist political filmmaking of this period, on both sides of the Atlantic.

And so here is where I offer an American analogy of my own, although I do so following a French critic. In his text on *Jonas* titled "Les huit *Ma*" (a reference to the fact that all eight of the characters' names start with the letters "Ma," which is the French word for "my" and thus emphasizes the degree to which the film is about individuality), Serge Daney writes that "Tanner, like that other film that also comes to us from the very heart of Capital, *Milestones*, only films *one* generation but on *many* stages, the generation that, having been born in 1968, will soon be ten years old" (48).[20] Daney is referring there to Robert Kramer's 1975 epic portrait of an American left in full-on disintegration mode, as militants of various stripes wander into other forms of activism, into young families of their own, into jail or deadly confrontations with police over petty crime, or onto the streets and under bridges. This film has a truly dizzying number of characters; its entry in the catalogue of MoMA's Circulating Film Library places the number at fifty, and their exact connections to each other are difficult to keep track of. That confusion is, of course, the point of Kramer's analysis of the 1970s; a community of activists that had once at least tried to present a united front was now fractured into a series of smaller, and often more self-centred and sometimes mutually exclusive, battles. They once spoke about "Our" or "Notre," but in Kramer's vision, they all now speak in terms of "Ma." The militants of the 1960s thus became, in essence, a group of isolated people talking past one another, and *Milestones* is about what that condition of disconnection and true political ineffectiveness looks like. That analysis of post-'68 politics, like that of *Jonas*, takes place on the level of narrative structure.

In contrast to politically minded critics in France, where *Milestones* was greatly admired (*Cahiers du cinéma*, 258–59, published a roundtable titled "*Milestones* et nous"; it also published a poem about Kramer's work), some segments of the American left hated the film, and their critique would resurrect itself with the release of *Jonas* two years later. The editors of *Jump Cut* (Chuck Kleinhans and Julia Lesage, plus Michelle Citron) may have published a basically friendly interview with Robert Kramer in their double issue 10–11 (1976), but in that same issue their review of the film said that *Milestones* "doesn't just deal in bad politics, which it does freely, but it is also basically dishonest and reductionist in its presentation of bad politics" (9). Now earlier, I used the phrase "Criticizing *Jonas* in the pages of the American film journal *Jump Cut*," but that didn't really do justice to the furor that the film provoked, a furor comparable to that provoked by Kramer's film. The magazine may have published Ying Wing Wu's favourable review of *Le Milieu du monde* in #7 (1975), but *Jump Cut* 15 (1977) had a photo from *Jonas* on its cover, with the question: "Tanner's JONAH: Subversive Charm or Reactionary Nostalgia?" That issue paired two *very* different essays on the film: Robert Stam's more or less positive piece (which was translated and reprinted in the French version of the film's published scenario) and Greene/Hess/Lakes' evisceration. The latter essay strikes a faux-conciliatory tone early on, stating that "Basically, we think that *Jonah* is a light-weight, slightly progressive, warm and charming film in which petty bourgeois actors and actresses pretend to be workers and peasants, but fail because neither they nor Tanner knows much about the daily lives of Swiss workers" (8). That's about as nice as it gets. The sheer ferocity of the critique here is actually refreshingly polemical, even if a lot of it also seems pious, prescriptive, and ill-informed. Greene/Hess/Lakes were responding not only to Stam's piece on the film but also to Todd Gitlin's review in *Film Quarterly*. Gitlin's review is, more than any of these other longer pieces, an attempt to put *Jonas* into the context of Tanner's work overall (that's where his criticisms of *Le Milieu du monde*, which I quoted in the last chapter, are to be found), although a lot of what he has to say about *Jonas* itself is descriptive. Greene/Hess/Lakes open by saying that both pieces "celebrate the film's warmth, charm, optimism, and intelligence, seeing it as a valuable contribution to radical film and politics," and they themselves say that "the film really does have charm." But then they pull the rug out and echo the *Jump Cut* editors' evisceration of *Milestones* a year earlier: "It seems to us that both of them miss or choose to ignore how bad the film's politics really are" (8).

What is remarkable here is that both Stam's positive piece and Greene/Hess/Lakes' negative piece criticize the film along the same grounds: it's sexist, it's insufficiently detailed about the lives of Swiss workers, especially migrant workers, and these problems come together in the subplot of Marguerite having sex with migrant workers for twenty francs a go. "Why, one wonders, have her initiate these relations, and why with immigrant workers?" Stam wonders. "Here Tanner takes two oppressed groups – women and Third World workers in Europe – and places them, for reasons that are not at all clear, in relations of mutual exploitation" (1). Remember, now, this is the writer that *likes* the film. Greene/Hess/Lakes, on the other hand, first criticize *Jonas* for paying insufficient attention to feminism: "Switzerland may be backward and lack a women's movement, but while Tanner was making this film, hundreds of women in Italy and Portugal were taking part in mass movements, as women for women's rights and as leftists for socialism" (9). I rush to point out that in Judy Klemesrud's *New York Times* article on Tanner, Tanner recalled how "My wife used to have women's lib meetings at our place in Geneva, and on those nights I'd go to a movie. When I'd get back I'd have to walk over 20 women in my living room. They'd ignore me" (B6). She was, presumably, part of the Mouvement de Libération des Femmes. Julie Dardel's history of the movement in Geneva notes that "Very active and often spectacular, the activists of the MLF quickly became one of the indispensable players of Geneva's political life" (43). She goes on to note how active and yet also self-governing it was throughout the confederation: "On the national level, the autonomous groups of women that sprang up in Geneva, Lausanne, Basel, Berne, Zurich, Locarno and Bellinzona, weren't connected by any formal structure, but managed to coordinate with each other on many occasions" (58).[21] So it's hard to know what could possibly lead Greene/Hess/Lakes to make such a statement about backward Switzerand lacking a women's movement. I also feel some obligation to point out, as I did in Chapter 1, that Swiss women only won the right to vote at the federal level in 1971. Critics who, a mere six years later, make allusions to "a women's movement" or the lack thereof but fail to mention that little historical tidbit do not inspire much confidence either in their knowledge of the relevant historical and political situations or in their moral authority to call the film's actors and crew onto the carpet because "neither they nor Tanner knows much about the daily lives of Swiss workers." For me this ignorance of the basic historical situation is more melancholy than anything else, given that de Dardel notes on several occasions how inspirational the Swiss movement found the work of its American sisters. There were certainly opportunities during the 70s for curious American feminists to discover the movement, via book-length treatments like Susanna Woodtli's *Gleichberechtigung: der Kampf um die politischen Rechte der Frau in der Schweiz* (published in 1975) or journals like *Le mouvement féministe* (published in Geneva from 1912 to 1960). Overall, the *Jump Cut* critics of the film strike me as not knowing much about the political lives of Swiss women.

The real meat of *Jump Cut*'s complaint, however, is in the film's treatment of migrant workers. Greene/Hess/Lakes go on to write that:

> If possible, even more offensive is Tanner's shabby treatment of the foreign workers from the Mediterranean countries. And damn it, John Berger, Tanner's scriptwriter, should know better. He put out a book on these exploited and brutalized people (*The Seventh Man* [*sic*], Viking, 1975). Berger's title refers to the fact that every seventh man in Europe is a foreign worker, and Switzerland has its share of these 20th century slaves.... What does Tanner do with them? While raising great sympathy for poor Marie, who must travel a few miles to and from work in Switzerland, he completely reinforces all the vicious Swiss stereotypes about foreign workers. Since none of them become characters themselves, they remain furtive, inhuman figures seen from a distance. Since Marguerite slips off to have sex with them, Tanner reinforces the idea that all they want to do is fuck upright Swiss women. Imagine the effect on a white American

audience if the female lead in a film slipped off to have sex with blacks in a nearby shantytown. Would that help the audience understand the lot of blacks or sympathize with black people? Or would it increase racism? (9)

The stills they are referring to here are among the film's occasional inserts of black and white imagery; these represent the fantasies or imaginary formulations of various characters. The only time the film uses black and white *stills* is just after the two long-serving farmhands (who Marcel calls "the zeroes") tell Marco about Marguerite's visits to the workers' barracks, and Marcel walks in to serve the evening soup; that's when the film presents these photos of migrant workers' barracks. The pictures are thus very clearly tagged as Marco's subjective imaginings of what those barracks must be like, imaginings which, since he seems a relatively au-courant, educated European leftist, could very credibly have been strongly influenced by Berger and Jean Mohr's photo-book *A Seventh Man*, both of whom are fellow citizens of Geneva. This quality of the insert as fantasy seems to fly past Greene/Hess/Lakes; they write "Tanner shows some stills of squalid rooms in which foreign workers live (leftover photos from Berger's book?)" (9).

Um, sort of. The first photo in the montage, of four workers lounging around in a dormitory, is nearly identical to Mohr's image of two of those same workers lounging in that same dormitory (127). The next image, of two men washing clothes in a trough, is nearly identical to images of men washing clothes that are part of a contact sheet of eight images that Mohr reproduces (165); it was probably part of the same roll of film. The final image, and the one that raises all this ire about negative stereotypes of hypersexualized migrant workers, is a photo of three men in a room that is covered with pornographic pin-ups; that photo is simply from *A Seventh Man* (174), although the reproduction in *Jonas* has black bars along the men's eyes where the photo in the book does not. Stam criticizes the inclusion of this image too, again along *exactly* the same lines as Greene/Hess/Lakes: "Still shots show us the workers' quarters papered over with photographs of nude women. Such an association runs the danger of confirming racist attitudes (the immigrant workers just want to sleep with 'our' women) while it obscures the oppression of these workers" (1).

Jonas qui aura 25 ans en l'an 2000 (Alain Tanner, 1976). Citel / SSR / Action Films / Société française de production. Pictured (clockwise from man facing camera): Jean-Luc Bideau, Pierre Holdener, Dominique Labourdier, Jacques Denis, Miou-Miou, Myriam Boyer, Rufus. Photo from The Kobal Collection/Art Resource, NY.

But anyone following up the film's inter-textual cue would find, in *A Seventh Man*, Berger's nuanced and sympathetic explanation of the ubiquity of pornography in barracks like these. Shortly after observing that "In situations where time is served (conscripted service, prison) and which involves absence and sexual deprivation, to sleep is a deliverance from time" (167), Berger writes:

> Nine inches above his pillow he has driven a nail into the wall. On the nail he has hung an alarm clock. From there it wakes him ninety minutes before the shift begins. Around the clock is a votive frescoe of twenty women, nude and shameless. The prayer is that his own virility be one day recognized. The vow is that he will not for an instant forget now what women are like. The pictures have been taken from posters or magazines published in the metropolis. The women are unlike any he has ever spoken to. They have instant breasts, instant cunts, which propose instant sex: the proposition as rapid as the action of the press that printed them. (187)

The language here is raw, but so is the vision of alienated labour in a culture defined top to bottom by consumerist capitalism. Reading Berger's text certainly helps to solidify that vision of alienation, but that vision is also contained in those still photos that Marco imagines. These are spare images, although they are also under-lit and slightly soft of focus. What keeps these effects from being lush and homey is precisely the sparseness of the dorm room, the concrete minimalism of the washing area, the grim plastic excess of a wall covered with porn. Migrant employment in the capitalist west, these images show us, is not about the "hard" violence of forced labour or militarily regimented production. Instead, it is about the "soft" violence of loneliness, deprivation, sadness. This sort of awareness does not exclude considerations of the economic inequalities that are at work, or of the dynamics of gender that figure into these transactions. *Jonas* evokes the weird power relationship here, after all, by having Marguerite charge something for the sex (so she remains unsentimental about what she's doing for these guys and the fact that she gets something out of it too), but not so much that workers can't afford it (and not so much that it would make any financial difference to her). Economic, gender, and material considerations are part of understanding, and they are all present here. What I object to is the idea that such analysis constitutes understanding itself, and that anything else is somehow politically suspect.

And so here, we can again see Marx giving way to Rousseau. Tanner and Berger's film is evoking the ineluctable paradoxes of society (with rich/female <> migrant/male replacing the country/educated <> city/unformed that I discussed earlier), rather than a more economically determinist vision. The film's overall analysis is that Marguerite going to have sex with migrant workers is, finally, *sad*. That sort of emotional response should not be dismissed as some sort of sentimental liberal weepiness. The film is explicit (however briefly) about the desperate *material* conditions under which this all takes place. But its analysis doesn't stop at economic materialism, just as *La Salamandre* evoked Rosemonde's alienation by iconic images of her both at the sausage maker and alone on her bed, just as *Le Milieu du monde* was about both sexual passion and economic and ideological normalization.

I linger on these *Jump Cut* essays, not only because they are the longest, most sustained analyses of the film in English (the Stam essay is quite a bit longer than most of the French-language material on the film), but because they seem to me symptomatic of the slightly ham-fisted way that political cinema was being been defined by many 1970s leftist critics. The perspective of both Stam's and Greene/Hess/Lakes' pieces sounds a lot like the criticisms from French-speaking audiences of *Le Milieu du monde* and *Jonas* that Tanner recalls annoying him. Echoing his sense of discomfort at audiences of *La Salamandre* who seemed to laugh at the revolutionary posturing a bit too knowingly, Tanner said in that 1977 *Cahiers du cinéma* interview accompanying the release of *Jonas* that "We didn't want to hold up a mirror for this or that group so that they could crowd in to admire themselves. The extreme radicals don't discover themselves there, and they are often the most mediocre interpreters of the film: they 'learn nothing,' obviously (and above all not *how to look at* images); I 'offer no solutions,' etc." (*Jonah who will be 25*, 166).[22] I wonder if Tanner has *Jump Cut* in mind here. He did seem to know of the magazine; there is, in the Cinémathèque Suisse's file on *Jonas*, a hand-written note on Tanner's stationery giving the magazine's address, along with that of *Film Quarterly* (which had published Gitlin's long and favourable review of the film) and mentioning that "Cahiers, tu l'as" (presumably this was addressed to someone assembling the French version of the film's published scenario, which was the Cinémathèque's project and which included French translations of Stam's and Gitlin's pieces as well as a reprint of Daney's "Huit *Ma*" text). Furthermore, Tanner's crack that leftist audiences learn nothing "surtout pas *à regarder* des images," is quite consistent with both *Jump Cut* essays, which make no mention of form whatsoever. This is actually quite unusual for the magazine, which has always had a serious commitment to non-conventional forms and has over the years given a lot of space to discussions of the political avant garde. But the pieces by both Stam and Greene/Hess/Lakes spend most of their time trying to figure out whether the film has good politics.

Indeed, what they are really trying to figure out is whether the film's characters have good politics, as though they were real people. "Although Marcel does seem politically aware in the scene with the land speculator," they write at one point, "there is not a shred of evidence that he ever participated in any progressive political activity, or ever will" (9). A bit later they describe Mathieu as "a skilled craftsperson, a typesetter, one of a group of European workers who have tended to struggle to maintain their own privileged position within the working class rather than for the working class as a whole." They then lament that "Clearly, this alone does not discredit Mathieu, but it does raise questions and doesn't allow us to accept his political work and union activity as automatically progressive. As with Max, Tanner denies us the information we need to assess Mathieu's politics – past, present, and future" (9). All this invocation of the future activities of these characters really does make it sound like they are real people, with lives that began before the film started and will continue after the film is over. To which it is incredibly tempting to say: relax, comrades, it's just a movie. That is to say, it is obviously essential to accept all films – and especially a film like *Jonas*, which works so hard at the level of visual form to resist easy, Hollywood-style identification with these characters – as constructions, not as reflections of an idealized reality.

That sort of idealized reflection is the stock in trade of illusionist narrative, of course; it's also the stock in trade of the segment of left film criticism informally known as "positive images." Positive images criticism was big in the 1970s, and it's certainly easy to see how it might have seemed useful in raising consciousness about the ways popular Hollywood representation distorted oppressed groups and led to undesirable political consequences (*Barbarella* made women look like simple-minded sex kittens and undermined the ERA! *The Deer Hunter* made the Vietnamese look mean and made the public think it had been right to keep fighting them all those years! A film with a subplot of a white woman having sex with black workers in a shantytown would increase racism!). But in retrospect its shortcomings seem equally clear: it is patronizing in the extreme, starting as it does from the assumption that audiences are basically at the mercy of the images on the screen, and thus need to be led along in politically positive directions, without the burden of contradictory or politically paradoxical behaviour on the part of any of the characters (a female farm owner fighting against capitalist developers but also having sex with migrant workers for twenty francs, say). Diane Waldman offered a critique of positive image criticism along these lines, in the pages of *Jump Cut* no less (about a year after the essays on *Jonas* appeared). Writing of Linda Artel and Susan Wengraf's 1976 book *Positive Images: A Guide to Non-Sexist Films for Young People*, she asserted that "The notion of 'positive image' is predicated upon the assumption of *identification* of the spectator with a character depicted in a film. It has a historical precedent in the 'positive hero' and 'heroine' of socialist realism.… Yet the mechanism of identification goes unchallenged, and introduces, I think, a kind of complacency associated with merely presenting an image of the 'positive' heroine" (9). Expecting left films to provide this kind of positive reinforcement, so close to the sort of coddling that, following Waldman, both Hollywood and Socialist Realist films specialize in, is anathema to the thematic and formal project of all of Berger and Tanner's work together and alone, and *Jonas* for sure. It was important to many sectors of left filmmaking in the 1970s, precisely because it was a blow against the sort of complacency that Waldman is identifying and that Artel and Wengraf are symptomatically taking for granted. "Critics have frequently called Mr. Tanner's films 'political.' Does he agree?" Klemesrud asked in her aforementioned *New York Times* article. "'In form, rather than content,' he replied. *Jonah* is an example of what I mean. It breaks up completely the sort of plot obsession of traditional filmmaking'" (B6). There were sections of the left that were just as prone to obsession over matters of plot, and prone to a blindness to matters of formal complexity, as mainstream interpreters were.

This doesn't have to be part and parcel of a left critique of the film. The French film magazine *Positif* – whose parochialism I groused about in Chapter 1 but whose leftist credentials are unimpeachable – didn't like *Jonas* either, but for very different reasons. After complaining a bit that the film is too sentimental about May '68, their reviewer, Frédéric Vitoux, wrote that "The tremendous rigours of the production – the careful layouts, the warm quality of the direction of actors – are here put at the service of a limp and simple writing that has only minimal effect" (73).[23] I don't particularly agree with that assessment, but I respect it inasmuch as Vitoux is mounting a critique of an aesthetic object that he sees as operating in an unsophisticated way, not of characters who have some sort of moral obligation to be pronounced and unambiguous in their radicalism. These *Jump Cut* essays seem to me exemplary of a literalist tendency that is too common in American political criticism generally, especially that of the 1970s. It is a vision of political cinema to which Berger and Tanner's work has always been vigorously opposed.

At the same time, the equally leftist Canadian journal *Ciné-Tracts* was paying close attention to Berger and Tanner's work, especially *Jonas*, and the difference there illuminates the tension in political film circles between a less concrete (or more theoretical) approach and one that was more explicitly activist. *Ciné-Tracts* published, in its very first issue, the English versions of the letters that Berger had written to the two lead actors in *Le Milieu du monde* (French versions appeared simultaneously in the Swiss film journal *Cinema*). Their third issue featured Ron and Martha Aspler Burnett's translation of part of the scenario of *Jonas* (before Michael Palmer's full translation was published by Berkeley's North Atlantic Books in 1983, which is the version I am using in this book), along with a short introduction by Martha Aspler Burnett. "The film leaves open the question of growth, change, political action," she writes. "Rather, it tries to point out the false scenarios that can be followed, scenarios which confuse the issues rather than clarify them" (8). The journal seems drawn to both *Le Milieu du monde* and *Jonas* because, like the best parts of film theory, they are intellectually and formally ambitious attempts to consider questions that can only be posed through the means of cinema, questions that are connected to the material world but still inseparable from the workings of a specific medium. *Ciné-Tracts*, during its brief existence (17 issues, some of which were double issues, from 1977–82), published a great deal of this kind of theoretical writing; Stephen Heath's "Film and Nationhood" essay, also published in the same issue that reproduced the *Jonas* screenplay, is an example, as is Bruce Elder's exchange with Bill Nichols on the possibilities and limitations of structuralism, also in that same issue (Elder criticized Martin Walsh's *Jump Cut* essay on Rossellini along some of the same lines I did their critique of *Jonas*).

Being honest, though, there isn't much more about formal matters in these *Ciné-Tracts* considerations of Berger and Tanner that there were in the *Jump Cut* essays. Indeed, these aren't really examples of interpretation at all; Martha Aspler Burnett's sense of *Jonas* as ambiguous and interested in blind corners is certainly true, but her note here is just that, a note on the film rather than a sustained analysis. That interest in ambiguity and blind corners was consistent with *Ciné-Tracts'* editorial orientation as a whole, and the way in which they "adopted" Berger and Tanner is similar to how *Screen* "adopted" Straub-Huillet in the 1970s. In an essay called "The Place(s) of Danièle," arguing that what each filmmaker brought to the collaboration remains something of a mystery, Jonathan Rosenbaum wrote that "I think the fact that their work provokes silence more often than discussion – a tribute in some ways to its continuing radicality and difference – may be partly to blame for this. The same sort of syndrome was responsible for magazines like *Screen* reproducing some of their scripts at the same time that they chickened out of grappling with any of their films critically." Something very similar was going on with the Berger-Tanner/*Ciné-Tracts* relationship. Films like *Le Milieu du monde* and *Jonas* provoke way more questions than they answer, and while I wouldn't call the journal chicken, I do think that this intense radicality and difference accounts for some of why the they chose to publish *materials* from the films – letters, screenplays – rather than sustained critical analyses.

One of the barriers to such interpretation may have been precisely Tanner's constant insistence that his films' politics are to be found on the level of form. The sort of complex tracking shot that I described earlier, where Mathieu, Mathilde, and Marcel all discuss the work he will do, requires work of the viewer too, and, most importantly, forces the viewer to recognize the usually hidden work of film interpretation, just as three of the "Ma"s are bringing to the fore the usually hidden work that surrounds food and its production. Recognizing interpretation as work need not include trivializing assumptions to the tune of "following a long sequence-shot with a complex sound-image relationship is just as much labour as shovelling horse manure onto cabbage patches," although it's easy to see how left critics would want to avoid the appearance of such conflation. But what is true of both visual interpretation and manure-shovelling is that capitalist modes of production try to conceal both, presenting the final product – the story, the cabbage – as something that has come about completely naturally, without the intervention of human, and thus ideologically formed, actors. Making both explicit, and doing so with a single cinematic gesture, does indeed constitute an oppositional stance, a stance that opposes not just a specific political or social problem (the use of chemical fertilizers in agriculture, say, or the hierarchical nature of farm work), but that opposes the naturalization of choices that, far from being natural, are at the core ideologically motivated. Such naturalization is, of course, the first step in that watchword of *Le Milieu du monde*, normalization. "You have to make that spectator who dominant cinema turns into a sleepwalker do some work," Tanner said in that *Nouvelle Critique* interview with François Albera. "The scene, the shot, I conceive of them in a way that will make the spectator active on the level of the 'why' of things" (47).[24] Naturalization under capitalism, be it on the level of cinematic form, agricultural production, etc., is all about obscuring that "niveau du pourquoi des choses."

An even better example of the intersection of form and content, of tracking shots and morality, to follow Godard's well-worn phrase, is when Marco delivers one of his first history lectures. This is a single tracking shot, lasting almost three minutes, with a very simple soundtrack (made up entirely of Marcel lecturing and some ambient noise of students shuffling). The camera follows him as he moves up the centre of the room, explaining that, although he is no determinist, "In an acorn are already present the creases which will give the oak its shape. What you are, each one of you, was present in the chromosomes at the moment of my conception. Excuse me, your conception!" (*Jonah who will be 25*, 41–42).[25] The real meat of the lecture, though, develops when Marco reaches the head of the room and draws a diagram on the chalkboard, to illustrate what he calls the holes that great thinkers create in time, holes that reach forward and backward to connect with other historical forces. At first the camera is still when he draws the diagram, and then pans only slightly to the left as he sits at his desk to elaborate. But then, in good "découpage sans ciseaux" fashion, the camera tracks towards him slowly, getting him into a medium close-up as he really makes his point about why prophets are always misunderstood: "They exist between times. No one understood much about Diderot until an entire generation screamed 'monster' at Freud. That much time was needed to pass through the hole." But as he gets into the overall relevance of the metaphor, the camera does not simply hold him in close-up for a visually simple emphasis, as would be common in a classical system. Rather, the camera moves *away* from him, up the middle of the classroom and into the student body, by way of visually emphasizing that Marco is speaking about everyone, not just about two specific historical figures like Freud and Diderot but about history, and indeed about the film's overall view of history. The camera slowly moves him into a long shot as he says: "The holes prophets make for looking into the future are the same through which historians later peer at the stuff of the past. Look at them leering through the holes dug by Jean-Jacques Rousseau in order to explain the eighteenth century to us" (all *Jonah who will be 25*, 42).[26] Here is an intensely Brechtian moment in the film, where the filmmakers' overall analysis, including their philosophical touchstone, is laid out explicitly. The words of that analysis are in the mouths of a character, in keeping with the limited cooperation with classical modes of narration that Tanner (like Brecht) has spoken of being willing to provide. But the most important of these words come as the camera is literally distancing us from that character, as it is physically moving away from him.

This sequence is not only important for understanding the film in terms of what Tanner brings (Brecht), but is *Jonas*'s most "Bergerian" moment. Tanner affirmed to François Albera that this part of the film was especially close to Berger's own thought; he said that "All that reflection on time belongs to John Berger, who works on these problems, especially political time, the absence of the notion of time in Marx's thought. Since we were headed towards the year 2000, he proposed to me that we integrate that into the film. The history teacher Marco's course was written completely by him" (48).[27] This is no surprise, for any devoted reader of Berger's work knows of his love of diagrams to illustrate abstractly philosophical topics. Towards the end of *A Seventh Man* (176–77), Berger (sounding a bit like he did at the beginning of *Mike ou l'usage de la science*) holds forth on time and space, writing that "Just as the measures of exterior times – hours, days, seasons, years – are dependent upon the solar system, so the self's time is constructed like a system rotating round a sun or a nucleus of self-consciousness. The felt space of a life's time may be represented by a circle." Below this is a (clearly hand-drawn) circle. Then he writes of how "the circle is filled at any given moment with past, present and future," and on the facing page there is the circle again, now filled with little lines, as well as tiny circles both hollow and solid, with text next to it reading "Elements of past and future free to form an amalgam with the present." At the bottom of the page is that circle again, with the lines now forming a smaller circle within the circle, and the smaller circles all clustered together at the centre; text next to that diagram reads: "In bereavement the past becomes fixed and the future withdraws." In his 1978 essay "Uses of Photography" (reprinted in *About Looking*), he writes that "Normally photographs are used in a very unilinear way – they are used to illustrate an argument, or to demonstrate a thought which goes like this:"; below is a long arrow pointing left to right. He goes on to write that "Memory is not unilinear at all. Memory works radially, that is to say with an enormous number of associations all leading to the same event. The diagram is like this:"; below is a circle made up of eight lines, all radiating out from a central point (60). Berger's 1979 novel *Pig Earth* concludes with a "Historical Afterword" that tries to explain the difference between modernity's "culture of progress" and the peasantry's "culture of survival." He writes of the former that "The future is envisaged as the opposite of what classical perspective does to a road. Instead of appearing to become even narrower as it recedes into the distance, it becomes ever wider." He writes of the latter that it "envisages the future as a sequence of repeated acts for survival. Each act pushes a thread through the eye of a needle and the thread is tradition." Below both, there are diagrams made up of lines and circles that illustrate these concepts; on the next page Berger puts two slightly different diagrams of each culture face-to-face to reinforce his point (all 204–5). So while Todd Gitlin, in his *Film Quarterly* review of the film, writes of this scene that "One finds a close similarity in Walter Benjamin's 'Theses on the Philosophies of History,'" it seems clear to me that the relevant intertextual connection is with Berger's own writing. For Benjamin may indeed have seen history as a series of interactions between, in the words of his famous formulation, angels facing backwards towards the future, Berger sees it somewhat differently. What is always at stake for Berger is a tension between the immediately present – material and historical reality, economic inequities, gender relations – and the ineffably time-bound – memories of the past, anticipation of the future, and misapprehension of the present. The tensions between these elements (which he seems to relish explaining via abstract line-diagrams) are what form our understanding of history; focussing on any one of them to the exclusion of the others can only lead to trouble (the existential malaise of the migrant worker, the misuse of photography in newspapers, the barely noticed disappearance of the European peasantry).

The connection between childhood and adulthood is, of course, the most basic, universal dialectic of history, and in many ways *Jonas* is wrestling with this fundamental problem and the questions it poses. What do the young and the old owe one another? What sort of society would insist that such debts be paid, and what sort of society makes it easy to forgive such debts? What do people retain of their youth when they age? George Orwell memorably evoked this connection between history and growing up when, in his 1940 essay "The Lion and the Unicorn: Socialism and the English Genius" he used it as a metaphor for the evolution of English identity: "What can the England of 1940 have in common with the England of 1840? But then, what have you in common with the child of five whose photograph your mother keeps on the mantelpiece? Nothing, except that you happen to be the same person" (13). Jim Leach sees a comparable search for continuity between childhood and adulthood as key to *Jonas*, writing that:

> ... the birth of Jonah testifies to the possibility of achieving the communal goal of creating conditions in which subjective desires can be objectivized. Childhood is seen as the time during which this harmony is achieved and normally destroyed; and through a network of interconnected images dealing with such issues as time, food, nature, education, and money, the film explores the relationship of nature and society and the struggle to re-define this relationship so that the harmony of childhood can be carried into adult life. (126)

Marco's professional evolution is one way that the narrative signals that this relationship between nature and society, between subjective desires and objective reality, could be realized via a reconciliation between adulthood and childhood. After admitting to his students that his fantasy is to sleep with two women at the same time, he is fired from his job teaching at the college.[28] The next time we see him he is working in a retirement home, leading old-timers in a song and telling Mathieu and Max, in another densely Bergerian reflection on time, that this is actually better than teaching children, which only allows you to influence the present. "Old people take time for what it is, because they have so little of it. Having a lot makes you believe that time is the future and the past. Of course, their present is full of memories of the past. All the world's memories are in the present. And all its hopes too. But these memories and hopes are a creation of the present, and not what destroys it. That's why I like old people and want to play with them" (*Jonas Who Will Be 25*, 135).[29] This is part of a sequence made up of three lengthy, complex tracking shots (in contradiction to Tanner's statement to Albera that "All of the scenes are in sequence-shot or in two shots maximum") where the three guys are making supper (it's the same sequence as where Mathieu sings his ode to the onion). But when Marco delivers this little soliloquy, the camera stops moving and holds him in a medium-long shot, emphasizing that this is an important part of the dialogue without resorting fully to a dominant film language. And it is important; this desire to *play* with the old is a paradox that sums up the film's ideology very neatly. Those who have experienced the fullness of life are more aware of the need to fully integrate the experiences of childhood: curiosity, openness, playfulness, freedom. These experiences are not all that there is to life, but they are important, and they are easily lost, especially in a capitalism-led culture where a sterilizing normalization is the dominant ethos.

Really, though, the fullest embodiment of this childhood-adulthood dialectic is the character of Marie, and the sequences where she plays with a retired French train engineer named Charles could be seen as icons of the film's search for a reconciliation of childhood and adulthood. This is most true of a scene late in the film, after Marie has served a year in prison for purposely undercharging senior citizens (and Marco) at the grocery store where she is a migrant worker of sorts (she has a work but not a residence permit for Switzerland, and so must go home to France every night). She goes to visit Charles, and he asks to resume the role-playing games that they had so enjoyed before her incarceration. She agrees, but when he goes to get his engineer's goggles, she says she only wants to play a game about prison. This sequence is made up of two shots of about ninety seconds each, and again it uses stillness (and thus a lack of découpage, with or without scissors) to emphasize the importance of what is going on. The only movement in the first shot is a pan as Marie gets up from the table to go into the living room; following a cut to a reverse angle, the only movement is a slight track in as Marie becomes horribly upset about her memories of prison. Both Charles and Marie throw themselves into the game, into the "pretending," in a way that is so complete as to seem utterly childlike. But there is something fully adult about this performance as well. Charles asks detailed questions about her life in the slammer and Marie gets impatient when he gets some of the details wrong in his performance. She is particularly annoyed that he plays the part of the priest as a doddering old man, telling him that "The chaplain wasn't an old fruitcake. He was young. Every time he was there I'd imagine him making love" (*Jonas Who Will Be 25*, 146).[30] Her final collapse into tears is childlike in its intensity but is preceded by her declaration that Charles can't possibly understand the sheer desolation of prison life, an adult senti-ment if ever there was one.

Seeing scenes like this one as the bearer of *Jonas*'s meaning, rather than more sentimental moments with actual children, seems to me crucial for understanding the film's overall analysis. Christian Dimitriu writes that "The film's central sequence-shot is a veritable redemption scene which unfolds through Max's crucifixion. The general theme of *Jonas* is ideology, or rather how ideology's fragments reorganize themselves, seven or eight years after May '68, into a new project. The undercurrent of this theme is naturally economy, to which is opposed, as a new possibility, ecology" (65).[31] Now, this is an important scene for sure. During the shot's three minutes of almost constant movement, all eight of the "Ma"s eventually gather around as kids paint an outline of Max, who has stretched out his arms onto a stone wall. As the camera cranes up slightly towards the end of the shot, both Max and then Marcel start to sing a song to the tune of non-diegetic accordion music, a moment of sound-image fracturing that recalls comparable scenes in *La Salamandre*, such as when Pierre and Rosemonde listen to the jukebox in a café and it becomes unclear whether the music is really supposed to be diegetic. From the standpoint both of subject matter (collectivity) and formal patterns (long take, complex camera movement, eccentric sound-image relationship), the sequence contains a lot of what is important about *Jonas*. But I do not accept the contention that film is basically about ideology, and I accept even less the idea that it is mostly about May '68 and the shift towards ecological sensibilities. Rather, the film is using occasional references to May '68 (and they are very occasional; Max is the only character with any lived experience of the strikes, and he is also the most politically cynical of the group), and frequently tongue-in-cheek references to ecological frameworks (recall Max: "All manner of virtue in vegetables. Eat your vegetables!") as *means* to evoke the way ideology changes over time. Seeing *Jonas* through the lens of childhood/adulthood rather than '68 or environmentalism as such actually allows us to see it as more ideologically sophisticated. The film is not so parochial as to see May '68 as some sort of transcendentally significant date; it's just one among many. Nor is it so romantic as to see ecological movements like organic farms as the new solution to everything; indeed, such romanticism is the subject of frequent jokes and is clearly laced with just as much irony as Voltaire's famous summary of self-satisfied defeatism "il faut cultiver notre jardin." What is instead at issue in the difficulty of finding a way of being in the world that is both aware of the socio-political realities around you, while keeping faith with both the historical forces that led to those realities and the hypothetical future which those realities will in turn help to form.

The quest to allow history, in the fullest sense of the word, to guide the assumptions that form our view of the world (assumptions which are also known as ideology) is what lies at the core of *Jonas qui aura 25 ans en l'an 2000*. As a subject for a film that is as *engagé* as anything (cinematic or otherwise) that emerged from the idealism of the 1960s, and it is a great deal more philosophically nuanced as well. It is also as true to the spirit of Brecht as anything to have emerged during this period. In an early essay on Brecht's theatre and an ideal Brechtian criticism (1956's "Le tache de la critique brechtienne," reprinted in *Essais critiques*), Roland Barthes sets out "les plans d'analyse où cette critique devrait successivement se situer" (84). These *plans* are sociology, ideology, semiology, and *morale*. This is a stunningly precise summary of the film's concerns: a film about the specific moment of the 1970s and the social conditions that led to it, a film about ideology's debt to history, a film whose visual language is rigorously constructed along non-dominant lines but which nevertheless remains lucid, and a film which is, finally, about responsibility. For *Jonas* is a film about the ways that time acts on everyone, and the responsibility that this action in turn demands of everyone: responsibility to the past (struggles and victories, half-forgotten though they may sometimes seem), responsibility to the present (to the people you live in community with now), responsibility to the future (to kids who are just being born, and whose experiences at the age on 25 can only be vaguely imagined). To see it as a celebration of dropping out could not be more wrong. It is, instead, a film about conscience, a conscience that lies in the synthesis of the dialectic between childhood and maturity.

1 "Pangloss disait quelquefois à
Candide : « Tous les événements
sont enchaînés dans le meilleur
des mondes possibles; car, enfin,
si vous n'aviez pas été chassé d'un
beau château à grands coups de pied
dans le derrière pour l'amour de
mademoiselle Cunégonde, si vous
n'aviez pas couru l'Amérique à pied,
si vous n'aviez pas donné un bon coup
d'épée au baron, si vous n'aviez pas
perdu tous vos moutons du bon pays
d'Eldorado, vous ne mangeriez pas ici
des cédrats confits et des pistaches. –
Cela est bien dit, répondit Candide,
mais il faut cultiver notre jardin. »"
(234).

2 The film's French title is *Jonas qui aura
25 ans en l'an 2000*. It was released
in English as *Jonah Who Will Be 25
in the Year 2000*. Almost all of the
discussion of the film in English
uses the spelling "Jonah," which I
don't really understand; that seems a
half-step away from releasing a film
like Godard's *Pierrot le fou* as *Crazy
Pete*, and then always referring to
the main character as Pete. Anyway,
I use the abbreviated title *Jonas*;
references to *Jonah* come only when I
am quoting discussion of the film that
is originally written in English.

3 "Toute notre sagesse consiste en
préjugés serviles; tous nos usages
ne sont qu'assujettissement, gêne et
contrainte. L'homme civil naît, vit et
meurt dans l'esclavage : à sa naissance
on le coud dans un maillot; à sa
mort on le cloue dans une bière; tant
qu'il garde la figure humaine, il est
enchaîné par nos institutions" (43).
The translation in the subtitles and
the English version of the published

screenplay (26) both vary slightly, and
in different ways, from Allan Bloom's
1979 translation, which I am using
throughout this book.

4 "... à vivre, s'il le faut, dans les glaces
d'Islande ou sur le brûlant rocher de
Malte" (43).

5 "... passer de Surinam à Bordeaux,
d'aller de Bordeaux à Paris, de Paris
à Dieppe, de Dieppe à Portsmouth,
de côtoyer le Portugal et l'Espagne,
de traverser toute la Méditerranée, de
passer quelques mois à Venise" (209).

6 "C'est encore ici une des raisons
pourquoi je veux élever Émile à la
campagne, loin de la canaille des
valets, les derniers des hommes après
leur maîtres, loin des noirs mœurs
des villes, que les vernis dont on les
couvre rend séduisant et contagieuses
pour les enfants ; au lieu que les vices
des paysans, sans apprêt et dans toute
leur grossièreté, sont plus propres à
rebuter qu'à séduire, quand on n'a nul
intérêt à les imiter" (115).

7 "On façonne les plantes par la culture,
et les hommes part l'éducation" (36).

8 "Les paysannes mangent moins de
viande et plus de légumes que les
femmes de la ville; et ce régime
végétal paraît plus favorable que
contraire á elles et á leurs enfants"
(64).

9 "Mais souvenez-vous que j'irai
labourerez vos fèves, si vous touchez à
mes mélons" (121).

10 "MATHIEU (il chantonne). L'oignon
est un légume superbe, démocratique.
Il pousse partout. Il a la peau dure
pour se protéger du froid. On le

trouve vulgaire. Il donne du goût à tout. Il dure. On peut le manger cuit ou cru. Il est doux et aussi un peu amer. Il tue les microbes. Il coûte pas cher. (*musique sur la 1ère partie*)

MARCO. Moi, c'est le chou.

MAX. Toutes les vertus dans les légumes. Mangez des légumes! Alors tu va te retirer dans un asile de vieillards ? Et devenir une sorte de poireau ?" (172).

11 "… plus l'homme est resté près de sa condition naturelle, plus la différence de ses facultés à ses désirs est petites, et moins par conséquent il est éloigné d'être heureux" (94).

12 "Or, les besoins changent selon la situation des hommes. Il y a bien de la différence entre l'homme naturel vivant dans l'état de nature et l'homme naturel vivant dans l'état de société. Emile n'est pas un sauvage à reléguer dans les déserts, c'est un sauvage fait pour habiter les villes" (267). Again, the translation in the film's subtitles and the English version of the published screenplay (162) vary slightly from Bloom's, and in slightly different ways.

13 I think that the whole Rousseau-derived idea of "the savage," "savage man," etc., has emerged because of an overly phonetic translation of Rousseauian concepts such as "l'homme sauvage," which is found in his 1755 text *Discours sur l'origine et les fondements de l'inégalité parmi les hommes*. It seems obvious to me that Rousseau means "sauvage" as being "wild" or "natural," akin to "les fleurs sauvages" or wildflowers. Translating "l'homme sauvage" into English as "savage" is to import a pejorative and often violent connotation that the French word does not possess. The English word "wild," of course, carries these connotations when it refers to a person (although not when it refers to a flower). I would thus prefer to see terms such as "l'homme sauvage" or "un sauvage" translated as something like "uncultivated man," which seems to me much closer to the spirit of these Rousseau texts. Nobody would translate the term "les fleurs sauvages" as "the savage flowers," so I genuinely do not understand why the widely accepted translation of "L'homme Sauvage" is "Savage man."

14 "Il faut qu'il sache y trouver son nécessaire, tirer parti de leurs habitants, et vivre, sinon comme eux, du moins avec eux" (267).

15 This was first published in the 27 November 1976 issue of *Voix Ouvrière*, the newspaper of the Swiss worker's party (Parti suisse du travail).

16 "Le premier principe est le choix du plan-séquence. De manière presque mécanique, il y a refus de couper dans une scène. Il y a cent cinquante plans dans le film, cent soixante-dix environ avec les plans en noir-blanc. Toutes les scènes sont en plans-séquences ou en deux plans au maximum…. Le plan-séquence implique et permet un travail de la caméra tout à fait différent, dans les mouvements d'appareil surtout, apparemment « incongrus ». Dans la scène du film située au début par exemple, où Rufus entre dans la cuisine de la ferme, il s'agit d'un plan-séquence de quatre minutes et demie environ. La caméra découpe la scène comme on le ferait avec des ciseaux puisqu'elle filme

d'abord un personnage, un deuxième, un troisième, puis deux, puis trois, puis elle passe derrière chercher la suite du texte, revient et finit en « totale ». On a donc un découpage sans ciseaux. Mais la première incidence sur le spectateur, c'est que le fonctionnement de ce découpage est complètement différent : normalement, on changerait de plan, d'axe, de focale au besoin pour un gros plan. Là, il y a déjà un effet de distance parce que ça traîne, il y a des trous, des moments où la caméra n'est sur rien, elle est entre les personnages et elle continue à bouger à la même vitesse, de manière autonome."

17   "… je fais appel à certains éléments relevant du code de représentation « classique » : effet de réel, personnages reconnaissables par exemple. Mais ces éléments n'interviennent que dans les limites précises qui leur sont assignées – en guise de repères pour le spectateur – et qui sont circonscrites avec précision dans les « morceaux » du film, à l'intérieur des scènes, mais n'opèrent jamais au niveau de la structure globale" (Heinic, 38).

18   "*Jonas* marque bien une nouvelle étape dans l'évolution du cinéma selon Tanner. Précédemment, de *Charles mort ou vif* au *Milieu du monde*, en passant par *La Salamandre* et *Le Retour d'Afrique*, le cinéaste, à travers l'étude du comportement d'une, de deux ou de trois personnes, nouait des liens solides entre elles à propos d'un fait précis…. Aujourd'hui, élargissant le récit à de nombreux personnages principaux, il fait littéralement éclater la narration, privilégiant plusieurs moments et les imbriquant les uns dans les autres sans former

nécessairement une histoire au sens traditionnel du terme."

19   "… toute la charge, signifiante et plaisante, porte sur chaque scène, non sur l'ensemble…. Même chose chez Eisenstein : le film est une contiguïté d'épisodes, dont chacun est absolument signifiant, esthétiquement parfait" (187).

20   "Tanner, lui, comme dans cet autre film qui nous vient aussi du cœur du Capital, *Milestones*, ne filme qu'*une* génération mais sur *plusieurs* scènes, la génération qui, d'être née en 1968, aura bientôt dix ans."

21   "Très actives et souvent spectaculaires, les militantes du MLF deviennent rapidement des actrices incontournables de la vie politique genevoise…. Au niveau national, les groupes autonomes de femmes qui ont fleuri à Genève, Lausanne, Bâle, Berne, Zurich, Locarno et Bellinzone ne sont reliés par aucune structure formelle, mais tentent à plusieurs reprises de se coordonner."

22   "Nous n'avons pas voulu tendre un miroir à tel ou tel autre groupe pour qu'il puisse se défouler en s'y admirant. Les ultra-gauches ne s'y retrouvent pas et ils sont souvent les plus médiocres lecteurs du film : ils « n'apprennent rien », évidement, et surtout pas *à regarder* des images, je « n'offre pas de solution », etc." (Heinic 38; emphasis in the original).

23   "La grande rigueur et les moyens importants de la production – le soin des cadrages, la qualité chaleureuse de la direction d'acteurs – sont ici mis au service d'une écriture limpide et simple qui se refuse aux moindres effets."

24 "Il s'agit de faire travailler le spectateur que le cinéma dominant transforme en somnambule.... La scène, le plan, je les conçois de telle sorte que le spectateur soit activé au niveau du pourquoi des choses."

25 "Dans un gland il y a déjà les méandres qui donneront la forme du chêne. Ce que vous êtes, chacun de vous, était déjà là dans les chromosomes au moment de ma conception. Je vous demande pardon, de votre conception !" (89).

26 "Ils sont entre les temps. Personne de comprit grand chose à Diderot jusqu'au moment où une génération entière cria 'Monstre' ! à Freud. Il fallait ce temps-là pour passer au travers du trou. Les trous que font les prophètes pour regarder le futur sont les mêmes par lesquels les historiens lorgnent ensuite vers les vieux meubles du passé. Regardez-les lorgner à travers les trous creusés par Jean-Jacques Rousseau pour nous expliquer le dix-huitième siècle" (89).

27 "Toute cette réflexion sur le temps appartient à John Berger qui travaille sur ces problèmes, notamment le temps politique, l'absence de cette notion de temps dans la pensée de Marx. Comme on était parti sur l'an 2000, il m'a proposé d'intégrer cela au film. Le cours du prof d'histoire, Marco, est complètement écrit par lui."

28 In a strange life-imitates-art side story, Tanner and Berger found themselves in a bit of hot water for the scenes involving the students. Marco's classes were shot at Geneva's Collège Calvin (Tanner's own alma mater), and upon the film's release, the daily *24 Heures* reported (on 3 February 1977) that Hermann Jenni, a councillor for the Parti vigilant, protested to Geneva's Conseil d'état that "There are scenes that are an insult to good morals, an invitation to sexual license" ["Il y a des scènes qui sont une attaque aux bonnes mœurs, une invitation à la licence sexuelle"]. On 3 March 1977 the daily reported that the Conseil had voted down his motion "to use all means at its disposal to have those scenes and references that deal with Collège Calvin cut from the film" ["à user de tous les moyens à sa disposition pour faire couper du film toutes les scènes et mentions impliquant le Collège Calvin"]. The paper went on to report that "The councillor responsible for public education, Mr. André Chavanne, responded that it wasn't Calvin College in Tanner's film, inasmuch as it was its theatre group who was doing the acting, and that there had been no complaints or attacks that had come from the parents of students, who had all given their approval to the filming" ["Le conseiller d'État chargé de l'instruction publique, M. André Chavanne, lui a répondu que ce n'est pas le Collège Calvin en tant que tel qui figure au générique du film de Tanner, mais son groupe de théâtre, et qu'aucune plainte ni attaque n'est parvenue de parents d'élèves, qui ont tous accordé leur autorisation au tournage"]. In other words: Relax comrade, it's just a movie.

29 "... les vieux prennent le temps pour ce qu'il est, parce qu'ils en ont peu. Quand tu en as plein tu fais croire que le temps c'est le futur et le passé. Bien sûr que leur présent est plein de souvenirs du passé. Tous

les souvenirs du monde sont dans le présent. Et tous les espoirs aussi. Mais ces souvenirs et ces espoirs sont la création du présent, et non pas ce qui le détruit. C'est pour ça que j'aime les vieux et que j'ai envie de jouer avec eux" (174).

30 "L'aumônier n'était pas un vieux gâteux. Il était jeune. Chaque fois qu'il était là je l'imaginais en train de faire l'amour" (183).

31 "Le plan-séquence central du film est une véritable scène de rédemption qui se réalise à travers la crucifixion de Max. Le thème général de *Jonas* est l'idéologie, ou plutôt les fragments d'idéologie qui se réorganisent, sept ou huit ans après May 68, dans un nouveau projet. L'arrière-fond de ce thème est naturellement l'économie à laquelle s'oppose, comme nouvelle donnée, l'écologie."

CONCLUSION

I began this book by asking what constitutes political cinema. I have tried to answer that by discussing work that John Berger and Alain Tanner did together, and sometimes alongside one another. Several crucial elements have emerged throughout that discussion: a rigorous but never uncritical relationship with the political and theoretical idealism of the 1960s and 70s, a period that was indeed very fruitful from a politico-aesthetic standpoint, and a parallel insistence that there is much important political work to be done on the level of form; a continuous intertwining of fictional and realist aesthetic patters, and a parallel instance on the inseparable and coequal nature of the political and the personal. The political sensibility of Berger and Tanner was always close to the ideals of the internationalist left, but this period in their work is marked by the strong influence of specifically Swiss ideas about politics and collective action. Their shared work shows, then, that there are basic problems both in cinema and political practice that must, and just as importantly *can*, be reconciled by way of creating an artistic practice that seeks a just society. Like all fully formed artists, they have found the answers to these basic problems by being part of the society that formed them and their work. To return to the quote from Berger's photo-book *A Seventh Man* with which I opened this book, "The subject is European, its meaning global" (7).

Tanner is especially slippery on this matter, and I have tried hard throughout to illustrate the degree to which these films are defined by concerns specific to Switzerland, despite what Berger identified as Tanner's love/hate relationship with the place (Appignanesi 302). Tanner has recently been making a lot of waves in Switzerland on this front. He said in an interview published in the Swiss national daily *Le Matin* on 8 February 2004 that "Swiss culture doesn't exist. We are neither a nation nor a people, nor for even greater reasons a culture. Besides, Switzerland has become an unfilmable country" (20).[1] This strongly echoed what he would go on to write in his memoir *Ciné-mélanges* (published three years later), which I quoted in the introduction: "The Swiss do not form a people, and do not have a culture, but attach themselves to a bunch of others" (84).[2] This kind of talk, predictably, drives Swiss pundits nuts, and that *Le Matin* interview prompted Jean-Louis Kuffer to reply (in the 23 February 2004 issue of the rival newspaper *24 heures*) that "Swiss culture is alive and well; moreover, we can see it … in the films of Alain Tanner" (ellipses in the original).[3] But he had harsher words as well: "If there is no Swiss culture, then we might as well dismantle institutions like the Office fédéral de la culture or Pro Helvetia, as we wait for the market to once again sanctify stars like Pipilotti Rist and Mario Boota. Alain Tanner is certainly the last one to think like the neo-liberals, and yet his disillusionment well and truly risks giving the game to them."[4] There is indeed an unfortunate intersection between grouchy talk about national identity meaning nothing and the desires of globalized capitalists to eliminate all impediments to their activities.

This is clearly unintentional on Tanner's part, but more importantly, grouchiness like this doesn't really represent the position he has staked out, especially the position he was staking out at the time he was working with Berger. In a very nuanced 1970 speech he gave in Paris (titled "Histoire du cinéma suisse"), he said that "under fire from Hollywood allies, Swiss culture was completely menaced by colonization." He went on to say that "Our streets, our houses, our compatriots, have started to transform into things that are seen, looked at, commented on. Swiss cinema, a national cinema, is of little importance to us in and of itself: we simply want that filmmakers who live in Zurich, Lausanne, or Geneva be able to express themselves, and Swiss cinema will follow" (Boujut, 170).[5] Tanner's real resistance is not to Swiss identity or national identity as such, but to sentimental patriotism; his desire for a Swiss cinema was driven not by nationalism but by anti-centralization. He is advocating for images that are autonomous.

This is discernable not only in the statements he has made but also in the films he made with Berger. The *Cahiers du cinéma*, in the considerable coverage they gave to *Jonas qui aura 25 ans en l'an 2000*, understood this well. Serge Daney, opens his text "Les huit *Ma*," by writing that the film is defined in part by Tanner's interest in "*topography* (Switzerland as the centre of the capitalist world, a mid-place where all borders meet, utopia)" (48, italics his).[6] But it is the text by Serge Le Peron, "Ici ou ailleurs" (an allusion to the Godard-Miéville film of 1974–76) that is more expansive on the way that *Jonas*, among other films, really is engaged with Switzerland itself:

> In Tanner's films Switzerland (what it *symbolizes*, the capitalist system: in that Switzerland is an unreal emblem), is present but, as in a mirror, nullified, reduced to appearances. There are no clear signs of Switzerland's customary existence (if you want to pretend that those exist): snow-topped peaks, banks and bankers, not even immigrant workers; when these signs appear (they are only, really, ghosts) they are emptied of signification; in *Jonas* the soft, fat banker in the nightclub, the immigrants "in passing," the red lights of Geneva; the Swiss countryside reduced to an unrecognizable space.... First of all Tanner refuses the code (this space of tacit collaboration with international capital) that constitutes Switzerland; his characters have all the space that they *want*. (45, ellipses in the original)[7]

Le Peron is getting at the central paradox not only of *Jonas* but of all the work Berger and Tanner did together: Switzerland is clearly, unmistakeably present, even if its familiar icons such as bankers (awfully important in *Jonas*) and mountains (the setting of a key sequence in *La Salamandre*) are stripped of their familiar meaning. Even though (and perhaps because) they resist the familiar iconography of Switzerland, these films are very clearly about the topography of Switzerland.

There is a similarly critical quality to the relationship that the films have with theoretical matters, both film theory as such and Marxism broadly. Both Tanner and Berger are men of the left, although there is very little orthodox Marxism to be found in the work of either. I tried to establish in the introduction the kind of humanist socialism that has formed Berger's world view (and which was voiced as early as 1958 by a Hungarian painter named Jonas in his novel *A Painter of Our Time*). While this politics shares a great deal with the internationalist left generally, there is very little in

Berger's work that could be considered part of a political orthodoxy or even doctrine, and this non-doctrinaire leftism characterizes the films he made with Tanner quite strongly. I also tried to establish in the introduction the degree to which Tanner's work was, since his very first days making commissioned documentaries for Swiss television, defined by a broad humanist engagement, one that was clearly influenced (both aesthetically and ideologically) by Jean Rouch. As he moved towards feature filmmaking, his political and formal touchstone became Bertolt Brecht, but this was less a matter of a turn towards the activist than a search for a new form of self-awareness. Rouch's documentaries were strongly self-aware inasmuch as they were frequently explicit about the degree to which the documentary image is always a spectacle; this is most clearly true in a film like *Chronique d'un été* but it's just as true of the films he made in Africa such as *Moi, un noir* or *Les maîtres fous*. As Tanner moved towards fiction filmmaking Brecht's writings were clearly more useful as aesthetico-political guide. But Brecht shares some common ground with Rouch, inasmuch as they were both, as was Tanner, searching for a socially conscious artistic practice free of coercion, one that placed the spectator in a dialogue with a work of art. Brecht wrote in a 1927 article published in *Frankfurter Zeitung* that "instead of sharing an experience, the spectator must try to come to grips with things" (23),[8] and that coming to grips was an ongoing process, not one simply based in political propagandizing or polemic. "The spectator must try to come to grips with things" is an excellent way of summarizing the politics of these films that Berger and Tanner made together.

In the way in which this push to "come to grips" occurs on the level of form, these films are also clearly connected to the theoretical practice of the post-'68 *Cahiers du cinéma*, of which Tanner was a habitual reader. It is quite possible to move through the key texts of this period – work like Jean Louis Comolli and Jean Narboni's two-part essay "Cinéma/idéologie/critique," Narboni's review of Costa Gavras's film *Z*, Jean-Pierre Oudart's two-part essay "Suture" – and connect them directly to the work that Tanner and Berger were doing. This is especially true of *Le Milieu du monde*, which I tried to show in Chapter 3. But it is more important to note a shared interest in the role of realist illusionism in creating a dominant film language, as well as a shared interest in finding workable alternatives to that dominance. When Tanner told the *Cahiers'* N. Heinic in a 1977 interview about *Jonas* (in the same issue where the Daney and Le Peron texts were published) that "I call on certain relevant elements from the 'classical' code of representation: a feeling for the real, for example recognizable characters" ("An Interview with Alain Tanner," 66),[9] he wasn't invoking any specific theorists or specific articles. But any regular reader of the *Cahiers* during this period would recognize the code-words of a politicized approach to form: "code de représentation « classique »" and "effet de réel" should definitely set off bells of recognition, especially given the impact of Roland Barthes' 1968 essay "L'Effet de réel" (published in *Communications*) on the *Cahiers du cinéma* and its affiliated theorists. Berger's aesthetic principles had more to do with the legacy of realism, a form whose renewal he saw as the best means to restore visual art to its proper place as a social agent. But the kind of realism Berger was advocating, the kind he helped create with the films he made with Tanner, was just as critical of the "code de représentation « classique »." *La Salamandre*, *Le Milieu du monde* and *Jonas* are all keenly interested in quotidian reality, but they are also defined by visual patterns and narrative structures that call attention to themselves, which encourage the viewer to consider them as aesthetic objects formed by ideologically aware artists. Roland Barthes, in his short text *Leçon* (delivered as his inaugural lecture at the Collège de France in 1977), explained this political understanding of form in terms that resonate strongly both with the post-'68 *Cahiers* and with the films of Berger and Tanner. He writes there that:

> No "literary history" (if we must still write it) would be complete if it only dealt with the historical connections between schools of thought without marking the break which went along with a new prophecy: that of writing. "Change the language," that phrase of Mallarmé, is concomitant with "Change the world," that phrase of Marx: there is a *political* sense to Mallarmé, for those who have followed his work and who follow it still. (23)[10]

The choice between changing the world and changing the language is a false one: language is part of the world, and the world can only be understood through language. No film history (and I believe there is still a lot of it left to write, a history that includes marginal practices) would be complete unless it recognizes that basic principle that nothing of ideological substance is ever accomplished without a parallel substance of form.

Just as these films are defined by a desire to reconcile formal and political rigour, they also try to reconcile the personal with the political. These are not simply narratives of leftist consciousness-raising or awakening; in *La Salamandre*, *Le Milieu du monde*, and *Jonas* alike, Berger and Tanner are presenting problems whose dilemmas are as strongly emotional as they are ideological. This is part of a desire to escape from the tyranny of reason, a philosophical approach that actually found some strong advocates in the pages of the post-68 *Cahiers du cinéma*. Recall Sylvie Pierre in the magazine's 1969 text on "Montage" calling some elements of Eisenstein's montage "dictatorial" because of "movements from one shot to another that preclude the spectator from ever escaping reason" (25).[11] Geoff Dyer's belief that Berger "vehemently refuses to succumb to a vulgar materialism which in its assertion of the primacy of the economic derides the claim of the spiritual and the cultural" (115) is key here. Materialism, like reason, is an important element of Marxism and of left politics generally, but to boil down all of existence to a matter of class relations is vulgar in the extreme. This kind of vulgarity was hiding just beneath the critique of *Jonas* offered in the pages of *Jump Cut* by John Hess, Linda Greene, and Robin Lakes, a critique that read the film solely in terms of adherence to orthodox, U.S.-led Marixism, feinting towards a culturally sensitive perspective by browbeating the filmmakers and actors "because neither they nor Tanner knows much about the daily lives of Swiss workers." In a later issue of *Jump Cut* (ironically the same one where Diane Waldman published her critique of "positive image" criticism), Hess returned to this particular fray and engaged Richard Kazis in a dialogue about *Jonas* and the American left's responses to it. He wrote there that "to call the film a great revolutionary masterpiece or some sort of model for political filmmaking is a little much. That calls for a closer look at the film's politics – which are sorely lacking" (36). To call the film a model for political filmmaking – which I think it is, along with *La Salamandre* and *Le Milieu du monde* – calls for more than that. It calls for an examination of the film's form, which I criticized the *Jump Cut* critics for neglecting in Chapter 4. But such a question just as urgently calls for an examination of the way that the film visualizes experience outside of politics as such. It calls for an examination of whether it is or isn't totalitarian in that Eisensteinian way identified by Sylvie Pierre. *La Salamandre* is about the alienation that is part and parcel of capitalist society, but it is also about *alienation*. *Le Milieu du monde* uses a passionate love affair as a metaphor in the service of its critique of ideological normalization, but it is also about *sexual passion*. *Jonas* uses the dialectic between childhood and adulthood to evoke the political confusion of post-'68 leftists, but it is also about *time*, and the effect that has on *individual conscience*. While such considerations are connected to politics (as each of these films shows), they are not simply synonymous with politics. Recognizing the diversity of human experience (including cinematic experience: dominant vs. non-dominant forms) and the way that those diverse elements are intertwined is what lies at the core of Berger and Tanner's project. This goes quite a bit beyond an attempt to be sure that the films' characters have good politics.

This was true of the films that Tanner made following his collaboration with Berger, especially those films that expanded on the work that they had done together. Because although their collaboration ostensibly ended with *Jonas qui aura 25 ans en l'an 2000*, that's not really the end of the story of John Berger and Alain Tanner. Their coexistence after their collaboration took two forms: work on a series of short, experimental films for the television service Société Suisse de Radiodiffusion (SSR, now TSR, Télévision Suisse Romande), and a resurrection of the characters that they created together. By offering a brief discussion of *Ecoutez voir*, a series of shorts works on Super 8 and ¾-inch video that aired on Swiss television in 1977 and 78, I want to show the degree to which Tanner was, at the end of the 1970s, becoming more experimental in his sensibilities, which, as I mentioned in Chapter 2, was one of the reasons Berger had given to Richard Appignanesi to explain why they didn't work together anymore. Berger said in that interview that "Alain, I think, was more interested in making films of a looser structure, films which, in a certain sense, were more experimental in their narrative, whereas I, because of my experience in writing stories not for the cinema, had come to a different position" (306). This move towards the experimental, though, was more or less temporary, and Tanner soon returned to a more straightforward narrative practice. Among the works he would make over the next years were: *Light Years Away* (1980), which is set in the year 2000 and has a twenty-five-year-old protagonist named Jonas; *Fourbi* (1995), which is a story about a young woman named Rosemonde selling her story of killing her rapist to a television station and the difficulties that the station's two writers and young actress have in understanding her; and *Jonas et Lila, à demain* (2000), which is simply about Jonas at the age of twenty-five, and his desire to make films. These feature films really are Tanner's; Berger is not credited on any of them. The degree to which they follow the concerns laid out by the films that they "remake" – *Jonas* and *La Salamandre* – varies considerably. What this post-*Jonas* work shows us overall is that Tanner not only remained significantly more invested in these cinematic narratives of Jonas and Rosemonde, he also became more invested in cinema itself than Berger ever was. Furthermore, what connects *Temps mort, Light Years Away, Fourbi,* and *Jonas et Lila à demain* is their shared interest in the technology of image-making itself. As Tanner became more meta-cinematic, Berger's work was becoming more broodingly novelistic, with his "Into Their Labours" trilogy (1979–90) embodying this. To a great extent, this later work turns the films that we had known as "theirs" into something else that is more clearly "his" – Tanner's.

The technology of filmmaking was quite literally the starting place for *Ecoutez voir*. In a 1977 article for *Sight and Sound* called "Alain Tanner: After *Jonah*," Michael Tarantino interviews Tanner as he works on a film that he was then calling *Contre Cœur* (and which became 1979's *Messidor*). Tanner described *Ecoutez voir* (which Tarantino calls *Ecoutez voir*) for Tarantino, and Tarantino suggests that it "may be seen as a sort of a bridge between *Jonah* and *Contre Cœur*" (40). He explained the genesis of the series as follows:

> It was Francis Reusser who started it. He was interested in three-quarter inch video and Super-8 film. Then there was Loretta Verna plus Anne-Marie Miéville plus myself. We decided to try something together and approached Swiss TV to find out if they were interested. They *were* interested, not so much in what we wanted to show or make but in so far as the technique was concerned. They know that Super-8 film is out there somewhere and so is three-quarter inch video, but they have no one who can really experiment with it. So they gave us a little money to work with, and they also gave us complete freedom to do what we wanted. (41)

There is a very concrete way, then, in which *Ecoutez voir* was a series about low-end image-making and the way that it can re-arrange perception; Tanner would return to this idea twenty-three years later, when he also returned to the character of Jonas in *Jonas et Lila à demain*. It was also a series that Berger was involved in, although at more of a distance. The Swiss TV guide *TV8*, in their 2 November 1977 summary of the series, noted that "As a sort of prologue, a first film by John Berger (author and Tanner's screenwriter) presents the four authors."[12] TSR has not been able to locate this "first film"; their crackerjack archivist Claude Zürcher speculated that Berger's contribution was probably aired live, and would thus have not been preserved. Gareth Evans' otherwise comprehensive catalogue of Berger's television work also does not mention the series.

Tanner's contribution to the series was called *Temps mort* (first broadcast 27 November 1977), and that film is made up largely, although not entirely, of images shot out of train or car windows on trips between Berne and Geneva. One early sequence begins with a shot showing a Super 8 camera mounted to a car window (presumably the camera whose images we have so far been seeing), and then follows with a reverse-shot of Tanner driving and smoking. The voice-over narration switches between a female and a male voice (Tanner's); the woman usually talks about broadly philosophical topics, the male about filmmaking itself. Tanner told Tarantino that he was inspired to make the film because he had made that trip so many times that "I can't even look out the train window, I hate it so much. It's familiar and boring and something that I know too well, so I wanted to see what would happen when I filmed it" (42). What happens is, partially, that the landscape is rendered visceral or exciting by virtue of the spectator plunging through it. Charles, the elderly train engineer in *Jonas*, alluded to this effect when he told Marco how much he liked riding the rails at the head of the train "Do you still sometimes travel by train? What do you see? The countryside going by, like in the movies. Myself, I don't go to the movies anymore. But in the locomotive, the countryside doesn't go by. You travel inside. Always: inside, inside, inside. It's like a kind of music. You go in front of yourself, right to the horizon, and then it goes right on, right to the place where the rails come together. And they never come together" (*Jonas Who Will Be 25*, 106).[13] This is especially true of a shot towards the end of the film, during a rainstorm on a fairly narrow road. There is only rain on the soundtrack, and the limited visibility created by the downpour is augmented by the graininess of the Super 8 image. It is a stirring sequence, partially because it is in such contrast to the relatively sedate, almost hypnotic road imagery that comes earlier in the film.

It is also startling because of the sequence that directly precedes it, which isn't road imagery at all. For although Tanner's interview with Tarantino gives the impression that the film is made up entirely of footage shot right out of car and train windows, there are other kinds of images here as well. The sequence right before the rainstorm is made of images shot in a train station café; there is a shot of two guys (one of whom playfully shakes his fist at the camera), followed by an interview (in synch sound, no less) with these two guys, and then a montage of close-ups of people eating. Just as the aforementioned flash of shot/reverse-shot involving the camera mounted on the car takes us close but not quite into the visual grammar of conventional narrative cinema, this brings us very close but not quite into the grammar of conventional documentary. But we don't stay there long; this is a very short interview sequence. Then Tanner takes us right back into the realm of the purely kinetic road imagery, and does so with a vengeance, as the rain pelts down and the soundtrack fills up with its sounds.

The closing words of the film's commentary are Tanner saying that "Le fabrication du film, c'est déjà le film": the way a film is made is already the film. This was an ongoing concern of the work that he made with Berger: the degree to which formal choices are the place where the real meanings of a film are to be found. It was also why he remained interested in television: following Marshall McLuhan, Tanner believed that it was the technology of television itself that contained its meaning. Three years later, he wrote in his essay "Télé-Aphorismes" (which I discussed in Chapter 1 and which I reprint and translate as Appendix 1) that "McLuhan understood the inner workings of television very early on, that is to say that the real message transmitted by television isn't the content of this or that broadcast, but the phenomenon of 'television' itself, in the sense that it transforms social habits, modes of perception and relating as it imposes a standard and homogenous vision of things through a completely confused language that neutralizes all content and transforms it into signs that only refer back to themselves" (29).[14] This is *Temps mort* to a "T." Tanner uses a repetitive form to emphasize the degree to which a sort of voyage has become banal for him; there are *a lot* of shots out car and train windows. But he chooses to break up this uniformity visually, and he never breaks it up in the same way; he inserts one and only one example of completely still imagery, shot/ reverse-shot, talking-heads documentary, and hand-held footage. And he even breaks up the shots out the window by overwhelming us with rain, but again, only once. What we have, on a purely visual level, is a lot of monotony that is interrupted by little bursts of different visual forms. These images shot out of trains and cars may look like dead time, but that illusion only hides the reality that many different forms of perception lie along this road, waiting to be discovered. Tanner's critique of the way that modernity dulls our senses begins with the simple choice to violate what he calls television's "completely codified language" by putting consumer-grade Super 8 film onto the national television service. But he also refuses to impose his own "standard and homogenous vision of things," even though you get the sense from the Tarantino interview that *Temps mort* is made up *only* of material shot out of trains and cars. In fact, the film is quite diverse visually, and it is in that *visual* diversity, and the challenge that poses to television as a medium, where its critique of homogeneous vision is to be found. To follow the old engineer Charles from *Jonas*, he is showing us the movie-like landscape of riding from trains, the music-like landscape of driving, and several other visual forms as well.

The series *Ecoutez voir*, and especially Tanner's contribution to it, is very close to the kind of work that his compatriots Jean-Luc Godard and Anne-Marie Miéville were doing at this time. Indeed, Miéville was one of the filmmakers who contributed a film to *Ecoutez voir*. She and Godard had just finished two very long, experimental series for French television: *Six fois deux : sur et sous la communication* (1976, about 6 hours in all) and *France/ Tour/Détour/Deux/Enfants* (1977, also about 6 hours in all). It's thus strange to see Jérôme Prieur, in France's *Quinzaine Littéraire*, offer the argument about *Jonas* that it "is sometimes curiously close to *Six fois deux*, Godard's series of broadcasts" (26).[15] Prieur has in mind a shared concern with broad philosophical issues like time, and that's a fair enough point. But if he had waited a few months, and tuned into Swiss television, he would have found a real companion for *Six fois deux*. These Godard-Miéville series are far more meta-cinematic than anything in *Jonas* and are built on the premise of exploring different forms of televisual communication. That's especially true of *Six fois deux*, which even includes an episode on a Super 8 filmmaker named René, who seems to have the same approach to filmmaking that many Sunday-painters have to oils and watercolours. This sort of exploration was the project for *Ecoutez voir* as well, and thus it's no surprise to see Miéville involved. These are television series about television itself, and the way that it was transforming our perception of the world and our ability to communicate. But they were also both series about the specific sorts of interventions that could be made by low-end image technologies, such as Super 8 or ¾-inch video. The possibilities for transforming a form of image-making that seemed increasingly close to consumer-capitalist domination seemed to be coming from consumerism itself; Tanner, like Godard and Miéville, saw Super 8 as a implement of struggle (one among many, but an important one) against a mass media whose strategy for expansion seemed, by and large, defined by homogenization.

The Super 8 experimental phase, though, was fleeting; Tanner turned right back to narrative filmmaking with 1979's *Messidor*, and following that he made another narrative film that revisited the most famous character that he had created with Berger. *Light Years Away* (1981, released in French as *Les Années lumière*) is a strange film, and there are few critics who see this as among his strongest work. The film is generally known as *Light Years Away* because it was Tanner's first film in English since 1957's *Nice Time*. Rather than the bustling Piccadilly Circus at midnight, the setting here is the west coast of Ireland, specifically the damp, rocky region known as Connemara. Its protagonist is a young man named Jonas, who we find out about halfway through the film (when he is at a lawyer's office taking care of a will) is twenty-five years of age, and born in 1975. You'd never know the film was set in the year 2000; Tanner remarked sardonically to the *Cahiers du cinéma*'s Serge Toubiana that "It's set in the year 2000 to show that nothing changes" (x).[16] For a film so self-reflexive (its protagonist having been so important to a film that Tanner had made just a few years earlier), it seems strange that it is actually adapted from a novel: Daniel Odier's *La voie sauvage* (Odier was interested in mysticism, and has also translated several Indian spiritual texts into French). The film, like the novel, tells the story of a young man who, searching for some kind of enlightenment and discouraged by a series of dead-end bar jobs in the city (unnamed, but in the film visibly Dublin), is taken in by a mysterious, flight-obsessed old-timer named Yoshka. Todd Gitlin saw the narrative as hopelessly banal, writing in his 1984 article on Tanner for *Harper's* that "Austerity got the better of Tanner, and we were left with a countercultural sorcerer's tale in the mode of Carlos Castaneda" (70). By this Gitlin presumably means that the spirituality embodied by Yoshka – who talks to birds and insists that Jonas, as a rite of initiation, restore and then man a gas station that lies alongside a road that literally nobody drives on and then turns out to have no gas anyway – is thin, sentimental and undemanding, and that sounds about right to me.

What is noteworthy about the film is its use of landscape. Gitlin's *Harper's* article also agues for the existence of "a sequence of five films, all lyric and melancholy explorations of ways out of complacent bourgeois Switzerland" (69). These were *Charles mort ou vif*, *La Salamandre*, *Le Milieu du monde*, *Jonas*, and *Messidor*. That seems like a reasonable way to understand Tanner's evolution throughout the 1970s, and, given that, *Light Years Away* really is the next step; Tanner leaves bourgeois complacency by actually leaving Switzerland. Geneva and its environs may have been following the patterns of city-swallowing-country that we see underway in *Jonas*, but the west of Ireland circa 1980 was still proving remarkably resistant to this.[17] The reason, of course, was the desperate underdevelopment that had characterized the region for centuries, both before and after independence. The way that this sort of underdevelopment appears in the film is slightly edgier than the basically congenial rural bohemianism that characterizes the farm of *Jonas*. Yoshka's compound, such as it is, is rendered by Tanner as dirty, rusty, cold, and wet, in a way that creates a very viscerally evoked misery for Jonas, a misery that is quite absent from *Jonas qui aura 25 ans*. But the politics of this misery, of this desolation, the reasons that Connemara has proven so resistant to integration by the metropolis, are absent. There is nothing in the film about British colonialism, nothing in the film about the often shocking indifference of the newly independent Irish state towards its hinterland, nothing about the long history of insularity and xenophobia that characterized a lot of the culture of western Ireland, nothing even about the linguistic specificity of the place (Connemara is home to the Republic of Ireland's largest and most intact Gaeltacht, or Irish-Gaelic-speaking area). The place becomes almost abstract – a bit like the landscape between Geneva and Berne in *Temps mort*, really. It is never even identified as Ireland; the only way anyone would know this would be by identifying accents (including that of the Irish actor who plays Jonas, Mick Ford), or by identifying visual cues (such as Dubin's River Liffey and Hay'penny Bridge, visible from the window of Yoshka's lawyer, or the stony, rainy landscape so distinctive to Connemara).

This is very different from the way that Berger was representing a similar landscape during this period, and Tanner's movement away from an engagement with bourgeois materialism was very different from Berger's movement away from an engagement with bourgeois materialism. *Light Years Away* was released two years after Berger published his novel *Pig Earth* (1979), the first of the trilogy of works about peasant life in alpine France that I have mentioned already. The text of the novel itself is highly detailed about the economic and political pressures that peasant communities faced. Berger asserts in the book's "Historical Afterword" (which I mentioned in the last chapter) that "No class has been or is more economically conscious than the peasantry. Economics consciously determines or influenced every ordinary decision which a peasant takes. But his economics are not those of the merchant, nor those of bourgeois or marxist political economy" (197). In addition to a vigorous engagement with economic complexity of Europe's margins that is missing in *Light Years Away*, Berger was also becoming interested in those margins' political paradoxes. Just as *Light Years Away* sees Tanner abandoning the politics of Switzerland for an engagement with a spare spiritualism, *Pig Earth* sees Berger abandoning the ideological wrangling between metropolis and village for an engagement with what he calls "peasant conservatism." He writes of this ideology that:

> Peasant conservatism, within the context of peasant experience, has nothing in common with the conservatism of a privileged ruling class or the conservatism of a sycophantic petty-bourgeoisie. The first is an attempt, however vain, to make their privileges absolute; the second is a way of siding with the powerful in exchange for a little delegated power over other classes. Peasant conservatism scarcely defends any privilege. Which is one reason why, much to the surprise of urban political and social theorists, small peasants have so often rallied to the defence of richer peasants. It is conservatism not of power but of meaning.

It represents a depository (a granary) of meaning preserved from lives and generations threatened by continual and inexorable change. (208)

Both Berger and Tanner were, then, breaking with the political project that seemed to reach a peak with *Jonas*. But even though Berger's break seems to invoke the dreaded spectre of the conservative, it really is Tanner who, at this time, was moving away from traditions of struggle and activism. Berger did become more conservative during this period, but this didn't mean that he started campaigning for Thatcher. Indeed, in addition to becoming more conservative, his work also became more intensely social-ist. The ability of tightly knit communities to resist the totalizing forces of capitalist-led modernization is the central topic of the "Into their Labours" trilogy, and of later novels such as *To the Wedding* (1995) and *Here Is Where We Meet* (2005). Tanner, on the other hand, was using a character that he and Berger had created as signifier of leftist redemption in a way that basically ignored economics, and which used modernization as a kind of ghostly spectre signifying either doom or the antithesis of dreams (through images of the decaying gas station which so impedes both his and Yoshka's spiritual evolution) rather than as a social force. I reject the idea that *Jonas qui aura 25 ans en l'an 2000* is about the defeat of politics. That is what we see in *Light Years Away*.

Tanner and Berger's characters then sat fallow for quite a few years, until Tanner's 1995 film *Fourbi* (which he co-wrote with Bernard Comment). This is less a re-make of *La Salamandre* than it is a telling of a similar story using the same basic characters. The most important of those characters, of course, is Rosemonde herself, and a young woman named Rosemonde is the protagonist of *Fourbi*. The two films have a basically identical open-ing sequence, a long shot that tracks alongside Rosemonde as she walks next to the Rhône in Geneva (Rosemonde looks slightly broody in *La Salamandre*; in *Fourbi* she is gesticulating wildly with her hands as she lis-tens to a Walkman). But rather than someone who shot her tedious uncle under circumstances that nobody can quite establish, *Fourbi*'s Rosemonde killed a man who raped her and was then acquitted of murder. And rather than Pierre, the *engagé* but relatively hard-nosed freelance journalist and his dreamy poet collaborator Paul (whose actors, Jean-Luc Bideau and Jacques

Denis, make cameo appearances in *Fourbi*, the former as a butcher and the latter as a barman), we have here Kévin, a pony-tailed TV producer (who offers occasional bursts of American-accented English) trying to get in on the ground floor of a new private television network, and his pal Pierre, who he hires to work up a show based on Rosemonde's story. The argument that *La Salamandre*'s Pierre and Paul have about Rosemonde and reality – where Paul spins a great story about Rosemonde being from a poor, ignorant and giant Catholic family and an exasperated Pierre replies "It's reality that interests me... ... things!" – recurs in *Fourbi* as Kévin saying to Paul that he should make the TV show "fiction, but based on reality; a film like any other!"[18] There are a lot of similarly minor changes to familiar parts of the narrative: it is not really the writers but the actress who is to play Rosemonde (played by Tanner's daughter Cécile) who tries and ultimately fails to befriend and understand her; instead of learning early in the story that Rosemonde had had a child and given it up for adoption, in *Fourbi* we learn in the film's final shots that Rosemonde is pregnant, etc.

But the key change is a matter of shifting from a critical sensibility regarding communication generally and mass media forms such as television secondarily to a more acidic and cynical indictment of televisual voyeurism. Kévin clearly plans to make Rosemonde's traumatic tale of being raped into a sort of reality-TV show, and at one point Paul tells Marie of a plan to allow the audience to vote as to whether Rosemonde is guilty or innocent. The show's major underwriter is a dog food manufacturer called Doggy Bag (the film's title is the name of the company's mascot, who the four main characters are walking along the Rhône as the film ends), and keeping them onside is a constant concern for Kévin. The hard, cold crassness of television is thus on constant display here, both in emotional and economic terms. It is no minor plot point that the show based on Rosemonde's life is being developed for a private television network; such networks had been relatively uncommon in French-speaking Switzerland, and their emergence throughout the 1990s did seem to be a harbinger of the loss of televisual idealism about communicating with the general public in new ways. In *La Salamandre* Berger and Tanner were critiquing such idealism along largely philosophical lines: the indeterminate nature of interpretation, "The object is not purely perceived, but it is *there*," etc. In *Fourbi* this sort of idealism is basically beyond critique; the idea that Rosemonde could be meaningfully represented is practically off the radar screen. The state-run service of the 1970s might not have been able to deliver on its promises of civic engagement via modern communication, but by the 1990s we are in an increasingly privatized landscape where words like "engagement" or "communication," or even "promises," are more or less irrelevant. The lone figure of engagement is Marie (who, being played by his daughter, is certainly readable as an autobiographical stand-in for Tanner himself), who tries to build the sorts of connections with Rosemonde that Paul had sought in *La Salamandre*. Furthermore, Karin Viaud's performance as Rosemonde is wonderfully vivid; she presents her as full as life and dynamism, but also just on the edge of what could be very real mental illness. Her performance is more technically demanding than Bulle Ogier's 1971 turn as Rosemonde, I would say, for the 1995 incarnation is a genuinely damaged person, and yet also someone who is verily overflowing with a zest for life. Ogier's Rosemonde was more detached (and more genuinely alienated), but the depth of that detachment made her a bit easier for the viewer to understand her. Viaud's Rosemonde, though, really is a quandary; she is passionate and broken in equal parts, as though these were two elements of a single dialectic. The final scene, where she lags perpetually behind Marie and the two guys as they walk the dog, finally confides to Marie that she is pregnant, and answers "of course" to her question of whether she will keep the child, is nothing short of luminous (and, of course, recalls the climactic scene of *Jonas*). The television of committed writers and directors is clearly dead; for Tanner in *Fourbi*, the medium's last hope appears to be in idealistic performers, who still believe that actors can, with enough commitment, present the mystery of everyday life.

More than any of the other films he made based on his collaborations with Berger, Tanner's *Fourbi* feels deeply pessimistic. This is especially so in the light of his "Télé-Aphorismes" essay. He wrote there that "one of the most interesting recent shows on TV Romande was done by an Italian feminist group which obtained authorization, as part of its standing, to re-enact a rape trial. Using lightweight gear and in black and white. Will 'great' TV enter into the courtroom?" (26).[19] Here, fifteen years later, is the travesty of that rigorous, tele-political engagement: a reality-show-style recreation of the trial where the audience gets to vote on *the rape victim's* guilt or innocence. For anyone who knows Tanner's work, the hardness of that fall, especially as it is realized through a re-telling of one of his best films, is discernable.

It took Jonas himself to pull him out of this funk. 2000's *Jonas et Lila, à demain* (also co-written with Bernard Comment) is the most hopeful of Tanner's "Berger sequels," and like *Temps mort* and *Fourbi* it uses the process of image-making to communicate this view of the world. Like *Light Years Away* this is another story of Jonas in the year 2000, but this is a very different Jonas. Instead of the alienated, mystically inclined, Irish-accented drifter, this Jonas is a film student, in love with a young African immigrant named Lila. His mentor is an elderly man named Anziano, an old film-maker who now lives in relative seclusion in Marseilles (in a possible nod to *Le Retour d'Afrique*, he tells Jonas at one point that he is at this house because an old friend of his is spending two years in Africa). When Jonas has his expensive, school-owned video camera stolen, Anziano gives him a tiny hi-8 camera, warning him that it is dangerous because it will free him.

Tanner does indeed present Jonas as freed because he is able to make images in a new way, and this affects his political as well as his emotional life; this duality is where the film's clearest debt to Berger is visible. The first images that Jonas makes with his camera are of garbage dumps and (in a clear nod to the imagery of *Temps mort*) landscapes shot out of windows of cars and trains. But then he and some friends decide to make what one of them calls "ciné-tracts, comme à l'époque," referring to the famous group of shorts that both were filmed and shown during the strikes of May '68. At first these are videos of pranks, most of which are simply chaotic: they first put on ski masks, kick a soccer ball in the china section of a department store, and then (in a clear nod this time to *La Salamandre*) they all go onto a Geneva tram and simultaneously light up cigars (as one woman protests vigorously, a well-dressed old codger comes over to join them). But they turn melancholically political as well. Jonas makes one video when Lila's perpetually broke father takes him for a ride on the garbage skiff that he pilots down the Rhône. Another sequence has Jonas showing Anziano his video footage of an anti-military protest in Geneva that had turned violent; he marvels at the images, saying "La police protègent l'armée de la population; c'est une belle métaphore, non?" And they are intimate: Jonas and Lila film each other in bed, and later on Lila and their actress friend Irena (who Jonas met when he interrupted the shooting of a Russian-mob-financed porno) shoot each other as they have sex with Jonas. This mixture of subject matter shows a diversity of concern, a real humanist engagement, that was largely missing from the original ciné-tracts "à l'époque." Those were, more or less, documents of an evolving series of strikes; they were highly functional. Not so the videos shot by Jonas. The way in which they mix material that is materialist (garbage), anarchist (cigars on trams), insurgent (street protests), and personal (sex), strongly recalls the concerns of the films Berger and Tanner made together, especially *Le Milieu du monde*. Geoff Dyer is one critic who has very keenly pointed to Berger's sense of radical politics as needing to encompass more than the economic single-mindedness of Marx. This is surely visible in *Jonas qui aura 25 ans en l'an 2000*, a film that I, in perverse agreement with its harshest critics in *Jump Cut*, see as defined by a preference for Rousseau over Marx. It is visible in *Jonas et Lila à demain* as well, and Dyer could very well be writing about that film when he explains how Berger's work overall rejects an apolitical formalism:

> At the same time, he vehemently refuses to succumb to a vulgar materialism which in its assertion of the primacy of the economic derides the claim of the spiritual and the cultural. The strains and creaks in his early work were the product of his having to maintain this refusal in the face of the rigid base superstructure model which was then dominant within Marxist thought. Recently, however, the model of base superstructure has been challenged, notably by Raymond Williams [in *Problems in Materialism and Culture*] as "essentially a bourgeois formula; more specifically, a central position of utilitarian thought." (155)

Escape from utilitarianism, an ideological cousin of normalization, is a big part of *Jonas et Lila*. Jonas is engaged with material concerns, but he in also longing for a fuller connection, if not to the spiritual and the cultural, then to the emotional and the cultural.

This is manifested not only through images that challenge Swiss culture's reputation as clean, orderly, and rational, but especially at the end of the film. This ending is dominated by grainy video images of Jonas and Lila's trip to Senegal. Lila is in most of this footage and Jonas can be heard off-screen, presumably holding the camera. The climax comes when Lila is reunited with her grandmother, who she surprises by knocking on the door of her crowded apartment complex. Like the ending of *Fourbi* there is a slightly overwhelming quality to the images ("bouleversant" would be the word in French). But whereas this quality in *Fourbi* came from a sense that any future for moving images lay with committed actors, here the sense of the sublimely emotional comes from the degraded video image, the simplicity of someone capturing the everyday with a distinctly unpretentious technology. These images are full of the sort of context which Berger has argued that photographs need to respect – the feeling of personal histories of immigration, or feelings of the loneliness of return (Lila laments on the voice-over how she doesn't remember much of the language, how these people consider her a European now), or the bustle and confusion of crowded markets when experienced by outsiders. Berger wrote in his 1978 essay "Uses of Photography" (published in *About Looking*) that:

> The private photograph – the portrait of a mother, a picture of a daughter, a group photo of one's own team – is appreciated and read in a context *which is continuous with that from which the camera removed it....* Nevertheless such a photograph remains surrounded by the meaning from which it was severed.... The contemporary public photograph usually presents an event, a seized set of appearances, which has nothing to do with us, its readers, or with the original meaning of the event. It offers information, but information severed from all lived experience. (51–52; italics his)

These videos feel like private images, demanding to be read "in a context which is continuous with that from which the camera removed it." But they are part of a public, fictional work, one that tries to represent political, social, and emotional experiences in all of their complexity. *Jonas et Lila à demain* thus sees Tanner coming full circle from where he found himself with *Temps mort*. Using low-end, consumer-grade imagery, his task is to recover the submerged expressiveness of the everyday: the landscape between Geneva and Berne, garbage boats on the Rhône, apartments in Senegal crowded with families. *Light Years Away* and *Fourbi* were less successful works, if for no other reason than that they were marked by an abandonment of the socio-political in favour of either abstract mysticism or cynical pessimism. *Temps mort* and *Jonas et Lila*, on the other hand, are films that, although made without Berger's collaboration, strongly reflect that greatest of postwar English writers' desire to find both a politics and an aesthetics that tightly integrates the ineffably quotidian. Berger and Tanner, no: but these films are made by Tanner, with Berger always in their philosophical shadows.

So perhaps this is what constitutes political cinema: a practice that tries to expand our understanding of both cinema (and so uses a non-dominant form) and politics (and so moves beyond vulgar materialist assumptions about human experience), and which does so by intertwining the two. The 1970s saw an experiment in this kind of filmmaking; it was not *sui generis* (it had important connections in work that had been done in the 1950s and 60s, in both television and literature), and it didn't simply vanish like an extinguished match (work in the 1980s, 90s, and 2000s attempted to continue elements of the project). But these three feature films that John Berger and Alain Tanner made together – *La Salamandre, Le Milieu du monde*, and *Jonas qui aura 25 ans en l'an 2000* – deserve a more central place in the history of European cinema than they have heretofore been afforded. Their vision is unified without being repetitive, and it is a vision of a society wrestling uncertainly with modernity, a vision rendered in a way that renews narrative film language but does so from *within* that language's traditions. Given the challenges that a globalized Hollywood cinema represents (and has represented, basically since the end of the First World War) for people engaged with political cinema, filmmakers and critics alike, discussion of these films could hardly be more urgent.

Notes

1 "La culture suisse n'existe pas. Nous ne sommes ni une nation, ni un peuple, ni à plus forte raison une culture. D'ailleurs, la Suisse est un pays infilmable."

2 "Les Suisses ne forment pas un peuple, n'ont pas une culture, mais se rattachent à plusieurs autres."

3 "Bref, la culture suisse existe bel et bien : d'ailleurs nous l'avons rencontrée … dans les films d'Alain Tanner."

4 "S'il n y a pas de culture suisse, autant démanteler les institutions telles que l'Office fédéral de la culture ou Pro Helvetia, en attendant que le marché sacre de nouvelles stars à la Pipilotti Rist et autres Mario Botta. Alain Tanner est sûrement le dernier à penser comme les néo-libéraux, et pourtant son désabusement risque bel et bien de faire le jeu de ceux-là."

5 "De plus, sous le feu de l'artillerie hollywoodienne et de ses alliés, la culture helvétique était carrément menacée de colonisation…. Nos rues, nos maisons, nos concitoyens commencent a se transformer en choses vues, regardées, commentées. Le cinéma suisse, le cinéma national, peu nous importe à la limite : nous voulons simplement que les cinéastes qui vivent à Zurich, Lausanne ou Genève puissent s'exprimer, et le cinéma suisse suivra."

6 "… la *topographie* (la Suisse comme milieu du monde capitaliste, mi-lieu où se recoupent toutes les frontières, utopie)."

7 "Dans les films de Tanner la Suisse (ce qu'elle *symbolise*, le système capitaliste : car la Suisse est d'emblée irréelle) se retrouve mais, comme dans un miroir, annulée, réduite aux apparences. Il ne s'y trouve aucun des signes pleins de l'existence coutumière de la Suisse (ce par quoi on prétend qu'elle existe) : sommets enneigés, banques et banquières, ni même travailleurs immigrés ; quand ces signes apparaissent (ils ne font effectivement que des apparitions) c'est vidé de leur signification : dans *Jonas* le banquier gras et mou dans la boîte de nuit ; les immigrés « en passant » ; les feux rouges de Genève ; la campagne suisse ramenée à un espace non reconnaissable.… D'abord Tanner refuse le code (cette espèce de convention tacite du capital international) qui constitue la Suisse; aussi ses personnages ont tout l'espace qu'ils *veulent*."

8 "Nicht miterleben soll der Zuschauer, sondern sich auseinandersetzen" (*Über Realismus*, 38).

9 "… je fais appel à certains éléments relevant du code de représentation « classique » : effet de réel, personnages reconnaissables par exemple."

10 "Nulle « histoire de la littérature » (s'il doit s'en écrire encore) ne saurait être juste, qui se contenterait comme par le passé d'enchaîner des écoles sans marquer la coupure qui met alors à nu un nouveau prophétisme : celui de l'écriture. « Changer la langue, » mot mallarméen, est concomitant de « Changer le monde », mot marxien : il y a une écoute *politique* de Mallarmé, de ceux qui l'ont suivi et le suivent encore."

11 "… les passages d'un plan à un autre ôtent au spectateur toute possibilité d'échapper au raisonnement."

12 "En guise de prologue, un premier film de John Berger (écrivain et scénariste de Tanner) présente les quatre auteurs."

13 "Ca vous arrive encore de voyager en train ? Qu'est-ce que vous voyez ? Le paysage qui défile, comme au cinéma. Mais dans la locomotive, le paysage ne défile pas. Vous allez dedans. Toujours : dedans, dedans, dedans. C'est comme une musique. Vous allez devant vous, jusqu'au horizon, et puis ça continue, jusqu'à l'endroit où les rails se rejoignent. Et ils ne se rejoignent jamais."

14 "MacLuhan [*sic*] avait compris très tôt le mécanisme profond de la télévision. Ce qui signifie que le message réel transmis par la télévision n'est pas le contenu de telle ou telle émission, mais le phénomène « télévision » en lui-même, en ce sens qu'il transforme les habitudes sociales, les modes de perception et de relations, qu'il impose une vision standard et homogène des choses à travers un langage complètement codifié qui neutralise tous les contenus et les transforme en signes qui ne renvoient qu'à eux-mêmes."

15 "… le film de Tanner est curieusement parfois très voisin de *Six fois deux*, la série d'émissions de Godard."

16 "Il est situé en l'an 2000 pour montrer que rien ne changera."

17 That's not true anymore, of course. In the *Cahiers du cinéma* interview with Serge Toubiana about *Light Years Away*, Tanner went on to say that "Really, here, in this region, it was like this in 1950, thirty years ago, so there's no reason that it would be different in the year 2000, in twenty years" (x) ["De toute façon, ici, dans cette région, c'était comme ça en 1950, il y a trente ans, donc il n'y a pas de raison pour que cela soit différent en l'an 2000, dans vingt ans"]. The Republic of Ireland actually underwent enormous changes in the 90s and 00s as a result of its "Celtic Tiger" economy, changes that did indeed reach into Connemara, parts of which have become a de facto suburb of Galway City.

18 "Un fiction, mais d'après la réalité. Un film comme les autres !"

19 "Par exemple, l'une des émissions les plus intéressantes de la TV Romande ces dernières temps fut le fait d'un groupe féministe italien qui obtient l'autorisation, à partir de son statut à lui, de rendre compte d'un procès de viol. En matériel léger et noir/blanc. La « grande » TV serait-elle entrée dans la salle du tribunal?"

APPENDIX

ONE

"TÉLÉ-APHORISMES"

by Alain Tanner

Translation Note: This text was originally published in the Swiss film annual *Cinema* (1980), in a special issue devoted to television called "Sieht das Fernsehen?" It appeared in both French and German (it was translated into German by Martin Schaub) but has never appeared in English. Because it was organized alphabetically, I have retained the French versions of each heading.

My desire to translate and reprint this essay was yet another part of this book that Tanner thought was a little strange, and, although he was happy to grant permission for my work, he was at pains to point out that he considers this essay a historical document of little relevance today. I want to present it here because it represents the high-point of his thinking about television, an intellectual process that began in the 1960s with extraordinary television films like *Docteur B., médecin de campagne* (1968) and went right on through to his contribution to the experimental television series *Ecoutez voir*, which aired in 1978, two years before this essay was published. Tanner's radical work in television (often done alongside Berger) is very much of a piece with that of his compatriots Jean-Luc Godard and Anne-Marie Miéville. Godard and Miéville's massive experimental series *Six fois deux : sur et sous la communication* and *France/Tour/Détour/Deux/Enfants* aired on French television in 1976 and 1980, respectively, and Miéville also contributed a Super 8 film (on family violence) to *Ecoutez voir*. Similarly radical work was going on, with varying degrees of success, all over the North Atlantic, at roughly the same time. Ireland of the 1960s and 70s would be an especially fruitful point of comparison; the key text there is Jack Dowling, Leila Doolan, and Bob Quinn's 1969 book *Sit Down and Be Counted*, which had a preface by Raymond Williams. This was written shortly after the three authors had resigned from the Republic of Ireland's state-owned television service RTÉ; their reasons for resigning had a lot to do with the station's increasing obsession with technical perfection, and their argument that this constituted an ideologically motivated form of censorship and social control is very close indeed to what Tanner is arguing in this essay. Television may have moved on from these sorts of debates and experiments, but the medium is much poorer for it.

Arme / Gun: As an armament, television is essentially a weapon of dissuasion.

Bouche / Mouth: When a politician speaks on television, cover his mouth with your hand and while still listening to what he says, look at his eyes. Oftentimes they'll be saying the opposite. Television is an art of the mouth, and it's not always very appetizing.

Consumation / Consumption: Television basically belongs to the sphere of consumption, and not the sphere of communication. In order to have communication, you need an exchange, some speech that circulates, asking for and obtaining a response. "Thus, all of contemporary media architecture is built on this last definition: *they are things that never allow a response.* That makes any process of exchange impossible (other than as *simulations* of a response, themselves integrated into the process of the broadcast, which doesn't change the uni-linearity of communication in any way). That is their real abstraction. And it is on that abstraction that the system of social control and power is built." (Jean Baudrillard, *Pour une critique le l'économie politique du signe*)

Démocratie / Democracy: In order to please everyone – and to displease no one – television cuts [*fait un découpe*] horizontally across the public, that is to say that it breaks things into categories according to other people's requirements; sportscasts, international politics, game shows, singalongs, etc. But all of these categories express themselves in the same way, in the same fashion. Instead the cut should be *vertical*, between those who want *this* type of televisual expression and those who want *that* other type.

Dialectique / Dialectic: In its terrible homogeneity, television is the antithesis of all dialectic thought.

Différence / Difference: Electronic dots or photographic image. The geometry of the gaze in comparison with the screen and their dimensions. Magic and fascination and indifferent consumption. Empty or full movie theatre and living room with its "related" activity. Cold image and hot image. State control or commercial control, with its gaps. Often-radical differences. Put an image of a TV presenter on a movie screen. Estrangement and comical effects guaranteed.

Dimanche / Sunday: Try (because it seems a lot of people do it) to spend an entire Sunday in front of the television. It's a fairly dreadful experience.

Dire / Say: Almost nobody wants to "say" cinema anymore. Nobody ever "said" television.

Disputes / Disputes: The groups that struggle here for the "democratization" of television, on the left and the right, have not for a second thought that the stage they're fighting on, or rather the stage (the place) that they're trying to be so invested in, is already *marked* in advance. And that a few minutes in the air knocked from a leftist or rightist MP won't change much: no more than a spot on the boards that govern TV. They've got to know that the content of television is television itself, within its system of signs (see **Message / Message**). They must also know that there's little or no difference between the image of a left-wing MP's mouth and a right-wing MP's mouth (see **Bouche / Mouth**).

Dormir / Sleep: Audience selection that operates on the basis of social standing (people who go to bed early or late, according to their profession and the hour their alarm-clock rings) proceeds from a curious vision of "workers" and "intellectuals." Do we really believe that intellectuals watch television late at night? And if so, why? For a Mozart quartet, lit up all candy-pink?

Doute / Doubt: Profound expression of doubt is fundamental in our system of thought today, whatever form you give it. Television, though, has no right to doubt. It has to know, because of its power-monopoly. Hence its boring speeches, its platitudes, and its sense of not being very truthful.

Durée / Length: One of modern cinema's major conquests is its work on duration, on the length of its shots, on dead time,[1] on time that is not systematically "filled up." This acquisition, even if it's been severely demolished in cinema, has always been inhibited in television as well as in fiction and documentary. You must always fill things up, pull the spectator along, so that he doesn't have time to get bored, and suddenly "move on to something else." These old Hollywood methods are now forever perpetuated by television's diktat.

Economie / Economy: Two totally contradictory propositions. One: television must be free (including the TV set, which will be provided by the state). Two: you have to pay every time you turn it on (by dropping some coins into a slot for that purpose). The result is the same: you watch a lot less. A certain re-valorization of images must come from that.

Entrée (Port d') / Entry (Port of): Working for television can be, in some cases, a passport, an "open sesame!" (it's the voice of power that's going inside). The reverse can also be true: that this voice of power stays at the door. For example, one of the most interesting recent shows on TV Romande[2] was done by an Italian feminist group which obtained authorization, as part of its standing, to re-enact a rape trial. Using lightweight gear and in black and white. Will "great" TV enter into the courtroom?

Etalon / Standard: The standard TV image is the presenter seated next to some flowers. All of the techie ideology of "quality" images, another form of censorship, develops from that.

Etat d'âme / Scruples: When the author of a TV show or a film is told to check his scruples at the door in order to hide entirely behind the all-powerful "good subject" and honestly serve the "average viewer," there is a gap. And this gap, created by the absence of *one* voice (judged too private and not anonymous enough to interest the audience – see **Spectateur / Viewer**) is also filled not by a little extra happiness from a "big audience," but by all the signals emitted by power.

Evênement / Event: It's harder and harder for television to "create an event." In the domain of information it can still try to do that by fictionalizing reality a bit (i.e., French TV's attempts to create an obsession with war at the beginning of the year). In the domain of fiction, this doesn't happen anymore, at least inasmuch as fiction stomps on the flowers of historical documents. In order to create a TV event, you must do nothing less than go to the grounds of the Nazi death camps (*Holocaust*: see **Mémoire / Memory**). But *Holocaust* was never anything other than a TV event, and in no way shape or form a historical event, as they wanted us to believe.

Farine / Flour: At the end of the week, the Geneva dailies publish a TV grid called "What's on for Six Days." It's a bit like how they used to reassure people by saying "there's enough flour for six days."

Fiction / Fiction: On television, fiction "fictionalizes" badly. The electronic image, deprived of its powers of fascination, of myth, tends to erase the border between fiction and documentary, and in order to make an image, the border between "a lie" and "the truth." This is why on television, documentary is much stronger than fiction. But just as fiction loses a lot of its powers, diluted bits of information that are, in the cinema, pulled apart from the fictional texture, come floating back to surface on television. Thus it occurs to some people with a weak cultural background to mix fiction and documentary, to take the "information" gleaned from fiction as money in the bank and to make stuff up for the news broadcasts. And as the voice that comes out of the little box is "them," "they," power, then the one who tells the truth and can't be fooled, well you see how this amalgamation could be a lie. This informative quality of fiction also stands for a kind of "retro" vision of the world, backward-looking inasmuch as overall, public TV is fed essentially by fictions that come from cinema and are finally broadcast, quite a while after their production.

Garanties / Guarantees: TV films cost a lot of money today, even when they're given a leg up, than do fiction films made for cinemas (at least in our country). It's a question of "guarantees." Guarantees for the script, for a "good subject" that will lead to a "classical" form of shooting, with a big crew (a guarantee of employment) that will guarantee the technical "quality." Guarantee of the means to get it all together substitutes for the idea and the work. Guarantee against that *madness* which is, in some part, filmmaking.

Godard (Jean-Luc): "If nothing happens on television, it's because everything is happening."

Grille / Grid: The organization of programs, for some years (!) called, with a ghastly accuracy: the program grid [*grille des programmes*].

Habitude / Habit: You get used to it. You get used to everything.

Histoires / Stories: Stories, stories, still more stories. Lives lived by procurement.

Idéologie / Ideology: Look elsewhere.

Imaginaire / Imaginary: "We must talk about the cold light of television, about why it's so offensive to the imagination (including that of children), for the reason that it does not animate any imagery, and for the simple reason that *it is no longer an image*. Cinema, on the other hand, is still endowed with an intense imagination, because cinema *is* an image. That is to say not only a screen and a form, but *a myth*, something that still has a double, a ghost, a mirror, a dream. None of this is in a TV image, which suggests nothing, which magnetizes, which is only a screen, and not even that: a miniature terminal that, in fact, immediately finds its way into your head – you're the screen, and TV is watching you – as it transistorizes all of your neurons and goes by like a magnetic tape. A tape, not an image" (Jean Baudrillard, *Cahiers du cinéma*).

Information / Information: Television has tried – in vain – to invent a language and form. All of that was very quickly abandoned when we understood that television is not a matter of forms but instead of signs – and of content. Television only works on the level of information itself, and at the second degree it goes back to the socio-political. Nothing else. This is the source of TV's obsession with the subject, of *what* it speaks about and never with *how* it speaks. Information overflows everywhere on television, which is still solidly in the grip of the dominant ideology. It's omnipresent; in series, commercials, TV films. To a Radical[3] MP who complained to me once day about the excessive influence of the left in political debates, I replied that his group already had 95 per cent of the airtime. Did they want 100 per cent?

Investissement / Investment: "Everything that is invested by the spectator in the image, with the look, the brain, and the body as well, isn't invested elsewhere. That is to say it's not invested in social relations without images, not invested in communication" (Serge Toubiana, *Cahiers du cinéma*).

Liberté / Freedom: Television's freedom, the spectator's freedom, is simply being able to switch off the show. Miserable.

Mandat / Mandate: Who charged the state, one sunny day, with the task of, in the words of the SSR's statutes, "Educating, informing, entertaining" the people, through this enormous, "dominant school" that is television? As a citizen, I have no memory of being consulted.

Mémoire / Memory: Memory is the centre, the base of all creative work. Television's methods, where everything winds up as part of an endless and homogenous chain, only to finally erase itself, represents memory's liquidation. It is forgetting. Nothing better than serializing the great historical events only to expel them from human memory. (Best example: *Holocaust*.)

Message / Message: "The medium is the message." McLuhan understood the inner workings of television very early on. What this means is that the real message transmitted by television isn't the content of this or that broadcast, but the phenomenon of "television" itself, in the sense that it transforms social habits, modes of perception and relating, as it imposes a standard and homogenous vision of things through a completely confused language that neutralizes all content and transforms it into signs that only refer back to themselves. There is little to no cross-referencing or feedback. TV's signs exhaust themselves as quickly as they are absorbed. To again cite Baudrillard (*La Société de la consommation*, Gallimard): "what is received, assimilated, consumed is less a spectacle than the virtuality of all spectacles." "Thus the truth of the mass media is this: their function is to neutralize the living character, eventually of the world, and replace it with an alternate media universe that homogenizes one form after another, each one only signifying the others. In the end, they become each others' reciprocal content, and this is the *totalitarian 'message' of a society of consumption*." "What animates TV, by way of its technical organization, is the idea (the ideology) of a world visualize-able at will, arrange-able at will, and readable as images. It animates the ideology of *the total power of a system that reads a world that has become a sign system*. TV images try to be the metalanguage of an absent world...." "... and it's the substance of the world – broken up, filtered, reinterpreted according to its code [...] that we 'consume.' All value as a cultural or political event has faded from all the world's material, all industrially treated, finished, sign-laden cultural products."

Olympiades / Olympics: Somewhere between Brezhnev, Carter, and Afghanistan, there is television, worldvision. If the Moscow Olympics' only spectators were the people sitting in the bleachers of Lenin Stadium, Carter never would have sabotaged the games, which only exist on television, like the rest of the Olympic industry (exclusive contracts with Coca Cola, athletic wear, all of the enormous PR impact that results from an association with the TV-Games). What this does is punish the majority of TV viewers and advertisers involved by pointing the finger at Russia. It's the great universal mediator (TV) that allows him to take this position. Maybe one day there will be no wars, if there is no space on the grid to show them.

Paradoxe / Paradox: Television, or rather the television-effect, functions mostly on paradox. The first, and the most important, is the transformation of news [*information*] into fiction. We've already seen (see **Information / Information**) how fiction threatens to take on the status of TV news. But the final, overall effect is that the mass is constituted by a qualitative change that resembles a chemical process: at the moment that the overflow occurs – and it occurs very quickly – all news [*information*] changes to fiction. This is where the real status of fiction on television is to be found, in this turnaround that winds up as a sort of fictionalizing of the world. A fictional world.

Patron / Boss: It's not true that television's bosses are bosses, banks, capitalism, political parties, or what have you. Television's boss is the overall consensus that also includes all of the people, whose tastes and ideas television follows rather than precedes. Thus, because of a near-total refusal to think about images and sounds, we have a middling rather than democratic expression coming out of the box. Power is thus exerted through a sort of circulation, a vicious circle, that dissolves the responsibility for alienation into a magma that everyone winds up in. Television is a sort of national brotherhood. A sophist might say that it's the beginning of the dictatorship of the proletariat.

Phases / Phases: There have been three phases in the development of television, three ways to look at it. The first was a period of creativity, of work, and of a bit of belief. The second was the discovery of what television really is, accompanied by a perverse gorging on codes and signs, and a sort of third-degree joy in those codes and signs, a joy that goes right on up to understanding, and then to the quick exhaustion of that understanding. The third phase is now: a piece of furniture, with a bit of soccer and some old movies late at night.

Politiciens / Politicians: Swiss politicians are fairly shrewd: they aren't on television much. It's probably an old peasant contemptuousness that makes them do that. In France, the political program has wound up totally ruining any credibility that politicians might have had, and is finally doing this for politics itself as well.

Pourcentage / Percentage: During the debates of the 1960s, about the right way to use the Loi sur le cinéma, some groups were worried about soon seeing signs of an "official art" and "official cinema." Today, nobody worries that 90 per cent of the images people see are state images, television images.

Prix / Price: Televisions are enormous, very expensive machines. The cost-value ratio is a bit imbalanced. If the same ratio were applied, for instance, to the vegetable trade, a kilo of potatoes would cost around 100 francs.

Publicité / Advertising: Commercials have a double function: simply commercial on one hand (selling things) but just as powerfully ideological on the other (selling a lifestyle, a behaviour appropriate to the sale). In a commercially logical way, ads ask for, and easily get, the best spots in the broadcast. They ask for privilege and they get it. Thus, its mixture with news-time brings it into a network that is strongly marked by ideology. To be democratic, we should give the same amount of airtime that the "dominant ideology" gets over to *silence*, or to very simple images, if possible still, but in any case *mute*.

Question / Question: Why read the news in the same voice that we hear in commercials: a lively, wily, sexy voice, soft like an airline hostess's? What is the source of this special power that a commercial's voice seems to have?

Reflet / Reflection: Now within its final and definitive phase, and created by a lanky bureaucratic machine, television (in all countries) has a harder and harder time creating its own original material. Work on TV today is a lot better than in the past. But the "moral" conditions of its creation are clearly degraded. This is why it must borrow from other fields of creative activity in order to make a televisual event, such as a soccer game, or something from Milan's La Scala. More and more, television reflects, borrows, distracts, ceremonializes. Harsher tongues say it steals or pillages. Or that it kills. Via its monopoly it enacts a process of *dispossession*, "thus, a song isn't really popular until the medium gives it a means to be via its buzz and hit-parades. Radio and TV sing for us, which is to say they sing instead of us" (Pierre Baudry, *Cahiers du cinéma*[4]). And still more: the makers of pop, disco or rock albums also make their own videos, videos of a distinctly promotional quality, which TV takes right up, all too happy not to have to make such things itself. In all of its programming, TV is happier and happier with advertising put in place by agents, press people, and other salesmen. The more television becomes "big," the more blubber it develops and the more it gives the sense of being powerless.

Règles (du jeu) / Rules (of the game): The television viewer is all-powerful (see **Patron / Boss**) but at the same time, the viewer's power is practically annulled by the rules of the game, which are the rules of the media (see **Message / Message**).

Réduction / Reduction: Television is an essentially reductive phenomenon.

Regard / Look: The direction of the look in television is a matter for experts. There are only two categories of people who know that they have to look into the lens, so they can address the viewer directly (which they completely fail to do; there is not the least amount of communication between the look and myself, who is looking at the look). The first group is made up of television people: journalists, presenters, newscasters. The second group is made up of politicians, who respond to a profession question from a journalist next to them by turning towards the camera (as they were so badly taught to do), in order to address the voters. This never fails to produce discomfort, in that it's tremendously rude to the journalist who asked you the question and who you then abandon to his fate as a simple foil. What's more, when the newscaster looks at *me* and says "now it's time for your show" (that's *my* show, which belongs to me), I feel diminished sitting there in my chair, and get the sense that the prefab smile that accompanies the address is semi-obscene.

Rentabilité / Profitability: I don't know why television is so preoccupied with the profitability of its programs, why it conceives of the 10:30 p.m. time slot as needing to be for a "big audience" (that is to say, the lowest common denominator). Television is performing the same calculation here that a film director makes when shooting a movie destined to turn a profit. Where is television's profit? Neither economic nor cultural in this case. So? In what rulebook do we find this obligation to pander to a "majority" at the expense of others? On TV Romande, we've recently descended to abysmal depths in the name of this policy.

Santé / Health: Television makes anyone who watches it for a long time hungry. This may seem strange at first, but it's easily proven psychologically. Whoever eats also drinks. An entire night in front of the TV leads to excessive drinking. This is not healthy.

Simulacre / Simulacrum: Television is the *site* of the simulacrum.

Solitude / Solitude: Not only is there no response to television's speech, but it deprives people of any communication they might have between themselves; you don't talk when the set is on. On one hand, it produces a fantastic unification of the social group; on the other, it atomizes everyone. We are more similar and more alone.

Son / Sound: On television, the entire message is conveyed through sound. Images, because of their overflowingness and their saturation, have their potential impact terribly devalued. Moreover, because of the laziness of those who make them and the strict censorship exercised upon signs, they end up by looking all alike, as though they were "taken" from the same material. Thus you're not really tied to the images; you look at them because they're there, but what really moves things along is sound. This is why the number one enemy of television is silence, a hole. A breakdown of the image is OK; you put up a card and play some music. But a breakdown of the sound creates a feeling of panic. Television is thus a sort of radio, but a radio where you have to be *here*, and not somewhere else. A big part of television's conditioning happens through this *here*, this couch in the family room. But when you say sound, you are necessarily saying speech, words. Television is a river of words more than images. Fear of silence, river of words: listen to the intolerable babble of soccer commentators, who supplant the sound of the players and the crowd, which can be quite lovely. The imagining of images no longer exists on television; sound has replaced it. And that sound is entirely made up of words. When you see a movie in the theatre, it's the story or the images that dance in your head. After an evening of TV, you surprise yourself by responding to an imaginary interview.

Spectateur / Viewer: *The* viewer, the *viewers*: doesn't exist. It's a massive, completely demagogic entity, which snuffs out any political conception of the audience. *The* audience: doesn't exist. It's everybody and nobody at the same time. You must say *a* viewer. Him, individual, compatriot, brother (who knows?), and then another and another and another, separately giving you, finally, the only audience possible: some (not *the*) viewers.

Sport / Sport: Everyone agrees that what "works" best on television is sport. There are two clear reasons for this. The first is that sport has no content. (It has some, sure, but only at the second degree, as a bit of "opium of the masses" and in terms of the extraordinary futility of sports reporting). But in the moment, during the actual sporting act, there is no content. The second reason is that it has a form, a there-ness, that even the worst productions can't miss. A runner who gets from point A to point B is a nearly definitive form. This lack of form and easily rendered content together mean that sport is less susceptible to censorship of the linguistic codes that it's always tripping over, since it has to disengage from content and fabricate forms.

Téléspectateur / TV Viewer: They say, "hey pal, have you thought of the average TV viewer?" Who is that, exactly? "It's the guy who works hard all day, doesn't like his job much, and, at night, plops down on his sofa and wants to be entertained." The state (TV) is charged with this responsibility, and the discourse of entertainment that it produces takes up more time than even the working day (while being part of the same ideological tissue).

Tonalité / Tone: Everyone who talks on television is obliged to adopt the tone of the average bourgeois. And his vocabulary.

Troubles (de la vue) / Troubles (with seeing): One day, working as a stadium assistant during a soccer match, I marvelled at the idea – just for a second, but in all sincerity – that when one of the teams scored, the players didn't right away replay it in slow motion.

Utopie / Utopia: Today television has fully replaced the sector of cinema that produces little B movies. Instead of these grim shows we have now, you dream of making little detective movies for TV: shot quickly and cheaply, violent, in black and white, in a system where you're always working. A guy can dream....

Valeur / Value: "My remark comes back to Baudrillard's thesis: this profitability of tuning in is no doubt solicited by the medium itself, which proposes that its spectator appropriate the imaginary value of the discourse. Nevertheless, while at the cinema, for example, you pay for your ticket to get two hours of spectacle, and if you leave the theatre in the middle of the screening, you really lose something. When you do or don't tune into the TV [*écoute la télé ou pas*], it's the same price, as they say. Furthermore, speech on TV is being devalued, dethroned (the proof of this dethroning can be found in the frequent disengagement of TV viewers; you walk around, you talk about something else....). In other words, we could suppose that this thesis also functions in another way: there's nothing to lose by not tuning into TV [*écouter la TV*]. Just as TV is an imaginary driver of value, and even *becomes* value, at the same time its value '*falls*'" (Pierre Baudry, *Cahiers du cinéma*[5]).

Vidéo / Video: There has always been a "plot" against communication, and more particularly against the image. Even more so against video, sequestered by television's monopoly and smothered by all its potential. Just as the little black and white Sony is struggling to become usable, everyone in TV declares that you have to use colour and sets technical norms that require heavier gear and bigger crews than 35 mm films. So what will TV do with the extraordinary potential of video? With its lightness, its ease of handling, its infinite adaptability? Everything interesting being done in video is being done outside of television (Armand Gatti, Godard, etc.), and when television shoots these swanky events in a big studio and on video, you feel like you're in a bakery. On the other hand, our corporations are starting to use video essentially as a means of surveillance (policing department stores and street corners), or now to sell pornography (videocassettes are coming....).

Voix / Voice: We've seen (see **Son / Sound** and **Bouche / Mouth**) that television is a medium of speech, of the voice – or the voice-over. The voice-over, omnipresent in documentaries and news, indicates (for television) that images are insufficient, that they don't say everything, or even, and often, that they say nothing at all and you can make them say whatever you want. Here's a story. As I was making a news clip for TV Romande, the journalist working with me said: "I'm going back to the hotel to write my script; get some shots that I can put between two interviews." What shots? "Doesn't matter, whatever you find. Shots." "Voice-over is a matter of double-grafting: graft a stronger sound onto other sounds, and onto images in a way that the first one becomes the general equivalent of live sound, the sound that gives the others value, by adding one of more sign less. Put in place a hierarchy of sounds, of voices that line up in a recorder that questions what the spectator hears, that wins over his engaged conscience. The other grafting: voice-over discourse presents the cinema as a mimetic practice and offers it a stage on which to speak. And a powerful voice-over in a film may very well be refused all power over the real. The power it has in a film (over the gaze of a spectator) is really the belief in being taken along the rails of power itself, in that it's not barred from representation" (Serge Toubiana, *Cahiers du cinéma*).

Yeux (Voir avec ses) / Eyes (See with one's own): The ideology of the visual, which in our society is confined to a sort of voyeuristic hysteria, has turned into a disbelief in what you see. It's almost as grave for a country that commits an act of violence to hold back the images of the act itself. A crestfallen-looking French newscaster at the beginning of the Afghanistan situation: he apologizes for not having *good* images to show us, and that we have to trust the words. The *proof* arrives a few days later, in the form of Russian soldiers in Kabul. Phew!

Zèbre (c'est la fin de l'alphabet, c'est pour conclure) / Zebra (it's the end of the alphabet, so this is to wrap up): After all that, what can you do? Adapting a slightly distant attitude surely won't do. Work from the inside? That would be absurd, given the solidity of the structures in place. In any event, the machine is heavy and its connections to power give it a sort of "negativity potential" [« *potentiel de négativité* »] that's difficult to avoid. But looking at it a bit more closely (which I've tried to do over these last few pages), you can see that it may still have something to ask of us and in a way we can answer, but by (when possible) putting an end to it. Except in very specific, and rare, socio-political circumstances, I think it's useless to give in to the temptation to go along, at whatever price, with TV's "message," however humanist it might be. It will be absorbed into the overall din and dissolve. So? Co-productions between film and TV? Sure, if the images break away from the habitual naturalism and bring a bit of "edginess" to television as it acts as a kind of financial support system for cinema. But what seems to me in the end most interesting is to realize that images made for television *do not have to address themselves* directly to *the spectator*, but to the medium itself, because the medium is the message.

****

Television functions by the continuous, infinite quality of its discourse, by its massive and always smooth quality, regardless of nature of the broadcast. And equally by the completely "frozen," stilted quality of its arrangement of the shot, its arrangement of the grid, its technique. That's why it's most surprising – and most interesting, or funniest – when the machine comes off the tracks, stumbles on an incident along the way. It's the newscaster who's baffled, the surprised and worried look of the presenter of a film that won't get underway, a guest who won't play the game of politeness or who's just straight-out drunk and is dragged out on a stretcher (Bukowski[6] – the American writer – on French TV). From a distance you can see – because elsewhere it's so compact – that the TV image is actually extremely fragile and that nothing must disturb it. That's why the images it creates must be about *television itself* (the little box) more than about the spectator. They must be made so that when they appear on the screen, they constitute an interrogation of television itself, as they infiltrate the ectoplasmic televisual tissue and make it vibrate. Of course you think here of the spots that Bob Wilson[7] produced for television.

You can thus imagine filmmakers producing an enormous quantity (365 per year) of very short little films (3 minutes maximum) on whatever subject, films that also take on *silence,* have no title, no credits, no author's name, and are never announced in the listings but are broadcast in prime time. That's a concrete proposition. That sort of TV would finally allow for some slips. And we'd see some little air bubbles float up.

Notes

1   "... sur les temps morts" in the original. "Temps mort" was the title of Tanner's contribution to the experimental television series *Ecoutez voir.*

2   Télévision Suisse Romande, formerly part of SSR (Société Suisse de la Radiodiffusion), headquartered in Geneva. The term "Suisse Romande," is shorthand for French-speaking Switzerland. Switzerland's broadcasters are split along linguistic lines, with limited amounts of Romansh-language programming appearing on the German-language television network Schweizer Fernsehen 1 (headquartered in Zurich).

3   Tanner is referring here to the Parti radical-démocratique (which, after a merger with the Parti libéral, became the Parti libéral-radical in 2009). Despite its name, this is a centre-right Swiss political party. It is descended from the Radicals, the political faction who triumphed over the conservatives to create the 1848 constitution and its federal structure; this constitution is, basically, the blueprint of modern Switzerland.

4   Pierre Baudry, "Economiques sur les médias : Remarques sur la télévision, la radio et le cinéma, 1," *Cahiers du cinéma* 274 (1977): 51.

5   Pierre Baudry, "Economiques sur les médias : Remarques sur la télévision, la radio et le cinéma, 2," *Cahiers du cinéma* 277 (1977): 27.

6   Charles Bukowski (1920-1994), the American poet and novelist famous for his hard-drinking ways and much beloved in France.

7   The American opera and theatre artist Robert Wilson (b.1941), who has worked in video since the 1970s. His 1978 work *Video 50* is made up of 100 mini "episodes" supposedly meant for television; each episode is 30 seconds long. Renato Berta, who was cinematographer on *La Salamandre*, *Le Milieu du monde* and *Jonas*, as well as on Tanner's *Retour d'Afrique*, is credited with lighting on the *Video 50* piece.

APPENDIX
TWO

"VERS *LE MILIEU DU MONDE*"

by John Berger

Translation Note: This text was originally written in English, but has only appeared in French as "Vers « Le Milieu du monde »" as part of Michel Boujut's published version of the *Milieu du monde* screenplay (the translator is not given). Basically all of the material in quotes, however, can also be found in Berger's letters to the film's actors, specifically to Phillipe Léotard (who played Paul). These letters were, as I mentioned in Chapter 3, published in English as "On 'The Middle of the Earth'" in *Ciné-Tracts* 1 (1977) and in French as "Le milieu du monde" in the Swiss film annual *Cinema* (1974). For this material in quotes I have copied from those letters directly. I give page numbers and descriptions of any variations in the endnotes. Because Berger informed me that he no longer had the original English version of the text, I translated the remainder from the version found in the Boujut book and sent my translation to Berger for editing and revision, which he very generously provided.

****

I had gone to the cinema. When I came out it was cold and damp. It was hard to see the cathedral's tower against the sky.

Between the cathedral and the station in Strasbourg, there are a lot of shabby cafés and bars. I went into one of these places; there was a crow in a hanging cage, next to the bottles behind the counter. Then I worked on my first ideas for the film *Le Milieu du monde*, and that led me towards an analysis of the nature of passion, something I had jotted a few notes about on a school tablet. My back to the wall and a rum tea on the table before me, I began to read what I had written.

> "The beloved is the self's potential; this remains mysterious, even though it has been written about thousands of times. The self's own potential for action is to be loved by the beloved again and again. Active and passive become reversible. The love of the beloved 'completes' — as though we were talking of a single action instead of two — the love of the lover."[1]

The waitress sat down to have supper. She had long hair, the colour of straw.

> "With all those with whom we are not in love we have too much in common to be in love. Passion is only for the opposite. There is no companionship in passion. But passion can confer the same freedom on both lovers. And their shared experience of this freedom — which is astral and cold — and gives rise to an incomparable tenderness. The dream of desire gives birth to its opposite every time"[2]

A man, whom by all indications comes in every night, enters. He is around 60. Civil servant. He heads for the cage to talk to the crow. He speaks bird language to him.

> "The actual modalities of the opposition are not, however, easily calculable from the outside by a third person. What is more they are continually undergoing processes of transformation within the lovers' shared and subjective relationship. Each new experience, each fresh aspect revealed of the other's character, makes it necessary to re-define the lines of opposition. This is a continual imaginative process. When it ceases, there is no more passion. Another kind of love may remain."[3]

I pay the waitress with the straw-coloured hair, I say farewell to the regular who was talking to the crow, and I head for the train station. Starless night.

> "To conceive of the loved one as all that the self is not means that together you form a totality. Together you can be anything and everything. This is the promise which passion makes to the imagination. And because of this promise the imagination works tirelessly drawing and re-drawing the lines of opposition."[4]

There is a twenty-minute wait at the train station. My eyes wander across the big departure hall. Three men find shelter there. One sleeps standing up against the ticket window, his head against a poster of a chateau in the Loire valley. Another, hands on his knees, sleeps sitting on a scale. Its rubber mat is colder than the floor. Even though there is no luggage on the machine it has registered a weight, and because he hasn't bought a ticket, two lights flash, relentlessly indicating a charge of 50 centimes. The happiest of the three men is sitting on the ground, his back pressed up against the only radiator. He is wearing a cap and a bright red jumper. The soles of his shoes have holes the size of eggs. As they sleep, the wind howls.

> "Subjectively the lovers incorporate the world into their totality. All the classic images of love poetry bear this out. The poet's love is 'demonstrated' by the river, the forest, the sky, the minerals in the earth, the silk worm, the stars, the frog, the owl, the moon."[5]

The man who was sitting on the ground puts his knees back up against his stomach.

> "The aspiration towards such 'correspondence' is expressed by poetry, but it is created by passion. Passion aspires to include the world in the act of love. To want to make love in the sea, flying through the sky, in this city, in that field, on sand, with leaves, with salt, with oil, with fruit, in the snow, etc., is not to seek new stimuli, but to express a truth which is inseparable from passion."[6]

The man in the red cap sits up and pulls himself to his feet. Without a word the man of the chateau takes his place by the radiator. As he heads for the exit, the man in the red cap stops to pull up his pants, which were slouching. He takes off his belt, several shirts, and a jersey. His stomach and torso are tattooed. He signals me to approach. He is fat, and his skin seems surprisingly soft. The tattoos are of couples making love in different positions; the contours are black, and the sexual organs red. On his stomach and waist are outlines of Michelangelo's Last Judgement. Next to his nipple a woman sucks a man, who is leaning back. The tattooed man shivers. Does that surprise you? he says. He doesn't bother to put the coin in his pocket, but closes his hand with it until he is before the café.

> "The lover's totality extends, in a different manner, to include the social world. Social action, when it is voluntary, is undertaken for the sake of the beloved. That action, that choice, is inevitably an expression of the lover's love."[7]

The man in the red cap comes on through the front door of the café. "However, passion is a privilege; an economic and cultural privilege."

The train enters the station. I settle in a compartment where two men are seated, one on each side of the window. One is young, with a round face and black eyes, and the other is a bit closer to my age. They are both Spanish. We greet each other. Outside, the rain becomes snow. I find a pencil in my pocket; I want to change some of the lines I just wrote.

> "Many attitudes are incompatible with passion. But this is not a question of temperament. A cautious man, a mean man, a dis-honest woman, a lethargic woman, a cantankerous couple may all be capable of passion. What makes a person refuse passion – or be incapable of pursuing a passion which has already been born, thus transforming it into a mere obsession – is his or her refusal of its totality. But within that totality – as within any – there is the unknown: the unknown which is also conjured up by death, chaos, extremity. If a person has been conditioned or has conditioned himself to treat the unknown as something exterior to himself, against which he must continually take measures and

be on his guard, that person is likely to refuse passion. It is not a question of fearing the unknown. Everyone fears it, it is a question of where it is located. In our culture today most things encourage us to locate it outside ourselves. Even disease is thought of as coming from the outside: which is a necessary, pragmatic truth, but an incomplete one. To locate the unknown as being out there is incompatible with passion. Passion demands that the unknown be recognized as being within."[8]

The Spaniard my age was playing with a piece of paper ripped from a magazine cover. With his big thumbs and nicotine-stained hands, he tore it up gently. The young man watched with the pride of an impresario. But there were no spectators. Only the small hours of the morning. As he tore up the paper, a silhouette appeared. Head, shoulders, bum, feet. He folded it out, long and large. Then, clearly delighted, he ripped a bit out of the centre of the figure and folded it out again. The paper became a man ten centimetres long. When he opened the folds, a penis stood up. When he closed them, the penis fell. He showed it to me, and I looked. All three of us smiled. He said he could do better than that. Almost painfully, he scrumpled up the paper figure in his hands. Under the little table was an ashtray; he threw the paper into it and let the lid fall down with a smack. Then, arms crossed, he looked out of the train window, deep into the night.

Notes

1 From Berger's letter to Phillipe Léotard: "But this is because the loved one represents the lover's completion. The beloved is the self's potential; The self's own potential for action is to be loved by the beloved again and again. Thus love creates the space for love. The love of the beloved 'completes' – as though we were talking of a single action instead of two – the love of the lover" (17).

2 This quote is found verbatim in Berger's letter to Léotard (17), except for the sentence "The dream of desire gives birth to its opposite every time," which is not found there.

3 This entire quote is found verbatim in Berger's letter to Léotard (18).

4 This entire quote is found verbatim in Berger's letter to Léotard (18).

5 This entire quote is found verbatim in Berger's letter to Léotard (18).

6 This entire quote is found verbatim in Berger's letter to Léotard (18).

7 From Berger's letter to Léotard: "The lover's totality extends, in a different manner, to include the social world. Social action, when it is voluntary, is undertaken for the sake of the beloved; not because the results of that action directly affect the beloved; but because that action, that choice, is inevitably an expression of the lover's love; anything that the lover changes in the world pertains to the beloved" (18).

8 This is from Berger's letter to Léotard (19), although the *Ciné-Tracts* version includes a few statements that are not found here.

BIBLIOGRAPHY

"Alain Tanner: trois films." *Journal de Gevève, Samedi littéraire*, 12 March 1961. n.p.

Albera, François. "Faire déraper la fiction: Un entretien de François Albera avec Alain Tanner." *La Nouvelle Critique* 101 (1977): 46–48.

———. *"Jonas qui aura 25 ans en l'an 2000."* *Voix ouvrière*, 27 November 1976. 10–11.

Appignanesi, Richard. "John Berger: The Screenwriter as Collaborator." In Dan Georgakas and Rubenstein, eds., *The Cineaste Interviews*. Chicago: Lake View Press, 1983. 298–306.

Barber, Benjamin. *The Death of Communal Liberty: A History of Freedom in a Swiss Mountain Canton*. Princeton: Princeton University Press, 1974.

Barthes, Roland. "Diderot, Brecht, Eisenstein." *Revue d'esthétique* 26:2–3–4 (1973): 185–91.

———. "L'Effet de réel." *Communications* 11:1 (1968): 84–89.

———. *Essais critiques*. Paris: Seuil, 1964.

———. "Le Grain de la voix." *Musique en jeu* (November 1972): 56–63.

———. *Image, Music, Text*. Stephen Heath, trans. London: Flamingo, 1977.

———. *Leçon*. Paris: Seuil, 1978.

Bas, Frédéric. "Tanner, ou, l'Optimisme." Postface to Tanner, *Ciné-mélanges*, 161–90.

Berger, John. *About Looking*. New York: Pantheon, 1980.

———. *G*. New York: Vintage, 1991 [1972]

———. *Keeping a Rendezvous*. New York: Vintage, 1991.

———. "Look at Britain!" *Sight and Sound* (Summer 1957): 12–14.

———. "Le milieu du monde." *Cinema* (1974): 71–83.

———. "On 'The Middle of the Earth.'" *Cine-Tracts* 1 (1977): 15–26.

———. *A Painter of Our Time*. New York: Vintage, 1989. [1959]

———. *Permanent Red*. London: Methuen, 1969. [1960]

———. *Pig Earth*. New York: Pantheon, 1980.

———. *The Sense of Sight*. New York: Pantheon, 1985.

———. *A Seventh Man*. London: Writers and Readers, 1982. [1975]

———. *The Success and Failure of Picasso*. New York: Vintage, 1993. [1965]

———. "Vers « Le milieu du monde »." In Boujut, ed., 8–11.

———. *Ways of Seeing*. London: BBC/Penguin, 1972.

Berger, John, and Jean Mohr. *A Fortunate Man: The Story of a Country Doctor*. London: Allen Lane Penguin, 1967.

———. *A Seventh Man*. London/New York: Writers and Readers Publishing Cooperative, 1982. [1975]

Bonnard, Laurent. "Entretien avec Alain Tanner." *Positif* 135 (February 1972): 29–38.

Boujut, Michel, ed. *Le Milieu du monde, ou, le cinéma selon Tanner*. Lausanne: L'Age d'homme, 1974.

Braucourt, Guy. "Propos d'Alain Tanner." *Écran* 29 (October 1974): 45–47.

———. "Une Regard idéologique." *Les Nouvelles Littéraires*, 9 September 1974. 12.

———. "La Suisse en question." *L'Avant-Scène du cinéma* 125 (1972): 7. [Originally published in *Combat*, 28 November 1971]

Brecht, Bertolt. *Brecht on Theatre: The Development of an Aesthetic*. John Wilett, trans. and ed. London: Methuen, 1995. [1957]

———. "Formprobleme des Theaters aus neuem Inhalt." In Ruth Berlau, Bertolt Brecht, Claus Hubalek, Peter Palitzsch, and Käthe Rülicke, eds., *Theaterarbeit*. Dresden: VVV Dresdner Verlag, 1952. 253–55.

———. *Über Realismus*. Werner Hect, ed. Leipzig: Phillip Reclam, 1968.

Buache, Freddy. *Le Cinéma suisse, 1898–1998*. Lausanne: L'Age d'homme, 1998.

———. "*Le Milieu du monde*." *Tribune de Lausanne*, 6 October 1974. 5.

Burnett, Martha Aspler. "Introduction." *Ciné-Tracts* 3 (1977–78): 8.

Canby, Vincent. "Tanner's 'Jonah' a Cerebral Film." *New York Times*, 2 October 1976. 11.

Chessex, Jacques. *Jonas*. Paris: Grasset, 1987.

———. *La Tête ouverte*. Lausanne: L'Age d'homme, 1992. [1962]

Citron, Michelle, Chuck Kleinhans, and Julia Lesage. "*Milestones*: White Punks on Revolution." *Jump Cut* 10–11 (1976): 8–9.

Comolli, Jean-Louis. *Cinéma contre spectacle*. Paris: Verdier, 2009.

———. "Le Détour par le direct." *Cahiers du cinéma* 209 (February 1969): 48–53.

———. "Le Détour par le direct (2)." *Cahiers du cinéma* 211 (April 1969): 40–45.

Comolli, Jean-Louis, and Jean Narboni. "Cinéma/idéologie/critique." *Cahiers du cinéma* 216 (October 1969): 11–15.

———. "Cinéma/idéologie/critique (2)." *Cahiers du cinéma* 217 (November 1969): 7–13.

———. "Cinema/Ideology/Criticism." Susan Bennett, trans. *Screen* 12:1 (1971): 27–36.

———. "Cinema/Ideology/Criticism (2)." Susan Bennett, trans. *Screen* 12:2 (1971): 145–55.

Daney, Serge. "Les huit Ma." *Cahiers du cinéma* 273 (January–February 1977): 48–50.

de Baecque, Antoine, Stéphane Bouquet, and Emmanuel Budeau, eds. *Cinéma 68.* Paris: Petite bibliothèque des Cahiers du cinéma, 2008.

Delahaye, Michel, Bernard Eisenschitz, and Jean Narboni. "Alain Tanner: *Charles mort ou vif.*" *Cahiers du cinéma* 213 (June 1969): 26–30.

de Rougemont, Denis. *La Suisse, ou l'histoire d'un peuple heureux.* Lausanne: L'Age d'homme, 1989.

Deslandes, Pierre, and Fred Schmid. *Milieu du monde.* Lausanne: Guilde du Livre, 1943.

Dimitriu, Christian. *Alain Tanner.* Paris: Éditions Henri Veyrier, 1985.

Dyer, Geoff. *Ways of Telling: The Work of John Berger.* London: Pluto Press, 1986.

Evans, Gareth. *John Berger: A Season in London 2005.* London: artevents, 2005.

Fish, Stanley. "Why No One's Afraid of Wolfgang Iser." *Diacritics* 11:1 (1981): 2–13.

Fokkema, Douwe, and Elrud Ibsch. *Modernist Conjectures.* London: C. Hurst, 1987.

Gitlin, Todd. "*Jonah Who Will Be 25 in the Year 2000.*" *Film Quarterly* 30:3 (1977): 36–42.

———. "The Lyric Odyssey of Alain Tanner." *Harper's,* February 1984. 68–71.

Greene, Linda, John Hess, and Robin Lakes. "Subversive Charm Indeed!" *Jump Cut* 15 (1977): 8–9.

Hauser, Claude. *L'Aventure du Jura.* Lausanne: Antipodes, 2004.

Heinic, N. "Entretien avec Alain Tanner." *Cahiers du cinéma* 273 (January–February 1977): 38–43.

———. "An Interview with Alain Tanner." In Tanner and Berger, *Jonah Who Will Be 25,* 165–74.

Hess, John. "La Politique des auteurs. Part One: World View as Aesthetic." *Jump Cut* 1 (1974): 19–22.

Hess, John, and Richard Kazis. "Critical Dialogue: *Jonah Who Will Be 25 in the Year 2000.*" *Jump Cut* 18 (1978): 35–36.

Iser, Wolfgang. "Talk Like Whales: A Reply to Stanley Fish." *Diacritics* 11:3 (1981): 82–87.

Kael, Pauline. "The Current Cinema: A Cuckoo Clock that Laughs." *The New Yorker*, 18 October 1986. 75–78.

Kané, Pascal. "L'Effet d'étrangeté." *Cahiers du cinéma* 254–55 (December 1974 – January 1975): 77–83.

Klemesrud, Judy. "Alain Tanner: 'Art Is to Break with the Past.'" *New York Times*, 24 October 1976. B6.

Kuffer, Lean-Louis. "Alain Tanner nie la culture suisse dont ses propres films sont tissés." *24 heures*, 23 February 2004. 12.

Leach, Jim. *A Possible Cinema: The Films of Alain Tanner*. Metuchen, NJ: Scarecrow Press, 1984.

Legrand, Gérard. "Autres distances longées (*La Salamandre*)." *Positif* 135 (February 1972): 25–28.

Le Peron, Serge. "Ici ou ailleurs." *Cahiers du cinéma* 273 (January–February 1977) 44–47.

Liogier, Hélène. "1960: vue d'Espagne, la Nouvelle Vague est fasciste, ou, la Nouvelle Vague selon Jean Parvulesco." *1895* 26 (1998): 127–53.

Maffezzini, Ivan. "Cher John ..." *Conjuctures* 39–40 (2005): 141–52.

Monaco, James. "Au Milieu du monde: Alain Tanner and Swiss Film." *Movietone News* 51 (1976): 30–33.

Narboni, Jean. "Le Pirée pour un homme." [Review of *Z*, by Costa-Gavras] *Cahiers du cinema* 210 (March 1969): 54–55.

Narboni, Jean, Jacques Rivette, and Sylvie Pierre. "Montage." *Cahiers du cinéma* 210 (March 1969): 17–35.

Orwell, George. *Why I Write*. New York: Penguin, 2005.

Oudart, Jean-Pierre. "Cinema and Suture." Kari Hunet, trans. *Screen* 18:4 (1977): 35–47.

———. "La Suture." *Cahiers du cinéma* 211 (April 1969): 36–39.

———. "La Suture (Deuxième partie)." *Cahiers du cinéma* 212 (May 1969): 50–55.

Paz, Octavio. *La Quête du Présent : Discours de Stockholm*. Édition bilingue; Jean-Claude Masson, trad. Paris: Gallimard, 1991.

Prieur, Jérôme. "Alain Tanner." *La Quinzaine littéraire* 247 (1977): 26.

Ramuz, Charles-Ferdinand. *L'Amour du monde*. Rezé-lès-Nantes: Séquences, 2005. [1925]

———. *Les Servants et autres nouvelles*. La Croix-sur-Lutry: Plaisir de lire, 1983. [1946]

Rosenbaum, Jonathan. "The Place(s) of Danièle." *Undercurrent* 3 (2006). http://www.fipresci.org/undercurrent/issue_0306/huillet_rosenbaum.htm (6 May 2010).

Rostan, Blaise. *Le Service public de radio et de télévision*. Lausanne: Éditions René Thonney-Dupraz, 1982.

Roud, Richard. *Straub*. London: Secker and Warburg, 1972.

Rousseau, Jean-Jacques. *Emile: or, On Education*. Allan Bloom, trans. New York: Basic Books, 1979. [1762]

———. *Émile, ou, de l'éducation*. Paris: Flammarion, 1966. [1762]

Rubenstein, Lenny. "Alain Tanner: Irony is a double-edged weapon." In Dan Georgakas and Lenny Rubenstein, eds., *The Cineaste Interviews*. Chicago: Lake View Press, 1983. 98–104.

Schaub, Martin. *L'Usage de la liberté : le nouveau cinéma suisse, 1964–1984*. Lausanne: L'Age d'homme / Pro Helvetia, 1985.

Schüpbach, Marcel. "Le Dernier film d'Alain Tanner, « Jonas », marque un étape dans son évolution." *Journal de Genève, Samedi littéraire*, 24 April 1976. 13.

Simsolo, Noël. "*Le Milieu du monde*." *Écran* 29 (October 1974): 45–47.

Sontag, Susan. *Against Interpretation and Other Essays*. New York: Picador, 2001 [1966].

Stam, Robert. "The Subversive Charm of Alain Tanner." *Jump Cut* 15 (1977): 5–7.

Tanner, Alain. *Ciné-mélanges*. Paris: Seuil, 2007.

———. "En Suisse, pas de place pour les poètes!" *Le Matin*, 8 February 2004. 8, 22.

———. "Le « pourquoi dire » et le « comment dire »" In Michel Boujut, ed., 12–38.

———. "Télé-Aphorismes." *Cinema* (1980): 24–38.

Tanner, Alain, and John Berger. *Jonas qui aura 25 ans en l'an 2000*. Lausanne: Cinémathèque Suisse, 1978.

———. *Jonah Who Will Be 25 in the Year 2000*. Michael Palmer, trans. Berkeley: North Atlantic Books, 1983.

———. *La Salamandre*. *L'Avant-Scène du cinéma* 125 (May 1972): 8-40.

Tarantino, Michael. "Alain Tanner: After *Jonah*." *Sight and Sound* (Winter 1978/9): 40–43.

———. "Tanner and Berger: The Voice Off-Screen." *Film Quarterly* 33:2 (1979–80): 32–43.

Todorov, Tzvetan. *L'Esprit des Lumières*. Paris: Robert Laffont, 2006.

Toubiana, Serge. "20 ans après, Jonas…." *Cahiers du cinéma* 320 (February 1981): xiii–x.

Trueba, Fernando, and Carlos S. Boyero. "Alain Tanner: 'El contenido de la obra de arta está en su forma.'" *El Pais*, 12 March 1978. 12.

Truffaut, François. *Le Plaisir des yeux : écrits sur le cinéma*. Paris: Petite bibliothèque des Cahiers du cinéma, 2000.

Vallon, Claude. "Groupe 5 et Télévision." *Cinéma* (1974): 5–15.

Vallotton, François. "Anastasie ou Cassandre? Le rôle de la radio-télévision dans la société helvétique." In Theo Mäusli and Andreas Steigmier, eds., *Le radio et la télévision en suisse*. Baden: Heir und Jetz, 2006. 37–76.

Vitoux, Frédéric. "Les Emblèmes de la nostalgie : *Jonas qui aura vingt-cinq ans en l'an 2000.*" *Positif* 189 (January 1977): 71–73.

Voltaire [François-Marie Arouet]. *Candide, or, Optimism.* John Butt, trans. New York: Penguin Classics, 1985. [1947/1759]

———. *Romans et contes.* Paris: Gallimard, 1972.

Waldman, Diane. "There's More to a Positive Image than Meets the Eye." *Jump Cut* 18 (1978): 31–32.

Williams, Raymond. *The Country and the City.* London: Chatto and Windus, 1973.

Willis, Paul. "The Authentic Image: An Interview with John Berger and Jean Mohr." *Screen Education* 32/33 (1979–80): 19–30.

Wood, Robin. "The New Queer Cinema and Gay Culture: Notes from an Outsider." *CineAction* 35 (1995): 3–15.

Zeender, Christian. "Quand Tanner ne tient pas ses promesses: *Le Milieu du monde.*" *Journal de Genève*, 19 October 1974. 10.

Zoller, Pierre-Henri. "Connaître John Berger." *Construire* 52 (24 December 1976): 5–6.

SOURCES
FOR THE FILMS ON VIDEO

Videos of most of the films that Berger and Tanner made together (or which follows on work they did together) have mostly fallen out of print, but they have all been released and can still be found through online channels such as various Amazon websites (.co.uk and .fr as well as .com and .ca). Details are as follows:

Une Ville à Chandiargh:

Trigon Films: DVD/PAL, region 0, optional English subtitles, AISN #7640117980616

[This is an extra on the DVD of *Les hommes du port*]

La Salamandre:

Éditions Montparnasse: DVD/PAL, region 2, optional German subtitles, AISN #B000EU1IKW

New Yorker Films: VHS/NTSC, English subtitles, AISN #6303139647

Le Milieu du monde:

Doriane Films: DVD/PAL, region 2, optional English subtitles, AISN #B000GB804Q

Jonas qui aura 25 ans en l'an 2000:

Doriane Films: DVD/PAL, region 2, optional English subtitles, AISN #B000GB804Q

New Yorker Films: VHS/NTSC, English subtitles, AISN #6302498244

Light Years Away (on DVD as *A años luz*):

Manga Films: DVD/PAL, region 2, optional Spanish subtitles, AISN #B000G8NZIK

Fourbi

AV Prod.: DVD/PAL, region 0, optional German and Italian subtitles, AISN
    #B000FWGWFA

Jonas et Lila, à demain:

AV World: DVD/PAL, region 0, optional English and German subtitles, AISN
    #B004HZL8WS

The difficulty of viewing the feature length work is in vivid contrast, ironically, to the short television work Berger and Tanner did together (or which
Tanner did on his own), which is very easily available at the website of
Télévision Suisse Romande for all to see. Details on the films discussed in
this book are as follows:

Les Apprentis: http://archives.tsr.ch/player/tanner-apprentis

Docteur B., médecin de campagne: http://archives.tsr.ch/player/integrale-tannermedecin

Ecoutez voir: http://archives.tsr.ch/player/reflexion-tanner

L'Identité galloise: http://archives.tsr.ch/player/perspectives-gallois

L'Indépendance au loin: http://archives.tsr.ch/player/jura-situations65

Mike, ou l'usage de la science: http://archives.tsr.ch/dossier-cern/cern-mike

Le Pouvoir dans la rue: http://archives.tsr.ch/player/integrale-mai68

Les Trois belgique: http://archives.tsr.ch/player/belgique-conflit

La Troupe de music hall: http://archives.tsr.ch/player/perspectives-danse

INDEX

1968, 3, 39, 112, 122, 152–54, 178, 191
  and cinema, 11–24, 41n13
  Tanner's film about, 25

A

Akerman, Chantal, 103
Albera, François, 156, 172, 173
Amour du monde, L', 32–34
Années lumières, Les. See *Light Years Away*
Another Way of Telling, 78, 119
Appenzell (Innerrhoden), 111, 112
Apprentis, Les, 60, 61
Arpenteurs, Les, 4
Artel, Linda, 169
auteurism, 6, 8, 56–57

B

Barber, Benjamin, 24, 26–27, 39
Barthes, Roland, 82–83, 93, 95, 123–24, 159,
  178, 189
Bas, Frédéric, 20, 37, 103, 108
Basel (Stadt), 111
Baudrillard, Jean, 210, 214, 215
Baudry, Pierre, 217, 221, 224n2, 224n3
Bazin, André, 6, 94, 103, 123
Belgium, 21–22, 28, 44n31
Benjamin, Walter, 174–75
Berto, Renato, 118
"Between Two Colmars," 22–23
Bideau, Jean-Luc, 4

Bonnard, Laurent, 111
Boujut, Michel, 225
Brandt, Henry, 61
Braucourt, Guy, 142
Brault, Michel, 40n2, 58
Brecht, Bertold, 1, 19, 39, 64, 91, 135, 173,
  178, 188
  and conventional forms, 13–15, 126,
  and *Jonas qui aura 25 ans en l'an 2000*, 173
  and *La Salamandre*, 104, 106, 108–10
  and *Le Milieu du monde*, 117, 119–20,
    123–25, 126, 135
  and realism, 83
British Film Institute, 55
Buache, Freddy, 7, 61, 111–12, 140
Bukowski, Charles, 223, 224n7
Burnett, Martha Aspler, 170

C

Cahiers du cinéma, 5, 12, 15–19, 23, 24,
  42n20, 122, 189
Canadian identity, 26
Candide, 37–38, 46–47n49, 89, 97, 109, 149,
  150, 151, 152–53
Carlisi, Olimpia, 129–31, 136–37
Césaire, Aimé, 64
Charles mort ou vif, 5, 8, 30, 81–82, 107, 112,
  118, 158, 197
Chessex, Jacques, 3, 25, 34–36, 46n44
Chronique d'un été, 58
Chronicle of Anna Magdalena Bach, 118

239

Ciné-Journal Suisse, 7
Cinema (Swiss film journal), 8, 170, 209, 225
Cinéma direct. *See* Direct Cinema
"Cinéma/idéologie/critique," 16–17, 19, 42–43n21, 123, 144n8, 188
Cinéma vérité. *See* Direct Cinema
Cinémathèque Suisse, 117–18, 144, 167–68
Ciné-Tracts (Canadian journal), 146n19, 170–71, 225, 230
Cine-tracts (militant film project), 21, 202–3
Citizen Kane, 110
Citron, Michelle, 160
Comment, Bernard, 202
Comolli, Jean-Louis, 16, 17–18, 42n20, 57–59, 69, 73, 75, 123, 188
conservatism, 6, 28, 107, 139, 198–99, 224
"Continents sans visa," 53
Costa-Gavras, Constantin, 14
Counter-Cinema, 3, 119
Country and the City, The, 155
"Courbet and the Jura," 29–30, 107

D

Daney, Serge, 68, 69, 159, 187
Dardel, Julie, 161
Découpage, 11, 18, 77, 79–80, 94, 156–58, 173, 177
de Gaulle, Charles, 12
de Rougemont, Denis, 24, 27, 28, 139
Deslandes, Pierre, 117, 119
Dimitriu, Christian, 14, 19–20, 29, 53, 65, 67, 177
Direct Cinema, 17–18, 49, 59, 67, 69, 73, 75, 77, 81
    sound-image relationships, 40n2, 55, 60–62, 72
Docteur B., médecin de campagne, 49–51, 54, 59, 72–82, 84, 209
Doolan, Leila, 209
Dowling, Jack, 209
Drew, Robert, 40n2
Droit au logement, Le, 52–53
Duplain, Georges, 117
Dyer, Geoff, 55, 57, 77–78, 190, 203

E

École, L', 57
Ecoutez voir, 191–96, 209, 224n1
Eisenstein, Sergei, 17–18, 39, 66, 123–25, 159, 190
Elder, Bruce, 173
Émile, 37, 150, 151, 153–55
Enlightenment, 3, 36–39, 71
États généraux du cinéma, 12, 41n14
Evans, Gareth, 193
"Ev'ry Time We Say Goodbye," 32–33

F

federalism, 24, 25, 28–29, 38–39, 108, 139, 224n3
feminist movements, 161–62
Fish, Stanley, 97
Fokkema, Douwe, 127
Fortunate Man, A, 51, 72, 75–82, 119
Fourbi, 109, 191–92, 199–202, 204
France/Tour/Détour/Deux/Enfants, 195, 209
Free Cinema, 4, 55–56, 61
French New Wave. *See* Nouvelle vague, La
Fribourg, 115–16n16, 119

G

G (Berger novel), 110, 111, 121
    as experimental narrative, 91, 92–93
    and history, 89, 96, 112
    and representation of women, 100–101, 104, 132, 136
Garrel, Phillipe, 103
Gatti, Armand, 221
Geneva, 25, 37, 46–47n49, 104
Ginnocchio di Artemide, Il, 118, 144n2
Gitlin, Todd, 135, 141, 160–61, 167, 174, 197–98
Godard, Jean-Luc, 66, 90, 123, 145n9, 172, 187, 209
    and militant cinema, 13–14, 120
    and right-wing anarchism, 5, 57
    and television, 195–96, 209, 213, 221
Goretta, Claude, 4, 8
Gorin, Jean-Pierre, 13–14

Greene, Linda, 155–56, 160–68, 170, 190
Griffith, D.W., 127
Groulx, Gilles, 40n2
Groupe Cinq, Le, 8
Groupe Dziga Vertov, 13–14, 90, 120

H

Hauser, Claude, 28
Hess, John, 155–56, 160–68, 170, 190
History Lessons, 118
Holocaust, 212, 215
Hommes du port, Les, 54–55
Huillet, Danièle, 17, 117–20, 123, 128–29,
    144n2, 171

I

Ibsch, Elrud, 127
iconicity, 101–2, 105–7, 109, 112, 124, 127,
    167, 176, 187
Identité galloise, L', 54–55, 69
Indépendance au loin, L', 29, 69, 107
Ireland, 107, 196–98, 207n17, 209–10
Iser, Wolfgang, 97
Itinéraire de Jean Bricard, 117–18, 144n2

J

Jonas et Lila, à demain, 192, 193, 202–5
Jonas qui aura 25 ans en l'an 2000, 1, 19,
    91–92, 93, 95, 149–84, 205
    and Jacques Chessex, 46n44
    and political film criticism, 189–92
    and Swiss culture, 186–87, 197
Jump Cut, 6, 155–56, 160, 167–68, 171, 190,
    203
Jura, separatism in, 3, 5, 28–30, 45n38, 107–8

K

Kael, Pauline, 14, 135
Kané, Pascal, 128
Kleinhans, Chuck, 160
Klemesrud, Judy, 161, 169
Kramer, Robert, 159–60
Kuffer, Jean-Louis, 186

L

Lakes, Robin, 155–56, 160–68, 170, 190
Leach, Jim, 13, 14, 16, 18, 94, 134–35, 154,
    156, 175
Le Corbusier, 59, 63, 64, 65
Legrand, Gérard, 89
Léotard, Phillipe, 136–37, 225, 230
Le Peron, Serge, 187
Lesage, Julia, 160
letters, from Berger to Carlisi and Léotard,
    136–38, 146n19, 170, 225, 230
liberalism, challenges to, 27, 36, 62, 186, 199
Light Years Away, 46n44, 190, 196–99, 204–5
Loi fédérale sur le cinéma, 7, 52, 217
Lumière Brothers, 127–28

M

Maîtres fous, Les, 182
Marxism, 81, 118, 137, 173, 187, 190, 198,
    203
McLuhan, Marshall, 194, 215
Messidor, 192, 196, 197
Miéville, Anne-Marie, 90, 123, 144n8, 187,
    192, 195–96, 197, 209
migration, 121–22, 162–67, 176
Milestones, 159–60
Milieu du monde (photo book), 117, 119–20
Milieu du monde, Le, 1, 30, 117–47, 158,
    160–61, 188, 205
    and Berger's art criticism, 23
    and Canadian cinema, 26
    and *Ciné-Tracts*, 170
    and eroticism, 19, 226
    and formal eccentricity, 92, 95
    and montage, 66, 189–91
    and normalization, 23, 93, 112–13, 150,
        151, 167, 172
Mike et l'usage de la science, 49, 50, 51, 54, 59,
    67–72, 84, 173–74
militant cinema, 13–14, 21, 42n17, 73
modernism, 127
Mohr, Jean, 74, 76, 78, 119, 121
Moi, un noir, 182
"Moment of Cubism," 22
Monaco, James, 26

Montage, 38, 66–67, 81, 94, 103, 124, 126, 141, 158–59
   text in *Cahiers du cinéma*, 17–18, 38, 79, 190
Moses and Aaron, 118
Mouvement de Libération des Femmes, 161
Mouvement féministe, Le, 162

N

Narboni, Jean, 15, 16, 18, 42n17, 123, 188
Nice Time, 55, 60, 196
normalization, 23–24, 120–22, 138–40, 172
Not Reconciled, 118
Nouveau cinéma suisse, 2, 3, 4–11, 34, 118
Nouvelle vague, La, 6, 8–9, 56–57, 89

O

Odier, Daniel, 196
Ogier, Bulle, 90, 98, 201
Orwell, George, 175
Othon, 118–19
Oudart, Jean-Pierre, 19, 125–26, 127, 129, 188

P

Painter of our Time, A, 9, 11, 70, 187
Parti democrate-chrétien, 139
Parvulesco, Jean, 6
Pasolini, Pier Paolo, 128
Paz, Octavio, 90–91
Peirce, Charles Sanders, 106
Pence, Michael, 67–72, 74
Permanent Red, 9, 10, 71, 77
Perrault, Pierre, 66
Pierre, Sylvie, 18, 38, 79, 190
Pig Earth, 31–32, 76, 78, 91, 152, 174, 198–99
Porter, Edwin S., 127–28
Positif, 16, 89, 170
"Positive Images" criticism, 168–69
Pouvoir dans la rue, Le, 19–22, 29, 69
Prieur, Jérôme, 195
Primary, 40n2, 61
propaganda, 9, 24

Q

Quand nous étions petits enfants, 61
Quebec, 7, 9, 28, 64
Quinn, Bob, 210

R

Radicals (Swiss political faction), 214, 224n3
Raidió Teilifís Éireann (RTÉ), 210
Ramuz, Charles-Ferdinand, 3, 4, 25, 30–34, 36, 91
Ramuz, Passage d'un poète, 34
Raquetteurs, Les, 40n2, 61
realism, 56, 71, 73–74, 79, 83, 95, 122–23
   discussion in *Permanent Red*, 9, 65, 71, 77
Rétour d'Afrique, 8, 50–51, 158, 202
Reusser, Francis, 192
Rohmer, Éric, 150
Rossellini, Roberto, 128
Rouch, Jean, 57–59, 66, 86n8, 188
Rosenbaum, Jonathan, 171
Roud, Richard, 128, 144n2
Rousseau, Jean-Jacques, 37, 64, 150, 153–55, 156, 167, 173, 181n13, 203

S

Salamandre, La, 1, 19, 30, 89–116, 142, 150, 158, 187, 205
   and editing patterns, 125–27, 177–78, 189–92
   and Jacques Chessex, 35
   reception of, 167
   remade as *Fourbi*, 199–202
   and representation of women, 132, 141
   and Swiss culture, 197
   and the Swiss military, 44n33
Schaub, Martin, 4, 34–35, 36, 118, 209
Schmid, Fred, 117
Screen, 12, 171
Seventh Man, A, 119, 121–22, 135, 162–66, 185
Simsolo, Noël, 120
Six fois deux: sur et sous la communication, 195–96, 209
socialism, 10, 70

socialist realism, 169

Société Suisse de Radiodiffusion (SSR), 8, 52, 191, 214, 224n2

Sontag, Susan, 23

Soutter, Michel, 4, 8

Stam, Robert, 160, 161, 163

Straub, Jean-Marie, 17, 79, 117–20, 123, 128–29, 144n2, 171

Streghe, Le, 118, 144n2

Success and Failure of Picasso, The, 10, 11, 22, 23, 100

Super 8 film, 191, 192–96

Suture, 19, 125–26, 129, 188

Swiss culture, 3, 24–36, 107–8, 111–13, 139–40, 161–62, 185–87

Swiss military, 44n33

T

Tanner, Cécile, 200, 201

Tarantino, Michael, 93–94, 96, 110

"Télé-aphorisms," 53–54, 68, 194, 201, 209–24

television

    Tanner's interest in, 53–55, 69, 82, 191–95, 209–24

    in Switzerland, 8, 51–59, 191–96, 201, 212, 214, 224n2

Temps morts, 192–95, 197, 202, 204, 205, 224n1

Tête ouverte, La, 35

Todorov, Tzvetan, 3, 38–39

Toubiana, Serge, 214, 221

Trieste, 112

Trois belgique, Les, 21–22, 69

Troupe de music-hall, Le, 69–70

Truffaut, François, 56, 90

U

United Arab Republic, 65, 86n15

Université catholique de Louvain, 21, 44n31

"Uses of Photography," 174, 204

V

Verna, Loretta, 192

Viaud, Karin, 201

Ville à Chandigarh, Une, 15, 37, 49, 50, 59–67, 69, 84, 94, 150

Vitoux, Frédéric, 170

Voltaire, 37–38, 46–47n49, 97, 113, 149, 152, 178

W

Waldman, Diane, 169, 190

Walsh, Martin, 171

Ways of Seeing, 100–101, 132–33, 136

Weill, Kurt, 83

Wengraf, Susan, 169

Williams, Raymond, 155, 203, 210

Wilson, Bob, 223, 224n7

Wintonick, Peter, 58

women

    acquiring voting rights in Switzerland, 111–12, 162

    visual representation of, 100–104, 132, 136

Wood, Robin, 14–15, 126

Wu, Ying Wing, 160

Y

Yeats, W.B., 63, 64, 90

Z

Z (Costa-Gavras film), 14, 42n17, 188

Zappa, Frank, 150

Zeender, Christian, 140

Zürcher, Claude, 192